The Green Consumer's
SUPERMARKET
SHOPPING GUIDE

John Elkington is one of Europe's leading authorities on the role of industry in sustainable development. He is a director of SustainAbility and has visited over 300 companies worldwide, acting as an environmental consultant for many of them. He sits on advisory panels at the Merlin Ecology Fund and the Nature Conservancy Council. He has authored or co-authored numerous books including *The Green Capitalists* and *The Green Consumer Guide* and has published several hundred reports, papers and articles for a wide variety of journals, magazines and national newspapers.

Julia Hailes is co-author of the bestselling *Green Consumer Guide* and of *Green Pages*. She is also a director of 'green growth company' SustainAbility, which aims to promote environmentally sustainable economic growth. She has made numerous television and radio appearances, and during 1989 presented a weekly television series called 'Green Matters'. She was responsible for organising Britain's first Green Consumer Week in 1988.

On World Environment Day in June 1989, John Elkington and Julia Hailes were named to the United Nations Environment Programme's 'Global 500 Roll of Honour' for their 'outstanding environmental achievements'.

The Green Consumer's
SUPERMARKET
SHOPPING GUIDE

*Shelf by Shelf Recommendations
for Products which
don't cost the Earth*

John Elkington & Julia Hailes

LONDON
VICTOR GOLLANCZ LTD
1989

First published in Great Britain 1989
by Victor Gollancz Ltd
14 Henrietta Street, London WC2E 8QJ

A Gollancz Paperback Original

British Library Cataloguing in Publication Data
Elkington, John, *1949 –*
   The green consumer's supermarket shopping guide.
   1. Great Britain. Environmentally safe household products
   I. Title   II. Hailes, Julia
   648

   ISBN 0-575-04582-5

recycled paper

Typeset in Great Britain by
Action Typesetting Limited, Gloucester
Printed and bound by Cox & Wyman Ltd, Reading

Contents

Acknowledgements

Putting together a book of this sort is never easy, but it has proved particularly challenging at a time of exploding interest and activity in the green consumer corner of the economy.

There is always a temptation, as one development and announcement follows another, to squeeze in yet another bit of information. But, even though we have carried out a much larger research programme for this book than for *The Green Consumer Guide*, we have tried to keep in mind the idea that the book should be of practical use to shoppers walking around their local supermarket.

We have been enormously helped in this task by three of our colleagues at SustainAbility: Fiona Byrne, Anne Dimmock and Isabelle Gore.

And we should also like to thank the literally hundreds of people around the country who were involved, in one way or another, in filling in the questionnaires sent out as part of our Supermarket Survey and Manufacturers' Survey. Several dozen people also commented on drafts of the various sections of the book, which proved tremendously helpful.

Among those who have been particularly helpful have been Jane Bickerstaffe of the Industry Committee on Packaging and the Environment (INCPEN), Robin Bines of Ecover, Alicia Clegg of the British Plastics Federation, John Dickinson and Chris Ash of Varta, and the editorial staff of *Supermarketing* magazine.

Once again, the team at Victor Gollancz invested a disproportionate amount of time in the book, working all hours. We should particularly like to thank Liz Knights, Elizabeth Dobson and Sara Scamell, who were directly involved in editing and producing the book, together with Alex Huggins, Jane Blackstock, Kate Hordern, Adrienne Maguire and everyone else at Gollancz who did so much to make this task a manageable one.

If you have any suggestions for future editions of the *Supermarket Shopping Guide*, or of *The Green Consumer Guide* (which we hope to update in 1990), write to us at SustainAbility Ltd, 49 Princes Place, London W11 4QA.

Authors' Note

The authors have prepared this work in good faith having invited the co-operation of many supermarkets and manu- facturers. Where answers have been supplied by supermarkets and manufacturers, these have been taken as truthful. Information is taken as being correct at the time the survey was conducted.

The omission of any particular brand, company or any other organisation implies neither censure nor recommendation.

Neither the authors nor the publishers, however, warrant the effectiveness or performance of any product set out in this work and the reader and consumer must exercise his or her own judgement when determining on what criteria to purchase a particular product, in respect of which this book is intended merely as a guide. Any reader requiring further information concerning the product should write directly to the supplier or manufacturer in question.

The authors and publishers will consider any matter which is held to be inaccurate and upon satisfactory factual and documentary confirmation of the correct position will use all reasonable endeavours to amend the text for the next impression or edition.

During the period we were researching this book **Bejam** was bought by Iceland Frozen Foods. Consequently, we refer throughout the book only to **Iceland.**

The Green Consumer

'The world is dying. What are
you going to do about it?'

There was no mistaking the intent of these words, which blazed
across the front cover of the Sunday Times's colour magazine
during the period when we were writing The Green Consumer's
Supermarket Shopping Guide. They were designed to shock.
Behind the words lay a smouldering vista of burned rainforest,
a living world reduced to ashes.

Like Time magazine, which had devoted its New Year 1989
cover to the 'Planet of the Year, Endangered Earth', the Sunday
Times left readers in no doubt about what is now happening
around the world.

'We are all polluters on this planet,' the paper said. 'We burn
fossil fuels, we create waste, we ravage natural resources with
little or no regard for the consequences. But time is running out.
Our planet is becoming despoiled, rotten, overcrowded and
barren.'

The danger in all this is that ordinary Britons will be so
panicked by the scale of the problems that they simply switch
off. 'The terrible part about these global environmental

problems,' as Prince Charles put it, 'is that they tend to fill our hearts with gloom.' Like rabbits, many of us sit transfixed by the oncoming threat. Part of the trick of waking us all up is going to be showing that disaster is not inevitable, that we can win through — and that there is something each of us can do to change history.

'As individual consumers we can play a very significant part,' Prince Charles stressed. 'The revolt of the consumer against the use of CFCs in aerosols was dramatic. Since that revolt supermarkets have been falling over themselves to prove that they are the greenest of the green and, in order to meet the consumer pressure, the supermarkets are having to put pressure on their suppliers to meet ever higher environmental standards.'

In the spring of 1989, some 2.3 million Britons demonstrated their awareness of environmental issues by voting for the Green Party. Even though the Greens won around 14 per cent of the vote, our electoral system ensured they won no seats — but the scale of the green vote certainly sent a powerful signal to politicians that the environment is now a top priority issue. The recent conversion of such leading politicians as Britain's Mrs Thatcher, America's President George Bush and the Soviet Union's President Mikhail Gorbachev should not be discounted. More legislation is needed to tackle the many environmental problems caused by our industrial societies and consumer lifestyles; and there is an equally pressing need for much stricter enforcement of both new laws and the laws we already have on the statute book.

At the same time, however, legislation is a slow, blunt instrument for achieving the change needed to save our planet. And politicians do not, in any case, control all the levers of power. Many key decisions are made — or heavily influenced — by business. Governments often turn to industrialists for advice on whether new measures are technically feasible — or affordable — and so we must also change their hearts and minds.

In commercial terms, the tide is in our favour. The Baby Boom generation, now aged between 25 and 45, represents the sector in society enjoying the most rapid growth in disposable income. The securing of this spending power is the key area in which manufacturers are competing.

Our decisions to buy or not to buy give us enormous potential power. It is not simply a question of cutting the environmental impact of the products we purchase, but also of creating, through the choices we make, a commercial climate in which manufacturers and retailers see new market opportunities in 'green' goods and are encouraged to invest in new products and services.

The Green Consumer has already triggered a major shift in the way that the business community views environmental issues. And in the wake of the media impact created in 1988 by publication of *The Green Consumer Guide*, and by Britain's first Green Consumer Week, the movement has gone into overdrive. By June 1989 a MORI poll concluded that nearly half the adult population of Britain — or more than 18 million people — had made at least one purchase where a product was selected instead of another because of its environment-friendly packaging, formulation or advertising. MORI chairman Bob Worcester told *The Times*: 'The Green Consumer is here, in seven-league boots.'

Why your supermarket vote counts

The potential impact of the supermarkets in the greening of industry is increasingly clear. From the point of view of Green Consumers, the supermarket is the place where we can exert our power most effectively.

Many of the leading supermarkets have already announced their intention to go green, following the lead of Safeway, Tesco, Sainsbury's and the Co-op. And there are more changes in the pipeline. Our research for the *Supermarket Shopping Guide* has uncovered — and helped to provoke — an avalanche of new green products designed to appeal to the Green Consumer.

To understand why the checkout has become so influential in the battle to save the planet, it's important to know how the business of supermarketing is already changing. How are environmental issues affecting the major chains — and what could happen next? The trends which are reshaping the supermarket business are outlined in 'The Greening of the

Supermarkets' (page 7), while a summary of the most pressing environmental issues can be found in 'Costing the Earth' (page 15).

It is important to remember that no product can be 100 per cent environment-friendly. Everything we do disturbs the environment to some extent. Increasingly, we need to consider a product's impact from the moment raw materials are extracted, through manufacturing, distribution and use to ultimate disposal. Nevertheless, some products are 'greener' than others. Wherever you see yourself on the Green Consumer scale and whatever you're looking for — from organic produce to green batteries or phosphate-free detergents — The Green Consumer's *Supermarket Shopping Guide* aims to make the choices as clear as possible and to leave retailers, manufacturers and growers in no doubt that more and more of their customers are now looking for products that are not going, quite literally, to cost the earth.

KEY ISSUES FOR THE 1990s' GREEN CONSUMER

In general, the Green Consumer should avoid products which are likely to:

- endanger the health either of the consumer or of others

- cause significant damage to the environment during manufacture, use or disposal

- consume a disproportionate amount of energy during manufacture, use or disposal

- cause unnecessary waste, whether because of over-packaging, an unduly short useful life or because they are not suitable to re-use or recycle

- use materials derived from threatened species or from threatened environments

- involve the unnecessary use of — or cruelty to — animals, whether this be for toxicity testing or other purposes

- adversely affect other countries, particularly in the Third World.

The Greening of the Supermarkets

The greening of Britain's supermarkets is now well under way. Many people assume that this trend emerged suddenly, but anyone who has been watching the supermarket sector carefully will know that it has been under pressure from environmentalists for many years. Indeed, it is worth asking why it took so long for supermarkets to start going green — and, now that they have begun, how far will the trend go?

The arrival of the supermarket triggered a revolution in shopping habits. To find the roots of this revolution, you have to go back at least 25 years. From 1964, when the retail price index was abandoned, retailers were able to sacrifice short-term profits by cutting prices — and thereby, they hoped, boosting their market share. The price war that followed helped to knock many small traders out of the nation's high streets.

Bakers, greengrocers and butchers all suffered. Between 1961 and 1984, the number of greengrocers dropped by nearly two-thirds, the number of butchers and poulterers was cut in half, and the number of bakers also fell by nearly a third.

Looking for Growth

The supermarkets have not, however, simply become super-grocers. The 1970s saw a great deal of experimentation. Supermarkets began to move into non-food markets, stocking clothing, household goods, DIY products and toys. Later, in the 1980s, the supermarkets began to move away from their previous concentration on processed products to stock a growing range of fresh foods — mainly fruit and vegetables, bakery goods, dairy products, delicatessen items and fresh fish. All these products not only enjoyed a healthy image but also offered much higher profit margins.

But if you think that competition between the chains has been fierce in the 1970s and 1980s, hold on for the 1990s. They now face a new problem: the imminent prospect that Britain will have too many supermarkets.

As a result, the major chains are looking for new markets that will sustain their growth. They are expanding into non-food areas again — and thinking in terms of providing what they call a 'total shopping environment'. They are increasingly moving towards the American approach of clustering a growing range of shopping, leisure and other services under the same roof, including dry cleaning, banking services, coffee shops, opticians and hairdressers. The aim will be to increase both the time and the money that we spend in supermarkets.

Like the dinosaurs before them, the big supermarket chains are getting bigger by the day. Five of them — Sainsbury's, Tesco, Asda, Argyll (which owns Safeway) and Gateway — now control over 60 per cent of all grocery spending. As they open scores of new stores and buy up smaller chains, the forecast is that by the year 2000 the top four chains alone will control nearly 70 per cent of the market. The Gateway take-over in July 1989 was a symptom of the escalating pressures in this area.

Each year, the competition intensifies as the major supermarkets recognise that quality is often now at least as important as price in selling products. They are all trying to attract better-off customers by improving the range and quality of the goods they offer, and by freshening up their images and brightening their in-store environments. Since the early 1980s, when Tesco decided to move up-market, all the top ranking supermarket chains have been involved in 'trading up'. They are showing much more interest in what individual groups of consumers — including Green Consumers — say they want.

Going Green

The big supermarket chains are desperately looking for new ways to make themselves stand out from the crowd. One way in which they are beginning to feel that they can gain an edge on their competitors is to show they understand, and are responding to, environmental concerns. Even companies which are less keen on the environment are being left with little option but to 'go green'.

In the late 1960s and early 1970s, it is worth recalling, the environment was already high on the agenda. So why has it taken so long for the supermarkets to begin to recognise the environmental challenge?

The main reason is that supermarkets have always said that their business was to supply what the customer demanded; they could only respond to environmental issues if their customers asked them to. Until recently, clearly, most consumers were simply unaware of the ways in which their shopping habits affected the environment. But now they are waking up to the scale of the challenge and the supermarkets are having to respond to changing patterns of demand in very short order. Environmentalists, too, are waking up to the massive leverage that green consumerism can give them in getting prompt action from industry.

Over the years, a succession of crises has helped wake up supermarket groups to the need for change. The first was the *energy crisis* of the early 1970s. The supermarkets responded by initiating the energy efficiency programmes described later on in the Supermarket Survey. Some of them have made major progress in this area.

The second crisis revolved around the *healthier eating trend*. Although consumer interest in health foods had been growing since the early 1970s, it really began to take off in the early

1980s. The supermarkets found that they were having to move very rapidly indeed to meet the demand for healthier, additive-free food and drink.

The third crisis, which hit the industry full blast in 1988, was the *environmental crisis*. Like the captain of the *Titanic*, the supermarkets had been given plenty of warning about the dangers, but had chosen to ignore them. Remember what happened with aerosols. When, as a result of a Friends of the Earth campaign, eight of the largest aerosol manufacturers announced they would phase out CFC propellants by the end of 1989, supermarkets suddenly realised they were moving into a market where the consumer would be able to choose between products on the basis of their environmental performance. This was new and uncomfortable territory.

Green in the Fast Lane

Looking back, it is clear that the success of the health food and get-additives-out-of-our-food campaigns helped open up a fast track for green issues. Publication of *The Green Consumer Guide* alongside Green Consumer Week made sure that a broad range of such issues roared on to that track. Indeed, the fact that two major supermarket groups — **Safeway** and **Tesco** — came in as sponsors of the launch of Green Consumer Week demonstrated their recognition that the world was changing.

Even so, Safeway and Tesco were completely taken aback by the pace at which events began to move. The media interest provided convincing evidence that new threats, and new opportunities, were emerging.

Safeway had been the first supermarket to stock organic food, but now others were following suit. A new generation of green products began to appear on the shelves. Environment-friendlier detergents and washing powders were stocked for the first time by **Sainsbury's** during the Week.

Even though the underlying trend must by now have been clear to many people in the industry, Tesco shook the supermarket sector in January 1989 when it announced an across-the-board plan to 'go green'. Four years to the day after it had launched its revolutionary Healthy Eating Campaign, Tesco stole a march on the competition with its 'Tesco Cares' campaign.

The Green Filter

'People understand the issues even more than they did the healthy eating issues,' explained Dr Richard Pugh, Tesco's Technical Director — and the man responsible for championing the company's new green strategy. Ranked third among the supermarkets in *The Green Consumer Guide*, after Safeway and Sainsbury's who shared the top slot, Tesco had decided it was not going to take that rating lying down. Everything the company does, buys or sells, Dr Pugh announced, will now be put under the 'green filter'.

As Tesco's competitors began to recognise the threat to their own business, with the green message appealing to exactly those customers whom all the leading supermarkets are now trying to attract, a spate of announcements and product launches followed.

Listen to Sainsbury's: 'Our trading philosophy is always to offer our customers the products they want, together with the best means of identifying them,' Joe Barnes, the group's joint Managing Director, told the press. 'Sainsbury's is renowned for its ability to respond swiftly to new trends and changing customer needs. Indeed, we have been doing so for some considerable time in this area and were given top rating among supermarketing companies in *The Green Consumer Guide*.' By early 1989, Sainsbury's were not only stocking growing numbers of green products, but also making sure that the consumer spotted them, by using special shelf-edge tickets.

The number of new lines that will be launched in the 1990s is enormous. Safeway alone are talking of the need to find 2,000 new products over the next couple of years. If as many as possible of these products are going to be environment-friendly, Green Consumers must keep up the pressure — not only in Britain but across Europe.

Nevertheless, the challenge we face in persuading the

supermarkets to green their entire product range should not be underestimated. One immediate way in which supermarkets can get to grips with this challenge is to carry out an 'environmental audit'. This may involve reviewing the performance of:

- suppliers, including growers, food processors and manufacturers

- warehousing, transport and other distribution operations

- store management, including energy efficiency measures

- all products stocked in any of the company's stores

- waste management and recycling operations.

The supermarkets can also help wake up the public to the importance of environmental issues generally. Are the green products made accessible and attractive, or are they consigned to a back shelf somewhere? Are the staff well informed about environmental issues — and about what shoppers can do to help? If not, they should be. Are there leaflets explaining the benefits of healthier eating, organic food, green consumer products and recycling? If not, ask whether they might be provided. There may also be potential for joint promotions with national or local groups such as Oxfam, the World Wide Fund for Nature, Friends of the Earth, CLEAR, Greenpeace or the Soil Association.

Most supermarkets are never going to be as innovative as specialist green shops. For the best service, seek out good health food stores and other green shops. The choice is constantly expanding. **The Land and Food Company**, for example, plans to open a chain of green supermarkets based on organically run farms. (See page 113.)

But the majority of shoppers will still frequent the big supermarkets. The first chains to launch green campaigns enjoyed a honeymoon period with environmentalists and the Green Consumer. Longer term, however, the pace of events in this field will be so intense that even top performers will have to look to their laurels if they are to gain — let alone maintain — the No. 1 slot in the green supermarket stakes.

Costing the Earth 1989

Most of the things we buy in the supermarket affect — either through their production or their use — the major environmental problems of today. While we will be analysing the implications of individual items in later chapters, we are giving here a brief resumé of the issues and the ways in which they relate to supermarket shopping. In some cases — the first hole in the ozone layer, the Greenhouse Effect, acid rain — the issues have been well aired elsewhere and so we will concentrate on current trends. In other cases — perhaps where circumstances are changing rapidly or where they are less often reported — we feel that a fuller explanation is necessary. For further background information consult pages 7–35 of *The Green Consumer Guide.*

The Disappearing Ozone Layer

While the thinning of the earth's protective ozone layer, most starkly illustrated by the discovery of the Antarctic 'ozone hole', has certainly been a dominating topic over the last eighteen months, the 'Saving the Ozone Layer' conference held in

London early in 1989 brought the key issues into much sharper focus. The EEC announced that it would seek to ban the use of all chlorofluorocarbons (CFCs) — the family of chemicals responsible for thinning the ozone layer — by the end of the century, though many environmentalists argued that the ban should come into force even faster. Although CFCs are at last being removed from most of the aerosols sold in Britain, they are still used in fridges, some plastics and the industrial solvents used for cleaning microchips. China, with more than 1 billion people, plans to supply every home with a fridge by the year 2000. The *Financial Times* has warned that 'the simple act of providing a refrigerator for every Chinese family could blow another mighty hole in the ozone layer.'

The supermarket connection

CFC-containing aerosols have long been top-sellers through supermarkets. And the supermarkets have also been using CFCs in refrigeration and air-conditioning plants and as foam-blowing agents for spongey plastic packaging used in meat, fruit and vegetable trays. The **Co-op** was the first supermarket chain to drop CFC-containing aerosols, but now the spotlight has inevitably moved on to packaging and refrigerants.

The Greenhouse Effect

This proved to be one of the key issues of 1989. It should not, incidentally, be confused with ozone depletion. Although incoming solar radiation and CFCs are involved in both, the problems are different. The earth's atmosphere acts like an insulating blanket around the planet, trapping some of the solar radiation reflected from the earth's surface — like a greenhouse. But increased discharges of certain gases mean that too much heat is being trapped and as a result the world is getting steadily warmer. This could lead to dramatic changes in climate and weather patterns and we may already have seen the first major results: severe droughts in the American mid-west and in China; record low temperatures in Alaska, the Lebanon and Jordan;

exceptionally mild winters in Western Europe, Scandinavia and the Soviet Union; and the highest rainfall in years in Australia. Future possibilities include the melting of the polar ice-caps, resulting in the flooding of low-lying cities like London, Bristol and Liverpool; more typhoons in India and Bangladesh; droughts in areas that were previously fertile; and intense rainfall in areas where the soils may be subject to erosion.

Living in the Greenhouse will not necessarily mean that Britain will bask in a Mediterranean climate. More likely, our weather will become even cloudier and rare events like the 1987 hurricane could become more frequent.

The main 'greenhouse gases' are carbon dioxide and nitrogen oxides (both produced by combustion processes, be they power station boilers, car engines or the burning of tropical rainforests); CFCs, each molecule of which turns out to be 10,000 times worse in terms of the Greenhouse Effect than carbon dioxide; and methane, or 'marsh gas'. Methane may be particularly important in the long term: not only does it have a powerful greenhouse impact, but it is produced by a wide range of sources — from rice paddies in Asia to flatulent sheep in Australia!

The supermarket connection

There are a number of ways in which supermarkets can help to reduce the emissions of greenhouse gases:

- by placing a much higher priority on energy efficiency in all manufacturing, warehousing, distribution and retailing

- by getting CFCs out of all their own-brand products and ensuring that manufacturers do likewise

- by moving to more ozone-friendly refrigerants in refrigeration and air-conditioning systems

- by providing recycling schemes for glass, paper, cans and plastics to promote material and energy conservation.

Tropical Deforestation

The loss of forests and woodlands around the world is one of the most profoundly worrying environmental trends, but the rapid destruction of the equatorial rainforests is now seen as particularly alarming.

Rainforests are one of the natural reservoirs which soak up excess carbon dioxide, storing it in trees, vegetation and soil. However, the burning of these rainforests means that they now produce more carbon dioxide than they absorb. Friends of the Earth estimate that 3 billion tonnes of carbon dioxide are pumped into the atmosphere each year from burning rainforests. Indeed, Brazil is now responsible for more than 10 per cent of world carbon dioxide emissions — more than the USA!

Apart from such global effects, rainforest destruction alters local rainfall patterns, accelerates soil erosion and flooding of rivers affected by the resulting silt, and threatens millions of species with extinction. Over half the world's species are found in the rainforests, which represent an extraordinarily valuable treasury of ecological and genetic diversity. As the rainforests disappear, so do the prospects of finding new crops, new foods and new medicines.

Many countries are to blame for what is happening. Japan alone, with one-fortieth of the world's population, now consumes 40 per cent of tropical timber exports. Some countries, however, are waking up to the threat: Indonesia and Thailand have already begun to impose controls on their logging industries.

The supermarket connection

If you see tropical hardwoods used or sold in your local supermarket (or any other shop), there is a direct link with tropical deforestation. But most of the connections are harder to spot. For example, the land left after rainforests have been cleared or thinned may be used for plantations growing cacao (used to make chocolate), coffee or palm oil, all of which find their way into a wide range of food products. Even though these plantations do not directly *cause* tropical deforestation they do act as a further economic incentive for the clearing of rainforests. Check through our listing on page 122 of some meat products which originate in countries that do not enforce strict controls on the clearing of rainforest for cattle ranching.

One of the few products on the supermarket shelves which will have come direct from an unspoilt rainforest is the brazil nut. Unlike the oil palm or rubber tree, the brazil nut has so far proved impossible to grow in plantations. So it is harvested in the wild and is thus both a product and a symbol of a healthy rainforest. From Autumn 1989, **Safeway** will be labelling its brazil nuts as 'rainforest-friendly'.

Acid Rain

Acid rain has become one of the most important issues in Europe, Scandinavia and North America. Power stations, factories and motor exhausts all produce chemical pollutants such as sulphur compounds and oxides of nitrogen. These combine with moisture in the atmosphere to form 'acid rain' which attacks plants (most obviously trees) and either washes valuable nutrients out of the soil, or locks them up. Whole forests can become sickly and die. In lakes and rivers, acid rain helps accelerate the leaching out of poisonous metals, like aluminium, which harm fish and other wildlife. The algae die, leaving the lakes sparkling clear — but dead.

Although attention has tended to focus on power stations as producers of acid rain, car exhaust fumes are an increasingly important part of the problem. European cities like Athens, Berlin and Paris, even London, are periodically wreathed in photochemical smogs.

Britain is the main acid rain polluter of Ireland and Norway, according to UN research. We contribute over 40 per cent of the sulphur pollution that falls on southern Norway and over 35 per cent the nitrogen pollution. Five thousand square miles of Norwegian lakes are now so polluted that they cannot support fish life. And we also contribute more to pollution levels in Denmark, Holland and even Switzerland than such countries receive from their own sources.

By 1993, if present trends continue, Britain should have achieved a 30 per cent reduction in sulphur dioxide emissions. But we could still be producing as much sulphur dioxide as France, West Germany, Sweden, Denmark, Norway, Austria, Switzerland, Luxembourg and the Netherlands put together!

The supermarket connection

Supermarkets are major users of energy, whether for manufacturing, distribution, heating, air conditioning, refrigeration, lighting or waste disposal. By locating on out-of-town sites, they also encourage — even force — customers to drive further afield to do their shopping, producing in the process more exhaust fumes and encouraging urban sprawl.

Water Pollution

The privatisation of Britain's water industry has put the state of the country's rivers firmly into the media spotlight. The picture that is developing in front of our eyes is alarming.

Sometimes, dramatic incidents bring the quality of our drinking water to public attention. In July 1988, 20 tonnes of aluminium sulphate were mistakenly poured into 300,000 gallons of purified water at South West Water's Lowermoor treatment plant, near Camelford. Water intended for 20,000 consumers was found to contain aluminium levels 6,000 times higher than EEC standards permit. Hundreds of consumers complained of sickness — and in some cases people's hair turned green!

But we do not need water authorities to add pollutants to the water they supply: in many cases the pollutants are already there because of widespread environmental contamination. We are polluting streams, rivers, lakes and the seas around our coasts.

The 1980s saw a rapid decline in the quality of our rivers for the first time since the 1950s. The number of reported pollution incidents rose from 12,500 in 1980–81 to 23,253 in 1987–88.

At least 10 per cent of our 27,500 miles of rivers and estuaries are so dirty and devoid of oxygen that they are unable to support fish. One in five sewage works is breaking the law by discharging sub-standard effluents into rivers. In 1988 alone, over 4,000 pollution incidents were caused by sewage.

Millions of consumers are drinking water containing unacceptably high levels of lead, nitrates, pesticides, aluminium sulphate, polycyclic aromatic hydrocarbons (PAHs) and other toxins. The Department of the Environment admitted that many water authorities will be unable to comply with EEC drinking water standards until 1995 at the earliest.

Intensive agriculture is also causing increasing problems. Undiluted farm slurry from intensive livestock operations is up to 100 times more polluting than untreated sewage. Silage liquor is up to 200 times stronger. And pollution incidents caused by farmers are increasing: in 1988, they were up 6 per cent on the 1987 figure. Farm pollution was responsible for 19 per cent of all water pollution incidents.

A much broader scale pollution is caused by artificial fertilisers and pesticides. By 1986, 1.3 million tonnes of nitrogen were being used nationally in fertilisers, double the figure 20 years ago. Fertiliser and sewage also contribute to phosphate build-up. The result: a 'toxic time-bomb' of chemicals is building up in groundwater sources, particularly in arable farming areas. In 1989, the Government admitted that almost 300 water sources were contaminated with pesticides and was promptly sued by the European Commission for breaching EEC drinking water standards.

The threat to our seas was dramatically demonstrated when an Indonesian vessel sank near Guernsey in March 1989. It was carrying containers of the pesticides lindane, cypermethrin and permethrin. The French Navy was soon hunting for a 40 ft container holding six tonnes of highly toxic lindane which went missing. Greenpeace talked in terms of a potential 'marine Chernobyl'.

While industry disputes such claims, the pressures on the marine environment are illustrated by what has been happening in Scandinavia. Chronic pollution helped to trigger several maritime plagues during 1988, including wholesale seal deaths due to a virus and an invasion of poisonous algae, which fed on agricultural pollutants in the water.

Marine pollution is not a remote problem. One in three bathing beaches in England, Wales and Northern Ireland are officially designated as dirty and unsafe because the sewage in the water exceeds standards set by the EEC.

Trends in marine pollution are causing growing concern around the world. Despite the *Exxon Valdez* oil disaster in Alaska, the pollution of our seas and oceans is generally a case of 'out of sight, out of mind'. But the message is finally beginning to get through: magazines around the world have been publishing cover stories on the theme of 'Our Dying Oceans'.

The supermarket connection

Many products that you buy from supermarkets can cause water pollution, from detergents, washing powders and bleaches to disposable nappies and loo paper. The food you buy may also have helped pollute our rivers and lakes. Pesticides and fertiliser run-off from intensive farms combines with the extraordinarily strong effluents produced by livestock units, used to raise animals which are turned into everything from veal to sausages.

Waste

Waste is unavoidable in any society, but the Consumer Society has outdone anything that came before. Whether we are unwrapping a biscuit packet or removing the packaging from a new stereo, each of us produces an ever-increasing volume of waste each year.

The problems of what to do with waste are moving towards the top of the political agenda. Waste in the wrong place causes pollution. Finding enough holes (industry calls them 'landfill sites') in which to dump our refuse is also becoming increasingly difficult. Incineration makes a good deal of sense for many hazardous materials, but incineration companies have still to persuade the public that their plants are sufficiently safe.

Waste is also an issue because so much of what we throw into holes in the ground is, in environmental terms, precious. The amount of non-renewable mineral resources available to us is constantly falling as we consume the more accessible deposits. To spend a tremendous amount of energy processing such resources and then to fail to re-use and recycle them makes no sense at all.

The litter in our streets is only the tip of a dirty iceberg. The tide of waste is sweeping around the world, reaching even to the upper slopes of Mount Everest. Toxic waste ships scour the oceans looking for somewhere to dump cargoes which no one wants, except for a few Third World countries for whom a bit of foreign currency in the hand is worth risking the death of the bush and any birds or beasts in it.

With over 50 million Britons, and around 100 times as many people now living on the planet as a whole, we simply cannot go on living in this way.

The average Briton throws away about ten times his or her own body weight in household refuse every year. The national total is around 20 million tonnes — and the trend is ever-upward. At the same time, other forms of waste, particularly the toxic wastes produced by many industrial processes, are likely to become top priority issues in the 1990s.

The Government has been fiercely criticised for the way Britain's landfill sites are run. A potentially deadly cocktail of domestic, commercial and industrial waste has been allowed to mix in almost 5,000 landfill sites around the country. As many as 1,400 rubbish tips could contain potentially dangerous quantities of explosive methane gas. Over half are close to housing. And the methane they produce contributes to the greenhouse effect: as a greenhouse gas, methane is 30 times more powerful than carbon dioxide.

A key Conservative-dominated House of Commons committee has described the current system of toxic waste controls as 'appalling', with unqualified officers left in charge at a time when waste imports to Britain have soared to over 180,000 tonnes a year, compared to just 5,000 tonnes in the early 1980s.

The supermarket connection

The supermarkets' role in fuelling the Waste Society has been clear since the late 1960s. In the early 1970s, the Conservation Society, one of the most effective environmental lobbying organisations of the day, put the spotlight on 'excessive and environmentally undesirable' forms of packaging. We were advised to: refuse paper bags whenever they were unnecessary; remove packaging and leave it in the shop; stick to returnable bottles — and complain bitterly when we could not find them on the shelves; and buy products in bulk.

The Conservation Society pointed out that, at the time, 7.5 billion paper bags were being thrown away every year. To make a ton of paper, it noted, industry needed 17 full-grown trees and 60,000 gallons of water, in addition to producing 275 pounds of sulphur pollution by burning fossil fuels.

Nowadays, the advice given to the Green Consumer is somewhat different, as later chapters explain, but the basic thrust of the argument is the same. What has changed is not only the scale of our problems, but the sheer volume of supermarket products that contribute to Britain's waste stream — and the extraordinary diversity of materials used, particularly in packaging (see Chapter 4).

The Disappearing Countryside

As more people spend more time in the open countryside or along Britain's coastlines, many of them are becoming alarmed about what they see there and the way in which our rural landscapes are disappearing.

By the mid-1980s, 95 per cent of Britain's lowland grasslands and herb-rich meadows lacked any significant wildlife interest, with only 3 per cent unaffected by agricultural 'improvement'. Something like 40 per cent of lowland heath had been destroyed, mostly by agricultural conversion, afforestation or buildings.

Somewhere between a third and half of all Britain's ancient

woodlands had been lost since the end of the Second World War, often replaced by conifer plantations. And the rate at which we have lost hedgerows, which were vital to the survival of many forms of wildlife, simply beggars the imagination. They have been lost at the rate of 4,000 miles a year since the early 1980s.

Many farmers and foresters argue that the loss of traditional farmscapes, and of the wildlife they harbour, is unavoidable. It is the price-tag, they say, on a world where our supermarket shelves are packed with a great diversity of affordable food and other goods. But growing numbers of people are sceptical.

The construction of reservoirs to supply our increasing demand for water is a less obvious way in which our consumer lifestyles place pressure on the countryside. We must be made more aware of the water efficiency of washing machines and dishwashers, for example. Industry, too, must change. Making one pint of beer can take over eight pints of water.

The supermarket connection

The supermarkets have eaten into Green Belt areas and developed a growing number of green field sites in recent years. And it is not simply a question of where supermarket developers want to go, but also of the size of what they want to build. The growth of the out-of-town supermarket and hypermarket has put intense pressure on inner-city and other urban stores. 'The small supermarket is an endangered species,' says David Sainsbury of the £3 billion supermarket empire.

Equally, the insistence of most supermarket buyers on a standard size, shape and unblemished quality of fruit and vegetables has been one of the pressures on the further intensification of farming. The trend towards organic food is a welcome step in the direction of a cleaner, greener countryside.

Endangered Species

No one knows how many species there are on Earth. A total of around 1.4 million have been identified to date. More than half of them are insects, while there are 250,000 plants and 41,000 vertebrates. The global total may be as few as three million or more than 30 million. The wide range is accounted for by the recent finding that a single tree in the tropical forest can house more than 1,000 beetle species unknown to science.

As the world's 'green belt' of tropical forests is destroyed, so the pace of species extinction accelerates. Many of the species that become extinct as a result will remain unknown to science. Nor is species extinction confined to the more exotic parts of the globe. The spread of cities, motorways and intensive farming methods have resulted in major species and habitat losses in Britain.

As the world's human population doubles over the next 50 or so years, the pressures will intensify even further. Future generations, who will inherit a biologically impoverished planet, will wonder why we let it happen.

The growing world demand for food and other products is helping to put pressure on threatened ecosystems like the tropical rainforests. Because of this rainforest destruction, 20 per cent of the 5 – 10 million species now known are likely to be extinct by the year 2000 — and in 50 years more than half will be gone if present rates of extinction continue.

The world we are creating is a world in which all sorts of familiar animals will be pushed aside, or over the precipice that leads to extinction. Among the animals we have lost from Britain are the beaver and the wild boar. More recently, modern farming methods have helped cut the numbers of the common frog in half over the last 30 years. And as field sizes have expanded and hedges have been stripped out, there has been a 70 per cent drop in the numbers of barn owls.

The supermarket connection

On occasion, new supermarket developments have cut into the habitat of rare or threatened species. Some of the products on your supermarket's shelves, particularly those produced by intensive farming methods, have also helped push threatened species towards the brink of extinction. Nor is it simply a question of the threat to the fish that ends up in your can, for example. Overfishing can threaten other animals — like seals, whales, dolphins or birds — that feed on the hunted species.

The supermarkets are basically concerned to get a product on to their shelves at a price which is equal to or less than their competitors'. The fact that hundreds of thousands of dolphins are drowned when tuna fish are caught by net could be of little interest to many supermarket executives — unless we ensure that they cannot ignore the issue.

Animal Welfare

Animal welfare is an important issue for the Green Consumer. Different policies are pursued by a variety of campaigning organisations, ranging from the Animal Liberation Front (ALF) — who are willing to break the law to bring animal abuse to an end — to the Fund for the Replacement of Animals in Medical Experiments (FRAME), who work with major manufacturing companies to develop alternatives to animal testing.

To ensure product safety, some form of animal testing will probably always be needed. However, a great deal can still be done to cut the number of animals used — and to improve conditions where animals are tested in properly managed programmes. Interestingly, the most important trend in the £2 billion-a-year cosmetics and toiletries market is the rapid growth of 'cruelty-free' cosmetics — worth an estimated £40 million in 1988. These are generally products that contain no animal ingredients and are not tested on laboratory animals. (See pages 203 – 5.)

The supermarket connection

Whether you are buying meat, poultry or eggs, animal welfare issues are rarely far away. Happily, supermarkets are increasingly interested in stocking free-range poultry and eggs, and are taking their first tentative steps towards hormone-free 'real meat'.

At the same time, however, many of the products stocked and sold by supermarkets are still tested on animals. Among the products and ingredients regularly tested are household chemicals, cosmetics and toiletries, and food additives. A growing number of manufacturers and retailers are now beginning to label products as 'cruelty-free'. Check what they mean by the phrase. Does it mean that there are no animal ingredients in the product? That the active ingredients have not been tested on animals? Or that the whole product has not been tested in this way?

SUPERMARKET POLICIES

Many of the environmental problems discussed in this chapter are affected by the way that supermarket groups run their businesses. We now look at seven main areas in which they affect the quality of our natural environment — and at some of the ways in which they can help to provide and promote environmental quality.

The first two areas relate to the trends in the size of supermarket developments and to the location of new stores, the third and fourth to how they are run, and the final three to what they offer to their customers.

Access and Transport

Trends and Problems
A number of basic trends are conspiring to make supermarket developments highly controversial.

Supermarkets are getting bigger. In 1971, the average size of British supermarkets was 8,000 sq ft. 1988, by contrast, saw the first 115,000 sq ft superstore, big enough to house aircraft carrier *Ark Royal* one and a half times over.

Doctors have even identified a new disease — a panic reaction which they say can strike shoppers confronted with the milling crowds and miles of shelves typical of the new hangar-sized supermarkets. Even more worrying, many smaller stores are being pushed into closure or bankruptcy.

Most supermarket designers put much more emphasis on the inside of a store than on the outside. As a result, many turn a blank concrete and glass face to the world. The growing scale of most supermarket developments simply aggravates this problem — and makes it more likely that green field sites will be used.

The larger supermarkets become, the more likely it is that they will seek out-of-town sites and build extensive car parking areas. Meadows and streams will be paved over and long-established trees felled to clear the way for our shopping trolleys.

Although out-of-town sites may help reduce inner city traffic congestion, they tend to serve customers who own cars, rather than those who depend on public transport. The area of land they consume is increased by the sheer scale of the car parks they need. And they often weaken already enfeebled inner city areas.

The trend towards larger supermarket and hypermarket complexes has spurred the trend away from rail transport to the heavy lorries which have become such an obtrusive and dangerous feature on our roads and in our villages, towns and cities.

Supermarket solutions

The basic trends driving supermarket development are so powerful that it is difficult to imagine how we might turn the clock back completely. But supermarket developers should certainly consider the following:

- Building on inner city or run-down sites, with underground car parks if necessary, instead of putting green field sites under concrete.

- Where out-of-town sites are used, public transport links should be developed. To cut the area of land used, car parks and other facilities may need to be put underground here too.

- Wherever possible, rail rather than road should be used for distribution.

- Where road vehicles are used, they should be converted to run on unleaded fuel if possible. The next step is to consider whether the vehicles can be fitted with catalytic converters, to cut the amounts of carbon monoxide, nitrogen oxides and unburnt hydrocarbons that they emit. Diesel vehicles may also increasingly need to be fitted with catalytic converters.

- Planners should do more to ensure that mature trees and other landscape features are preserved. If possible, extensive planting programmes should be undertaken, both to help blend the new development with its surroundings and to provide new wildlife habitats. 'Creative conservation', which produces new habitats for wildlife, is now becoming well established.

Energy

Trends and Problems

There are two enormous problems with our energy resources: first, there are only limited supplies and we are running through them at an unsustainable rate; and, second, every form of energy production has an environmental impact of one sort or another.

The impact of future pollution problems such as the Greenhouse Effect or acid rain will be determined by the mix of energy supply technologies we end up using.

World supplies of oil, at present the most popular fuel, are likely to be severely depleted within 30 years and though there may be enough coal in Britain to last another two or three hundred years, its extraction causes considerable environmental problems. Furthermore, when burned, coal is the worst contributor to acid rain and to the Greenhouse Effect.

Even so, nuclear power remains the least popular energy technology with environmentalists and with the public. Not the least of its problems is the safe disposal of radioactive waste.

Renewable energy also has its problems. Because it is more diffuse than that found in fossil fuels or in uranium, the facilities needed to capture the energy tend to be more extensive. A solar installation able to produce as much energy as a nuclear reactor, for example, might take up to 20 square kilometres (5,000 acres), compared to about half a square kilometre (150 acres) needed for a nuclear plant.

In short, there is no such thing as a totally 'green' source of energy. Some may pose less of a problem as far as acid rain or carbon dioxide build-up are concerned, but any form of energy supply will damage the environment. So the less energy we use, the better.

Supermarket solutions

The most important thing supermarkets can do in this area is to give energy efficiency top priority. Supermarkets are much more aware of the need for energy efficiency than they were, but it often ranks well behind customer convenience and the sheer pressure of keeping the store stocked and ship-shape.

Despite the 'oil shocks' of the 1970s, the general thrust in this sector has been towards styles of development — such as out-of-town superstores — which are tailored more to volume selling and easy car parking than they are to energy efficiency. The supermarkets are relatively large energy consumers, so we should expect them to take the lead in promoting energy efficiency.

So what can you do personally to cut the amount of energy you use while shopping and consuming?

- Shop locally wherever possible.

- Ask your local supermarket what it is doing to improve its energy efficiency.

- Buy in bulk if you shop by car, to minimise the number of trips you have to make and to reduce the amount of packaging used.

- Buy products that save energy, whether it be light bulbs or washing powder.

- Ask for energy-efficient products if they are not on your supermarket's shelves.

- Recycle waste material wherever possible: this saves much of the energy used in the initial manufacturing of new products.

Green Products

Trends and Problems

If supermarkets are to play a genuinely constructive role in the green movement, they will need to move beyond bland statements of intent. Even major conservation sponsorship programmes are only part of the answer. Increasingly, Britain's supermarkets will need to integrate environmental thinking into the heart of their development planning, day-to-day management, purchasing, staff training, customer information, public relations and waste management activities.

The main problems in this area revolve around determining exactly what sort of product is 'environment-friendly' or 'environment-friendlier' at any stage of the game. Can a mercury-free battery be described as 'green' if it takes up to 50 times as much energy to make a battery as you ever get out of it? The supermarkets are having to wrestle with these issues — and the answers are not always straightforward.

Consumers, too, often find that the information they are given is contradictory, whereas what they want is a combination of convenience and clear selling-messages for green products. While supermarkets have tended to view green products as premium items, which can bear a higher price than competing goods, most consumers want to find such products easily — and do not want to spend more money on them if they can possibly help it. The supermarkets have an enormously important role to play in ensuring that green products are as 'green' as they can be, are properly distributed, cost-competitive, attractively presented and convenient to use.

Supermarket solutions

Where supermarkets can be persuaded to turn into Green Purchasers, they can have a dramatic impact on growers, manufacturers and other suppliers. Manufacturers, for example, find it relatively easy to ward off new legislation, or at least to adapt to it over an extended time period. But when the message comes through from the market that environment-friendly products are in demand, things can move very much faster.

Where a given supermarket supplies own-label products, things can move even more quickly. The importance of own-label products is indicated by the fact that when **Tesco** announced its plans to go green, own-label products accounted for £2 billion of its £5 billion annual turnover. And a recent Euromonitor research survey showed that nearly half of **Sainsbury's** customers 'always choose own brands where there's a choice'. No longer is this simply a matter of relative cheapness: own-label products are increasingly seen as competitive in quality, too. Since supermarkets can directly specify the performance of own-label products, their ability to 'green' them quickly is that much greater.

Tesco was the first supermarket chain to announce that it would be passing all its policies, products and activities under a 'green filter'. And the potential for green pressures to influence new product development, whether in terms of supermarkets' own-label lines or of nationally known brands, is clearly very considerable indeed.

Once a given supermarket has managed to get more environment-friendly products on to its shelves, it is then faced with the question of whether it should develop a 'green stripe' through its advertising and other promotional activities. More and more, supermarkets are recognising that growing consumer awareness of environmental problems and issues means that well-produced and honest green advertising campaigns can pay real dividends.

Packaging and Recycling
(See also pages 41 – 63)

Trends and Problems

One of the ironies of the greening of Britain's supermarkets has been the sight of green products or produce, for example organic fruit and vegetables, presented in environmentally unacceptable types or quantities of packaging.

Despite their growing contribution to Britain's waste disposal problems, the major supermarket groups have been very slow indeed to accept that they have any responsibility for recycling and other forms of environmental protection. With the advent of the Green Consumer, however, they have changed their minds in short order. The performance of the major supermarket groups is covered in detail in Chapter 5.

Supermarket solutions

The 1990s will see mounting pressures on both retailers and manufacturers to use packaging materials more sparingly and more intelligently. As in so many areas of 'green design', the aim must be to 'do more with less'. At the same time, manufacturers should look at the opportunities for re-usable packaging, such as the refillable containers now used for fabric conditioners in West Germany.

On the recycling front, there are a number of key obstacles which get in the way of supermarket recycling programmes. The first is the attitude, frequently found among supermarket executives, that recycling 'is none of our business'. That may have been the consensus in the 1970s, but it simply will not do in the 1990s.

Health

Trends and Problems

There are many direct and indirect links between the quality of our environment and the health of consumers. In most cases, a better environment leads to improved health. Organic food, to take just one case, is both healthier for you and healthier for the environment. Sometimes, however, environment-friendly solutions may raise a number of issues in relation to human health. Cut back too far on packaging, for example, and you may end up with higher levels of food contamination. So it is essential that health and environmental issues should be considered in tandem.

The scares about salmonella in eggs and listeria in cheeses emphasised the fact that those who undertake to produce, prepare, cook and pack food products on our behalf simply cannot be too careful. Bacteria are prolific breeders: in half a day a single bacterium can generate 7 billion offspring. A number of studies, including one by the Public Health Laboratory Service, have shown that a significant proportion of prepared, cook-chill products are contaminated by listeria.

Nor is it simply a question of contamination. Many food and drink products currently sold by supermarkets are scarcely designed to provide a healthy diet. Instead, they are intended to meet the dictates of price, convenience or fashion.

Mercifully, however, the so-called fads of a small minority of 'health food freaks' triggered widespread changes in the nation's diet in the 1980s. Concerns about traditional high-fat, low-fibre diets, for example, led to an enormous increase in consumption of brown bread and reductions in consumption of white bread, eggs, red meat and butter. The average Briton now eats half the white bread and only a third of the butter that he or she would have eaten in 1961.

The growth of the health food business initially took place outside the supermarket sector. The number of health food stores grew from 850 in 1978 to 1,500 by 1986, with turnover almost quadrupling to £200 million over that same period. Not surprisingly the supermarkets decided they wanted a share of the action. The healthier eating trend, launched in the supermarket sector by **Tesco** four years before it announced its plans to go green, has had a considerable impact, but wander around any supermarket and you can still see an enormous amount of 'junk food'.

Supermarket solutions

The salmonella and listeria scares underscored the deep-seated concerns many people have about what is in their food. Environmental issues have the potential to cause similar concerns, as they have in the United States. To defuse such pressures, supermarkets will have to learn to sell environmental quality as well as product quality and customer convenience.

Those supermarkets that are sincerely interested in going green already recognise the strong links between healthier eating and many environmental issues. The Green Consumer looks for supermarkets that recognise the need for a quality environment, both inside and outside the store.

The major supermarkets can do a great deal to promote healthier, green diets.

- Does your supermarket offer information sheets and brochures on how to find, prepare and cook healthier food?

- Does it test food for chemical residues?

- Does it stock organic produce? If not, does it plan to do so?

Farming

Trends and Problems

Much of the farming industry is now effectively 'programmed' by what your supermarket decides to stock. Some of the impacts of intensive farming methods have already been described. If your supermarket simply orders cheap products without taking an interest in how they are produced, the chances are that we will end up with cheap, low quality farmscapes and industrial landscapes.

Supermarket solutions

If, on the other hand, supermarkets order more organic produce, this is an important boost for farmers who are working hard to produce quality food without contaminating the environment with chemicals. And, if supermarket buyers decide to stock free-range eggs, they send out a signal to battery hen farmers that providing their birds with better conditions could well mean increased profits.

Organic farmers do not use artificial fertilisers, synthetic pesticides or feed additives. They concentrate instead on building up healthy soils by using compost, animal manures and crop rotations. Plants grown organically are better able to resist disease — which crop rotations also help to discourage. Foods grown organically are not only healthier for you, the consumer, but are also healthier for the land.

Ten years ago, you could only find organically grown produce in a small number of health food stores, but the organic sector has made astonishing progress in recent years. No longer is it seen as the preserve of 'cranks'. Supermarkets are now competing to break into the market. Even **Marks & Spencer**, which scored a very low rating in *The Green Consumer Guide* partly because it did not stock organic produce, decided to do so from the spring of 1989.

Unfortunately, the word 'organic' on a food label can mean different things to different people. This variability in standards has been a major problem for genuinely organic producers and for consumers. The 1980s saw a growing range of partially competing symbols, as illustrated below:

- The **Soil Association** symbol is the most widely recognised and is awarded to producers who do not allow the use of synthetic fertilisers, pesticides, growth regulators, antibiotics, growth stimulants or intensive livestock operations.

- **Organic Farmers and Growers** combines a marketing role with standard-setting and inspection. Standards are more permissive than the Soil Association's. It has a second label, 'In Transition to Organically Grown', for those growers who have embarked on the process of weaning their land from chemical inputs — which takes a minimum of two years.

- The **Organic Growers Association** helps members switch to organic growing, and encourages them to apply for eventual Soil Association membership.

- Companies like **Jordans** produce a range of 'organic' and 'conservation grade' products, the latter denoting membership of the **Guild of Conservation Food Producers**, which allows the use of fertiliser compounds containing ground rock phosphate and potash.

The new UK Register of Organic Food Standards (UKROFS), based on a voluntary code of practice, has been introduced by the Government to ensure that we move towards a single scheme and label. The UKROFS label is shown below:

If this section has whetted your appetite for organic foods, you may want to buy a copy of Alan Gear's *New Organic Food Guide* (Dent, 1987). It lists suppliers of organic foods, from small producers with a little surplus produce for sale to large 1,000 acre farms, and from wholefood shops to supermarkets.

Third World Issues

Trends and Problems
Third World countries are likely to be hardest hit by many of the key environmental issues discussed earlier. These are among the most difficult problems for the supermarkets to tackle, but it is important that they take responsibility for the way the produce and products they sell are grown or manufactured in poorer countries.

Quite apart from a sense of global responsibility, the way natural resources are exploited in the Third World has direct implications for all of us. Whether we want bananas or fish, the abuse of pesticides in the developing countries can boomerang on us, with chemicals banned here turning up in foods imported from the Third World. Cash crops grown in Third World countries to earn foreign currency can displace local farmers, forcing them on to more erosion-prone soils or slopes.

Ultimately, soil erosion may undermine not only the environment in such countries, but also their economies. It is increasingly clear that such trends can lead to political extremism as the competition for shrinking natural resources grows — and they may threaten to damage Third World economies to the extent where they are even less able to afford our exports.

Supermarket solutions

The results of our supermarket survey suggest that some supermarkets are beginning to wake up to the impact on the Third World of what they do and buy. While there may be little they can do directly to help tackle problems such as tropical deforestation, their power as Green Purchasers should not be underestimated.

At the same time, environmental sponsorship links offer an extraordinarily powerful way both of attracting the Green Consumer and injecting much-needed funds into conservation and sustainable development projects in the Third World.

Unwrapping the Packaging Issue

Every single day of the year, Britain produces enough domestic rubbish to fill Trafalgar Square up to the top of Nelson's Column. Each year, the average British family throws away over one tonne of waste. There are around 21.5 million households in the UK, and among the things each throws out in the course of a year are, on average:

- waste paper equivalent to six trees, or 156 kg of waste paper per person

- 32 kg of metals

- over 510 cans, of which 300 are food or pet food cans

- 47 kg of plastics

- 74 kg of glass

- 45.5 kg of food.

In the United States, the problem is even worse. Each year, Americans produce enough domestic refuse to fill a convoy of 10-tonne garbage trucks 145,000 miles long, more than half way to the moon.

The fact is that at least 30 per cent (by weight) of the domestic waste each of us produces is made up of packaging materials. If you consider waste by volume, packaging is likely to be even more significant. Most of the food we eat comes out of some sort of pack, whether it's a packet of cornflakes, a can of beans, a frozen pizza, a bag of potatoes or a pot of cream. And many of the non-food products we buy come wrapped in layers of paper, foil or plastic films and foams.

According to INCPEN (Industry Committee for Packaging and the Environment), the weekly shopping done by the average household is packed in 1.6 kg of glass, 1 kg of plastics, 2.4 kg of paper and board and 0.7 kg of metals.

As the volume of packaging waste that each of us produces grows, so do litter problems and so do the problems of finding enough holes around the countryside to put all the rubbish in. The question of what to do with domestic refuse is becoming an increasingly pressing environmental issue in most industrial countries. As a result, some of the more far-sighted people in the packaging industry are beginning to think about ways in which re-use, recycling or reclamation for heat-from-waste schemes can be promoted.

One thing is indisputable: packaging plays a vital role in our supermarkets. It helps to preserve and protect food and drink, ensure hygiene, cut food spoilage, and identify quality standards, helping consumer choice. The issue is not so much whether we need packaging — we do — as which packaging materials we decide to use and how we use them.

In choosing packaging materials it is worth remembering that their production can directly or indirectly damage the environment during: the initial extraction or harvesting of raw materials; processing (for example, the energy which produces all metal, glass and plastics packaging used in Britain amounts to about 2 per cent of total national energy consumption); transport to the production plant and thence to the packager, retailer and purchaser; consumer use; and disposal.

Sadly, we are behind many other countries in dealing with the environmental implications of packaging. In West Germany, for example, this is now considered to be a top management issue. Many companies are committed to cutting down on the resources used in packaging, maintaining existing returnable systems, creating recycling systems and highlighting environmentally unfriendly packaging.

Since 1970, Sweden has had a tax on non-returnable beverage containers — although the main reason for introducing the tax was to finance a freeze on food prices. When aluminium cans were introduced a voluntary recycling scheme was set up, now replaced by a deposit scheme.

The political pressure is building even in southern Europe. In Italy, over 200 communities have banned the use of plastic bags. Also under pressure are plastic plates, containers and other disposable items. Following court action, Italian industry is now required to move towards fast biodegradability or workable recovery and recycling systems.

Increasingly, industry needs to design for re-usability or recyclability from the outset. In the States, **Pillsbury** actively encourages the re-use of its microwavable dish — and sells cake mixes without the baking dish for those consumers who already have a suitable container.

On the recycling front, it is crazy that Britain imports recycled Scandinavian newspapers and broken glass from Europe because our own recycling initiatives cannot produce enough! Even Leeds City Council, a pioneer in recycling, so far recovers only around 2 per cent of its rubbish. Friends of the Earth calculate that it costs £720 million a year to dispose of Britain's waste and that £750 million worth of reclaimable materials are discarded in Britain during the same period. But the Government's Warren Spring Laboratory also estimates that it could cost at least £1.5 billion to collect and clean all these materials.

Recycling is desirable, clearly, but we have a very long way to go before we can 'close the loop' on most materials. So what can the consumer do?

Green Consumer *action points*

- Avoid products that are over-packaged. Often the manufacturer will add packaging to make the product look more appealing or better value.

- Search out products that are packaged in more environment-friendly materials. Unfortunately, there is no totally environment-friendly packaging material. Check through our material profiles to see how different packaging materials contribute to different environmental problems — and which are the best alternatives for particular products.

- Re-use or recycle every material you possibly can. If no recycling facilities are available, ask your local council and supermarkets to provide them.

PACKAGING PROFILES

Paper and Cardboard

Issues: On average, every one of us consumes at least two trees' worth of paper and board every year. Some 90 million trees are cut down each year to meet UK demand for paper and board: only 10.7 per cent comes from home-grown trees.

Pulp and paper production are generally highly polluting and energy-intensive activities. Indeed, the paper and board industry is one of the most energy-intensive in the UK. Paper and board are manufactured by mixing cellulose fibres in a very large amount of water. The initial mix would be typically one part fibre to 99 parts water, a high proportion of which is then removed. Some is extracted by mechanical means or by gravity; the greater part is dried off by heat.

However, paper is a highly convenient material for many types of packaging. The Tetra-Pak, for example, used to hold many liquid products, is light, easy to pack tightly in large quantities and therefore economical in transport costs. Many cartons, though, are made from a mixture of foil, plastics and paper and cannot be recycled.

White paper products were in the media spotlight during 1989 following concern about the chlorine bleaching process used in their production. Not only were people worried that dioxins left in the paper might leach into foods, or cause health problems when used in hygiene products like tampons (unnecessarily, as it turned out. See page 202), but there was also the danger of dioxins and other toxic effluents being discharged into rivers. Recycled paper products are not totally innocent in this respect, but that is still no reason for not buying them.

Re-use: This is not generally an option with paper products. But it *is* often worth re-using cardboard boxes.

Recycling: Between 40 and 50 per cent energy savings can be made if paper is produced from waste paper rather than virgin pulp. Waste paper accounts for about half of the total materials now used by the UK paper and board industry, but only around 30 per cent of the paper and board we use in the UK goes on to be recycled.

Any given wood fibre can be recycled a number of times, but it tends to get shorter every time, thereby weakening the paper. Recycled paper products can be of high quality and range from stationery, paper towels and loo paper through to egg boxes and newspapers. However, at a time when most newspapers have increased in size, it is worrying that less than 20 per cent of household newspapers and magazines are recycled. It is particularly difficult to find people who can recycle your magazines.

Biodegradability: Although paper products generally break down in the environment, it is worth remembering that one way scientists can tell the age of landfills they dig up is by reading the newspapers they find there. Most of the papers are quite readable 20 to 30 years later. Another fly in the ointment is the discovery that paper is a major contributor to the methane gas which seeps from landfill sites — itself a major contributor to the Greenhouse Effect (see Chapter 3).

PACKAGING MATERIALS

Packaging material	Re-usable?	Recyclable?	Recycled in the UK?	Biode-gradable?
Single-trip glass bottle	◆	Yes	Yes	No
Regularly re-usable glass bottle e.g. milk or beer	Yes	Yes	Yes	No
Paper bag	*	Yes	*	Yes
Recycled paper bag	**	Yes	**	Yes
Plastic bag	Yes	Yes	No	No
Biodegradable plastic bag	††	No	No	††
Tetra-Pak carton	No	No	No	○
Aluminium can	No	Yes	Yes	No
Tin-plate can	No	Yes	Yes	No
PET bottle	○○	Yes	○○	No

Energy-efficient to produce?	Energy-efficient to transport?	Resource efficient?	Pollution issues
No	No	Yes	Glass production involves a degree of air pollution.
Yes (if re-used	No	Yes	The benefits of a re-usable bottle only apply if it **is** re-used. Bottle-cleaning can produce high strength effluents.
*	Yes	*	Pollution from pulp mills and bleaching processes is a problem.
**	Yes	Yes	Less energy needed in production and less pollution than with bags made from virgin pulp, although bleaching process still used.
Yes	Yes	†	The petrochemical industry is polluting, but it is also efficient at producing a large volume of product from any given petroleum feedstock.
††	Yes	††	Technology for biodegradable plastics is poorly developed.
○	Yes	○	Tetra-Pak have been particularly assiduous in investigating possible pollution problems and have taken the issues seriously for a number of years.
No	□	No	Bauxite mining and aluminium smelting can be an environmental problem.
△	Yes	△	Smelters and recycling plants can cause pollution.
Yes	Yes	Yes	Litter and recycling problems

Continued overleaf

PACKAGING MATERIALS (continued)

Packaging material	Re-usable?	Recyclable?	Recycled in the UK?	Biodegradable?
PVC bottle	●	Yes	No	No

◆ **Single-use glass bottle**   Glass bottles become a much more efficient form of packaging if they are re-used or recycled. Single-use glass bottles are obviously not designed for repeated use and you are not encouraged to return them to the supplier. They are resource-efficient because they are made from sand and limestone, which are readily available — but do not fare so well under the transport heading because they are heavy, bulky and fragile. These factors compromise their overall energy-efficiency.

Re-usable glass bottle   Glass bottles which are typically re-used are milk bottles and beer bottles. They are usually heavier than one-trip bottles but become energy-efficient if re-used a number of times.

* **Paper bag**   Paper bags are re-usable, but only in a limited way because they are not very sturdy. They are recyclable, but this is not generally done in the UK where collections for paper are scarce and not directed at all types of paper. While the energy used in their production is less than, say, an aluminium can, it is more than a plastic bag. Although wood is a renewable resource, paper cannot be considered to be resource-efficient. The quantity of trees we need to satisfy our paper demand is immense and the harvesting methods used by the forest products industry have caused concern.

** **Recycled paper bag**   Only re-usable in a limited way but preferable to a paper bag made of virgin pulp because it uses less energy in its production. Often presented as more environment-friendly than plastic bags. It is as well to note, however, that it is not as energy-efficient to produce as plastic bags. It is also bulkier, but is biodegradable, which is a considerable asset in environmental terms.

† **Plastic bag**   Plastic bags are not liked by environmentalists. Although they fare well in energy terms, their chief problem is that they are not biodegradable and in many cases are used unnecessarily. A shopping bag would be a better option. The petrochemical industry does make a large amount of plastic in relation to the amount of petroleum used so plastic is quite efficient in that respect — but remember that petroleum is not a renewable resource.

†† **Biodegradable plastic bag**   This might seem the perfect solution to the problem of plastics, but there are discrepancies. It is not as durable as an ordinary plastic bag and so has less potential for re-use. It also takes more energy to produce. The technology for biodegradable plastics is, as yet, poorly developed. This means that, although it breaks down it still leaves remnants in the ground which may be damaging. Although there are improved versions, they are prohibitively expensive for most supermarket-related uses.

Energy-efficient to produce?	Energy-efficient to transport?	Resource efficient?	Pollution issues
Yes	Yes	Yes	Can contribute – in a small way – to acid rain and dioxin contamination if burnt in poorly operated incinerators.

○ **Tetra-Pak**   While this performs quite well in terms of energy efficiency, it is probably not as good as, say, the returnable glass bottle. On the other hand, if used Paks are burnt, energy can be extracted from the process, making it a useful energy-from-waste fuel. But as this is not practised yet in this country a main benefit of this form of packaging is wasted. It is only partially biodegradable but is light and easy to transport.

☐ **Aluminium can**   Producing aluminium is a very energy-intensive business. This does mean that recycling aluminium cans is particularly worthwhile — making an aluminium can from scratch uses 95% more energy than making it from recycled aluminium. **British Alcan** have announced plans to set up a can recycling plant and will be encouraging greater recycling of aluminium cans. To tell if a can is aluminium or not, simply put a magnet against it — if the magnet will not 'stick' it is aluminium. The alumimium can gets a low rating for transport because of the distance its raw material, bauxite, has to travel. It is also worth recalling that the mining of bauxite from which aluminium comes has been implicated in causing problems with tropical deforestation.

△ **Tin-plate cans**   Most food cans and 50% of drinks cans are made from tin-plate. They can be recycled through can banks, like aluminium cans, although because less energy is needed to make the cans in the first place, energy-savings are less from recycling. But you still save around 95% of the energy used to make a tin-plate can. Tin, however, is a metal in short supply and pollution from tin-smelters can be a problem.

○○ **PET bottles**   Plastic bottles are not generally re-usable although in Germany, **Procter and Gamble**'s *Lenor* fabric conditioner comes in a plastic bottle that you can re-fill from sachets. It is possible to recycle most plastics, but there is a problem in identifying the many different types. PET is likely to be the first type of plastic to be recycled in the UK. It is most commonly used for soft drinks and already some supermarkets have started labelling their PET soft drinks bottles to identify the type of plastic. This sort of labelling encourages the plastics industry to start recycling facilities because it shows that the problem of identification could be overcome with retailer and manufacturer co-operation.

● **PVC bottles**   These are not generally re-usable. See also page 56.

ENERGY USED IN DIFFERENT FORMS OF PACKAGING

Material and volume	Energy used in producing one container (megajoules*)	Average amount of energy used (megajoules)	Average energy use per 1 litre of product packed (megajoules)
PET bottle (1 litre)	13 – 19	16	16
Glass bottle, non-refillable (1 litre)	20 – 26	23	23
Glass bottle, refillable (1 litre)	30 – 40	35	35
Tinplate can with aluminium end (330 ml)	6 – 9	7.5	23
All-aluminium drinks can (330 ml)	10 – 13	11.5	35

* 1 megajoule = 1 million joules, a measure of energy.

Source: Industry Council for Packaging and the Environment (Incpen); SustainAbility

NOTE: These figures show that the energy used to produce a PET bottle is much less than that of the refillable glass bottle or of the three aluminium cans needed to pack the same volume. But the energy used to make a refillable bottle ensures that it is strong enough to stand up to a multi-trip life, during which it provides a much better return on the materials — and energy — invested in it.

Unfortunately for the consumer, no single packaging material stands out as extremely environment-friendly. The acceptability of different materials depends to a considerable degree on the extent to which they are recycled. On this basis, choose glass in favour of plastics and aluminium — but make sure you put bottles in the bottle bank and keep an eye out for developments in plastics and aluminium recycling.

Glass

Issues: Some 6 billion glass bottles and jars are used every year in Britain, and over 1.5 million tonnes of waste glass are produced. Glass-making has always been an energy-intensive business, with 50 – 80 therms used for each tonne of glass, depending on the size of furnace. And it can have a considerable environmental impact. It takes a total of 1.1 tonnes of sand, limestone and soda ash to make 1 tonne of glass, as well as a great deal of energy and water.

Re-use: The returnable bottle is a highly environment-friendly form of packaging, as long as the bottle *is* returned. Milk bottles are re-used an average of 20 times, although some may be re-used as many as 40 or 50 times. Supermarkets and off-licences generally discourage returnable bottles, however, because they take up valuable space.

Recycling: Unlike materials such as paper, glass can effectively be recycled forever. At the moment only 14 per cent of all glass used in the UK is recycled. Every tonne of crushed glass (or 'cullet') used saves the equivalent of 30 gallons (135 litres) of oil and 1.2 tonnes of raw materials, representing a 25 per cent saving. Over 1.45 million tonnes of glass have been recycled in UK bottle banks over the last 10 years. Unfortunately, though, Britain still lags a long way behind much of the rest of Europe.

In Switzerland and the Netherlands, for example, there is one bottle bank for every 2,000 people. Here there are plans to boost UK bottle banks to one for every 10,000 people by 1991, just 20 per cent of the Swiss and Dutch figures, instead of the current situation of 1 for every 17,000.

Biodegradability: As any archaeologist will tell you, glass doesn't biodegrade. It's also dangerous to children, pets and wildlife if left around in the open environment.

Cans

Issues: More than 9 billion food, pet food and drink cans are bought every year, with most homes using about ten cans every week. Some 5.5 billion drinks cans are used each year in the UK. 4 billion cans are used for food and pet food, while 2 billion are used for paint and other goods — a total of over 11 billion cans. Placed end to end, just the drink cans would reach the moon. More prosaically, cans make up about 6 per cent of the rubbish in your dustbin — and 10 per cent by weight.

The main materials in cans are steel and tin (used to make tinplate) and aluminium. Metal production is energy-intensive and can be highly polluting, as well as environmentally damaging. For example, it takes 4 tonnes of bauxite to make 1 tonne of aluminium. However 'lightweighting', which involves cutting the amount of material used to make a product or its packaging, has already come a fair way in can production. Since 1957 there has been a 30 per cent reduction in the body plate thickness of soup and bean cans, and the tin coatings are now 50 per cent thinner.

Re-use: Not really an option.

Recycling: Other than lightweighting, this is the most important way in which the use of metal containers can be made environmentally acceptable. All cans could be recycled, but less than 2 per cent are. If you recycle aluminium, you save 95 per cent of the energy that would be used to make the metal from bauxite. However, aluminium recycling schemes have had a poor record to date; they prove viable only when the scrap value of aluminium is high.

The most successful can recycling scheme to date has been Save-a-Can, launched by can makers in 1982. By 1987, there were over 180 can banks in over 60 towns and cities, usually sited in supermarket or municipal car parks. These banks take any type of can, with the sorting done later. **British Steel** aims to be using 100,000 tonnes a year of burnt steel cans by 1990 – 91. A more recent initiative was launched in 1989 by the Aluminium Can Recovery Association. They are encouraging people to take all waste aluminium to their local official recovery centre and will pay a small amount of money per kilo collected.

In 1986, the European Aluminium Sheet Makers sponsored a recycling trial in combination with a number of **Safeway** stores in the Birmingham area, using reverse vending machines (where you 'post' a used can into a machine and are credited with a small amount of money). Although it provided good public relations value, Safeway dropped the project because it felt it didn't fit in with the store's image as a fresh food supermarket, handling clean, fresh merchandise in hygienic conditions. Among the firms active in this area — which will be increasingly important — are **Rockware Reclamation** and **Tomra**. The evidence suggests that recycling will only take off with concerted government action. The opening up of the Single European Market from 1992 may help boost our limited recycling efforts.

Biodegradability: Metals are not biodegradable to any great extent. Some metals are very long-lived (e.g. some alloys and aluminium), others rust away, eventually. When we lose metals to rust, we also lose the energy that went into making them. So, wherever possible, they should be recycled.

Plastics

Issues: Around 36 per cent of the packaging we use in the UK is made up of plastics. They also account for about 5 – 7 per cent, by weight, of all the domestic refuse we produce. A *Fairy Liquid* bottle weighs some 35 grams, while a large plastic bag weighs 15 grams. US evidence suggests that 20 – 30 per cent of landfill volume is accounted for by plastics. And the trend is towards greater use of plastics in packaging.

There are over 50 main types of plastic, based on raw materials such as oil, natural gas, coal and salt. Some plastics are more environment-friendly than others. Among the more common plastics you will find on our supermarket shelves are the following:

Plastic	Typical products	Environmental factors
Cellophane	Wrapping on cigarette packs	Made from cellulose, the most abundant plant material. Biodegrades fairly easily. Is being replaced by polypropylene, a stronger plastic.

Plastic	Typical products	Environmental factors
Polythene or **low density polyethylene (LDPE)**	Bags, sacks, bin liners, squeezable detergent bottles. Keeps produce fresh by allowing it to 'breathe'. Used by manufacturers of many 'green' detergents.	Around 50,000 tonnes of polyethylene film (or 10 per cent of UK production) are recovered each year to make products such as builders' sheeting and black refuse bags. The British Plastics Federation is organising the recovery of LDPE bottles as part of the UK 2000/FoE Recycling City project in Sheffield.
High density polyethylene (HDPE)	Bottles for pharmaceuticals, disinfectants, milk and fruit juice, bottle caps, closures	At least 2,500 tonnes of HDPE are recycled every year, mainly from processors' scrap and used bottle crates. Also being recovered in the Sheffield Recycling City project.
Polypropylene	Tubs for margarine and salads, bottle caps and closures, film wrappings for biscuits and crisps, microwave trays for ready-made meals, clear jars for pickled onions	At least 25,000 tonnes of polypropylene are recycled annually, or about 7 per cent of UK production.
Polystyrene	Yoghurt pots, clear egg packs, bottle caps, lids, closures	Polystyrene can be recycled to make injection-moulded products, including recycled versions of the original products, or new products, such as flower pots.
Foamed polystyrene	Food trays, egg boxes, fresh produce cartons, disposable cups, protective packaging for electronic equipment	Most recycling firms only take solid polystyrene, not foamed. Watch out for use of CFCs as foaming agents — although very few products now found in supermarkets contain CFC foaming agents. Some foamed polystyrene seed trays and plant pot holders sold in the high street are made from recycled materials.
Acrylonitrile Butadiene Styrene (ABS)	Lids, tubs for salads and margarine, electrical appliances, protective helmets	Most ABS is used in long-life automotive and electrical or electronic appliances, the most familiar being telephones. Around 2.5 million ABS telephones are recycled every year.

Plastic	Typical products	Environmental factors
Polyvinyl chloride (PVC)	Food trays, lids, cake and sandwich packs, bottles for fruit squash, mineral waters, body care products, shampoo, household cleaners, DIY blister packs, credit cards	See Box, pages 56–7.
Polyethylene terephthalate (PET)	Fizzy drinks bottles, ovenable ready meal trays	Often seen as the most environment-friendly plastic, perfect for recycling. But PET recycling schemes have been very slow to take off in the UK. The British Soft Drinks Association is collecting PET bottles as part of the Sheffield Recycling City project.

PET has been showing rapid growth. European PET consumption is expected to double by the early 1990s. 1.2 billion PET bottles were sold in 1987, representing 60,000 tonnes of plastic, with the result that £60 million of PET alone ended up in our dustbins that year! With PET recycling embryonic, where it exists at all, the result is a great deal of PET in the environment. By 1988, some 5 billion PET bottles had already been dumped in landfill sites in Britain alone. PET has the potential to be a relatively environment-friendly plastic, provided recycling schemes can be got off the ground.

Interestingly, plastic may on occasion be more environment-friendly than paper! West Germany's Federal Office of the Environment (Umweltbundesamt or UBA) has concluded that carrier bags made from *polyethylene* are less harmful to the environment than paper bags. The UBA took into account the input of raw materials and energy, damage to the environment during manufacture and waste management, and the potential for recycling.

Another issue which has been taxing the plastics industry revolves around the environmental impact of the CFCs used as blowing agents during the manufacture of many foamed

IS THERE A FUTURE FOR PVC?

At a time when energy efficiency is assuming rapidly growing importance, perhaps we should be looking again at PVC. It turns out to be the most energy-efficient plastic to produce. So, for example, it takes seven times as much energy to make a cast iron pipe as it does to make the same pipe out of PVC — and the PVC pipe will last a great deal longer.

Also on the plus side, discarded PVC is fairly easy to identify when it is mixed up with other rubbish. (Its chlorine content can be detected by chemical analysis.) PVC is therefore particularly suitable for recycling. The Soft Drinks Association is now collecting PVC bottles as part of the Sheffield Recycling City project. Currently, this is the only PVC recycling scheme in the country.

Of all the plastics we use, however, PVC has been under the greatest environmental pressure in recent years. Initially the concern was that vinyl chloride monomer (VCM), the basic material from which PVC is made, can cause cancer. It is worth pointing out, though, that nowadays the VCM stage of the PVC manufacturing process is completely enclosed, to protect worker health, while PVC itself does not pose a cancer risk.

More recently, the spotlight has shifted to the possibility that burning PVC in domestic waste incinerators can produce hydrochloric acid air pollution which could help cause acid rain. This last possibility has been a particular worry in countries like Switzerland and West Germany, where acid rain is a major issue and a higher proportion of domestic waste is incinerated.

Although Swedish research suggests that burning PVC in a well-run incinerator can be done perfectly safely, many UK manufacturers and retailers are now nervous about using PVC in their products or in packaging. As a result, growing numbers are switching to other plastics in environmentally sensitive applications.

Despite all these concerns, the use of PVC in packaging continues to grow. And, while we would not like to bet on it, the new interest in energy efficiency means that it is at least on the cards that the 1990s will see PVC resurrected as an 'environment-friendly' material. But if it is ever to have a chance of being represented in this way, PVC will need to be recycled — rather than being burned or landfilled — in very much larger quantities than is currently the case.

plastics. The foam plastics industry has been a significant user of CFCs. In 1976, it accounted for 17 per cent of EEC consumption of CFCs -11 and -12, which have the greatest ozone depletion effect, a figure which had risen to 33 per cent by 1985. Foam plastics have many applications, including building construction, food packaging, vehicles, refrigeration and furniture. But at least most supermarkets have abandoned the use of CFC-containing polystyrene, the spongey plastic used in some egg cartons, meat trays and the 'clam cup' insulators that keep hamburgers and other fast foods warm. Some, however, have switched to CFC-22, which is only one-twentieth as ozone-depleting as the original CFCs. This is a step in the right direction but means that these supermarkets still have some way to go.

By no means finally, some plastics, particularly those coloured orange or yellow, may contain cadmium pigments. Being heavy metals, these are ecologically undesirable. Over the last five years, the UK plastics industry has voluntarily made substantial reductions in its use of cadmium pigments and stabilisers. Virtually no cadmium pigments are now found in food packaging and very few items found in the supermarket today contain such pigments in their packets. The use of cadmium stabilisers is mainly confined to outdoor applications.

Re-use: Plastic's long life is inappropriate for most of the throwaway products made from it, although some plastic products can be re-used. An interesting pointer to the future is the 'cruelty-free' soap called *Puressa*, made by the **House of Bentley**. It is sold in a transparent plastic pack which can be re-used as a soap dish. Although most homes have a limited need for soap dishes, the idea might usefully be applied elsewhere.

Recycling: There are 30 different types of plastic in daily use. These fall into two broad groups: the thermoplastics (used in bottles, wrapping film and other forms of packaging), which can be recycled, and thermosetting plastics (used in plugs, sockets and toys, and in the handles of kettles and saucepans), which cannot.

Although the plastic processing industry recycles around 99 per cent of the plastic waste it generates in the factory, very little plastic is recycled after the consumer has used it in the UK. The voluntary PET-A-BOX scheme, launched in 1981, was abandoned in 1987. This was partly because too much PVC turned up in the reclaimed plastic, and partly because no market was found for the reclaimed PET.

One problem for recyclers is that plastics, while light, are bulky, although compaction equipment is now being introduced in countries like Italy. Another problem is that it has often been impossible for consumers to identify particular plastics. **Tesco** showed how easily this problem can be overcome when it started labelling the various plastics it uses for packaging in 1989. The **Co-op** has followed suit.

In Germany, a new law will force companies to provide arrangements for recycling through retail outlets and pay up to 50 pfennigs (16p) per returned bottle, as they already do with most glass bottles. **Coca-Cola** protested that the regulation was neither ecologically nor economically justified and that the law was adopting the wrong approach to the problem. Coca-Cola has subsequently taken the lead in promoting the establishment of a European recycling association. Some manufacturers are now pulling out of plastic bottles, rather than accepting the deposit approach.

While it may be inappropriate to use recycled plastics to package soft drinks, in the States **Procter & Gamble** recently started selling the liquid version of one of its leading cleaner brands in recycled plastic bottles. The growing pressure on such companies is indicated by the ban due to come into force in Minneapolis by mid-1990, which will prohibit all grocery and restaurant food packaging that is not biodegradable, returnable or capable of being collected for recycling.

In Britain, all eyes will be on Sheffield, now dubbed 'Recycling City', where the British Plastics Federation, the soft drinks industry, UK 2000 and Friends of the Earth are collaborating on a plastics recycling project, involving both plastic-bottle banks and door-to-door collections.

Biodegradability: Conventional plastics are composed of repeating hydrocarbon molecules, called polymers, which are derived from petroleum. These polymer chains are too long for microbes to eat, which is what makes plastics so resistant to decay. There are three main forms of degradability in plastics:

Photodegradation relies on ultraviolet light from the sun to break down the structure of the material. So photodegradable materials take longer to break down in Norway than, say, in the south of France.

Biodegradation involves the breaking down of and consumption of materials by bacteria and other living organisms. Plastics are often highly resistant to biodegradation and even if they do biodegrade, the speed of the process depends on environmental conditions such as moisture, temperature, acidity and the availability of nutrients needed by the bacteria.

Biodegradable plastic typically costs about 15 per cent more than conventional plastics. US manufacturers report interest from companies making refuse bags, disposable nappies and cosmetics. ICI, which uses a soil microbe to produce *Biopol*, a biodegradable natural polymer, says it has had 'terrific unsolicited interest in the material from all areas of plastics uses'. But Biopol, the scientific name of which is polyhydroxybutyrate (PHB), costs around $15 a pound, compared to 65c per pound for conventional plastics. A good deal more work is clearly needed.

Biodestruction means that the process results in smaller clumps of polymer which may persist in the soil. If they are described as 'biodegradable', it should mean that they break down completely into water, carbon dioxide and other harmless materials. Unfortunately, some decomposing plastics produce chemicals that can contaminate groundwater.

Overall, while degradable plastics will certainly find some important applications, the consensus is now that recycling is the best way forward.

WHAT YOU CAN DO

1 Don't litter.

2 Wash and return all returnable bottles, e.g. milk bottles and deposit bottles.

3 Recycle all other glass bottles in your local bottle banks.

4 If there is no bottle bank nearby, ask your local authority — or supermarket — to provide one.

5 Squash cans and put them in the local can bank.

6 Save ring pulls and clean aluminium foil for local charities, e.g. Oxfam.

7 When buying products, take great care to avoid over-packaging.

8 Don't discard plastics in the environment — apart from the litter problems, they can kill wildlife. Plastic wrappers and six-pack plastic rings can suffocate or strangle fish and birds. If you are disposing of a six-pack ring, cut all the rings before throwing it away.

9 Save all degradable rubbish for composting in the garden, if you have one.

10 Join or start a local recycling or clean-up group.

11 Attempt to use re-usable packages wherever possible.

12 Use recycled paper products at home and work. Suggest that your employer reviews the way waste materials are handled — and the opportunities for using recycled materials.

WHAT MANUFACTURERS AND RETAILERS CAN DO

1 Cut over-packaging and choose raw materials to ensure that products and packaging can be recycled.
2 Wherever possible, use single materials, rather than mixing materials — which complicates recycling.

3 Label products and packs to show the content of recycled materials and to inform the consumer on the best way of recycling the product or pack.

4 Promote recycling by installing bottle banks, can banks, paper banks and other suitable facilities.

5 Provide customer education information on recycling and resource issues at all stores.

WHAT GOVERNMENT CAN DO

Green Consumers can do a great deal to tackle the packaging problem, including helping to persuade retailers to become Green Purchasers by swinging in behind the campaign to cut down on packaging and boost recycling. But the failure of a number of the recycling schemes launched with much fanfare by major retailers suggests that Government action is also essential.

The following is an initial checklist of the actions the Government should now take:

1 Introduce mandatory deposit legislation, to provide a financial incentive for recycling and reuse, coupled with kerbside collection schemes.

2 Raise the cost of landfill disposal, to encourage waste minimisation and recycling schemes.

3 Ensure that public recycling centres are easily accessible, well publicised and efficiently run.

4 Require the packing of some liquids in materials which, even though they may be more expensive, can be more readily recycled.

5 Require the packing of more liquids in glass, which is already recycled fairly effectively.

6 Require all retailers to collect re-usable materials.

7 Require planning consents for retail stores to include adequate provision for the collection of re-usable materials.

8 Increase the cost of energy in real terms, making recycling more economically viable.

9 Introduce a rebate for every tonne of waste taken out of the waste stream and used for recycling.

10 Tax the use of virgin materials.

(These suggestions are based on work done by, among others, Friends of the Earth, Gateway Foodmarkets Ltd and Sheffield City Polytechnic.)

Our 99-page questionnaire prompted an extraordinary response from the supermarkets. All were keen to reply, although **Waitrose** had difficulty in doing so because it has a policy not to answer questionnaires. Even so, they sent us a detailed letter describing some of their activities in this area, part of which is reproduced on page 98.

Our analysis has been organised under the headings listed below and the responses we publish here detail the situation at the time of the survey early in 1989. We have used the same five-star ranking system developed in *The Green Consumer Guide*, although this time we have been able to apply tighter standards. In terms of this survey, five stars represent the top rating. Heading the league-table this time are **Safeway** and **Tesco**. We would emphasise that this rating does not denote perfection, rather it means that these companies have consistently broken new ground — and recognise that this is an area that needs long-term, unrelenting commitment.

Green Consumer Guide status is an indication of how things have changed, since this was the ranking given to each supermarket in *The Green Consumer Guide* in 1988. **Safeway** and **Sainsbury's** mentioned their rating in full-page national press ads.

Introduction summarises the supermarket's scale and style of operations.

Written Environmental Policy   Most of the supermarkets have only started addressing the issue of the environment within the last year and therefore most have not yet developed a formal environmental policy statement. Such policies represent a statement of intent, directed both at employees and external audiences, including customers, consumers, environmentalists and the media. A number of supermarkets have announced their policies in the wake of our Green Supermarket Survey.

Green Field Sites and Green Belt Areas   All the supermarkets insist that they operate responsibly in this area, yet it is common knowledge that there are many out-of-town developments which involve supermarkets, including a number of green field sites. Some supermarket developers have moved wildflower meadows to new sites, to save them from destruction, but this is — at best — only a 'fire brigade' operation. Instead, wherever possible, the supermarkets should be strongly encouraged to locate on already degraded out-of-town or urban fringe sites, or in neglected inner city areas.

Transport and Cars (Transport):

1) **Public Transport Facilities**   If a supermarket is in the centre of town, public transport should already exist. For new urban fringe or out-of-town sites, however, new public transport links should be provided, to cut the number of car trips generated by such developments.

2) **Company Cars**   Most companies now have a commitment to move towards unleaded petrol. The speed at which they made this commitment is a good indicator of how seriously they are taking the environmental challenge.

3) **Rail Transport**   The Supermarket Survey revealed that almost none of the supermarkets presently use the rail system for freight transport. This is understandable, given that the railways have not been modernised to cope efficiently with the expanding need of industry. But this declining trend in the use of rail freight links is nonetheless to be deplored, since it simply adds to the desperate congestion problems on Britain's roads, to road pollution problems and to the need to build new roads.

Energy Efficiency   This is a key consideration for the Green Consumer. As far as the supermarkets are concerned, we would expect them to consider the energy implications of their locational and distribution decisions, their store operations and their product stocking policies. There is tremendous scope for energy saving in most companies, as a number of the supermarkets have already demonstrated. Indeed, the 1990s are likely to see a renewed emphasis on energy efficiency, akin to that prevailing in the early 1970s during the first OPEC oil crisis, as we wake up to the implications of energy use for such key environmental problems as acid rain and the Greenhouse Effect.

Management of Production and Distribution Sites (PDS Management)   Most of the supermarkets seem to have done little in relation to reviewing their production and distribution sites through a green lens. This would be the logical next step.

Waste Management and Recycling (Waste and Recycling):
   1) **Bottle banks** should be provided in all supermarket car-parks.
   2) **Can skips** are designed to take both aluminium and steel cans and should become as familiar as bottle banks. Again, the supermarkets have an important role to play in ensuring adequate coverage and servicing of such recycling facilities.
   3) **Bulk packaging waste**   Most supermarkets say they bale their cardboard boxes and send them to be recycled. A few also recycle the plastic wrappings used to package boxes of goods during transport. Such approaches should become standard practice in the supermarket sector. Alternatively, the idea of using plastic boxes is a good one. They can be used again and again.
   4) **Plastics recycling** is as yet in its infancy, but it must become more common in the future. The supermarkets could encourage a speedy journey towards plastics recycling by committing themselves to collection schemes as soon as they are operable.

Litter may be one of the more pressing items on the Government's environmental agenda but it would be unfair to lay the problem at the door of the supermarkets. One way they can encourage less littering is to ensure that the 'Keep Britain Tidy' symbol appears on packs. They also have a role to play in educating the public in environmental care.

Packaging   The main problem here is over-packaging. Many products on the supermarket shelves come in packets which have more than one layer of packaging — a plastic bottle in a box in a cellophane wrapper for example. The supermarkets should look at the materials used in packaging to make sure they are the best available in environmental terms. Introducing labelling to identify them would help in recycling. Waste has to be sorted to be recycled effectively and at present this has to be done by the consumer. **Tesco**'s initiative in labelling the materials used in much of the packaging on its own-label products has been enormously useful, helping consumers to identify particular plastics — a key step towards comprehensive plastics recycling.

Bags at the Checkout   All supermarkets provide plastic bags at the checkout. Indeed, it is difficult to leave any supermarket without carrying one — or several. It would be better to take your own shopping bag.

Some supermarkets provide recycled paper bags which, although bulkier, do have some advantages (see page 46). A number of supermarkets have investigated the option of biodegradable plastic bags, although the current consensus is that their use will be limited.

CFCs (chlorofluorocarbons): 1) **Aerosols**   By the end of 1989, 90 per cent of aerosols will be CFC-free. The various supermarkets switched their own-brand aerosols away from CFC propellants at different speeds. Some then went further and put a time limit for manufacturers to remove them from their aerosols.

2) **Packaging**   The foam-blown packaging used for egg-boxes and meat and vegetable trays can contain CFCs. Most of the supermarkets have changed to CFC-free packaging, but some still have packaging containing CFCs on the shelves. Many imported products have been slower to switch to CFC-free formulations.

3) **Refrigeration**   CFCs are also used as refrigerants. Unfortunately, there is a dearth of viable ozone-friendly alternatives. Ammonia, which was once used in this role, is not usually practical for supermarkets because it requires bulky equipment and is highly toxic. As a result, supermarkets are switching away from CFCs -11 and -12 (which are the most ozone depleting) to CFC-22 which is one-twentieth as depleting. This should only be an interim stage before a completely ozone-friendly option is available.

Vegetarian Range   Some of the supermarkets offer an extensive range of vegetarian products which are specifically labelled. Others feel it is up to the individual to look carefully at the ingredients and decide if the product is suitable for vegetarians.

Environmental Promotions   Supermarkets can help to improve the environment by publishing leaflets or other materials giving consumers advice on the issues and choices open to them. They can also help promote the cause by developing sponsorship links with conservation or environmental organisations. We asked in the survey what they had done to date.

Supermarket Star Rating

★ ★ ★ ★ ★   Safeway
Tesco

★ ★ ★ ★   Sainsbury's
Co-op

★ ★ ★   Iceland (incorporates Bejam)
Marks & Spencer

★ ★   Asda
Spar

★   Gateway

ASDA ★ ★

(Green Consumer Guide Status ★ ★ ★)

Number of Stores: 126

Introduction   Asda are not particularly innovative in their approach to green issues. They have responded, but are not attempting to lead the field. They say that any innovations they might achieve in this area will be imitated by their competitors quite rapidly.

In the way they responded to our survey Asda appeared to be one of the least informed about operations in the country of origin when they buy direct from suppliers. The spirit of green consumerism, of course, extends responsibility for the environmental quality of a product from harvesting or manufacturing, right through to use and disposal.

Written Environmental Policy   No

Green Field Sites/Green Belt Areas   The majority of their stores are on the edge of towns; they say they have a policy of 'no development on green field sites'.

Transport   *Public Transport Facilities*: Provide free or subsidised transport to most stores.

Company Cars: Operate a car fleet, but have not disclosed details of their policy towards unleaded fuel or said how many of their cars are able to run on it.

Rail Transport: Do not use rail transport for freight.

Energy Efficiency   Appointed an Energy Manager in 1979 and have achieved over £2m per year in energy savings since then. Heat reclaim units in stores. Have received Energy Awards.

PDS Management   Say they take into account local needs in relation to planning of their distribution. It is not clear what this means in practice.

Waste and Recycling   *Bottle Banks*: 67 stores have bottle banks (53% of stores). Claim they are a leading bottle bank operator.

Can Skips: None.

Bulk Packaging Waste: Waste cardboard from boxes is re-used by specialist operators.

Plastics Recycling: Say they would help in recycling of plastics if there were clear agreements on collection and safety. Would also use recycled plastic for containers where practicable.

Litter   No own-brand products carry the 'Keep Britain Tidy' symbol.

Packaging   Biodegradable trays and non-plasticised wrapping have been introduced. Environmental effects of packaging are under review and therefore, at the time of our survey, they did not have much to say.

Bags at Checkout: There are no recycled paper bags at the checkout in Asda stores, but this option is under review.

CFCs   *Aerosols*: All own-brand aerosols have been CFC-free since 1988. They seem to have confused the labelling of 'ozone-friendly' aerosols by introducing three different wordings: 'This product is CFC-free'; 'Ozone-friendly'; 'Contains no CFC alleged to damage ozone'.

Packaging: Some foam-blown packaging still contains CFCs. They have a policy to move to CFC-free foams, which they are trying to implement as soon as possible.

Refrigeration: Researching alternatives to CFCs.

Vegetarian Range   Say they have developed a vegetarian range, but did not supply details.

Environmental Promotions   Have never carried out any own-label on-pack promotions with environmental themes. But have worked with the Rossendale Groundwork Trust.

BEJAM *see* ICELAND

CO-OP ★ ★ ★ ★

(Green Consumer Guide Status: The Co-op was not included in the survey)

Number of Stores: 5,000

Introduction   The Co-op is structured very differently from the other supermarkets. There are 80 independent retail Co-operative Societies whose activities are extensive. They operate in retailing, manufacturing, wholesaling and banking. The Co-op is the biggest farmer in the UK and also the largest undertakers!

The questionnaire was filled in by The Co-operative Wholesale Society Ltd and The Co-operative Retail Services Ltd. They have tried where possible to include general practice. The

3,000 different Co-op brand products are available to all Co-op stores.

It was because of this complicated structure that the Co-op was not included in *The Green Consumer Guide*. It seems they may have been worth including because they have been quite progressive in many areas. As mentioned below, for example, they were the first supermarket to remove CFCs from all their aerosols.

There is no doubt that in certain areas of the Co-op organisation there is a commitment towards 'going green'. It will be interesting to see if they manage to implement fully some of their intentions throughout the company. They could play an important role in educating the consumer.

Written Environmental Policy   Yes.

'We have redefined our "product quality" policy to say that not only must Co-op Brand products look, taste, smell, perform right and be safe, wholesome and consistent — they must also have origins, raw materials, additives, and ingredients and processing methods which are environmentally sound and that neither they nor their packaging should damage our customers or the environment in any way.'

Clearly, they are setting themselves extraordinarily high standards. It will be interesting to see if they manage to achieve them.

Green Field Sites/Green Belt Areas   71 Superstores (over 25,000 square feet), including Co-op Leo stores, most of which are 'out of town'.

Co-op superstore sites are generally located on the edge of towns. They have not undertaken any superstore projects within designated green belt areas. Also claim to try and avoid the use of green field sites wherever possible. In siting new units, they try to build on established industrial estates.

Transport   *Public Transport Facilities*: Approach varies around the country, but often provide a free bus service to their stores.

Company Cars: No figure was given for the

percentage of company cars able to run on
unleaded, but Co-op say they are 'supporting the
move towards unleaded petrol' and that their
largest fleet of over 1,000 cars is being converted
to run on unleaded 'as quickly as possible'.
Because the Co-op is composed of a number of
retailing groups, they have several car fleets. We
do not have any information on whether the other
car fleets are converting to unleaded.

Rail Transport: Do not use rail transport for
freight as yet and say they are unlikely to do so
'unless British Rail provide a comprehensive
service to meet modern distribution demand.'

Energy Efficiency   Regularly review energy use and have recently
reduced electricity consumption in head office by
21%. Managed to do this partly by installing low-
energy equipment and fitments. Have also
introduced more energy-efficient lighting and
heat reclamation systems for new and refurbished
stores. Most Co-op supermarkets and superstores
incorporate energy recovery systems.

CRS (one of the Societies) have received a number
of energy-efficiency awards in their dairy, food
and non food businesses.

Comment: If Co-op can achieve the same sort of
reduction in energy use in their stores as they
have managed at their head office, this would be
a significant achievement.

PDS Management   Claim to comply with, and improve upon,
legislation for atmospheric emissions.

Waste and Recycling   *Bottle Banks:* At least 110. Actively working with
local authorities on bottle bank schemes.

Can Skips: None.

Bulk Packaging Waste: Arrangements made
locally with waste paper recycling agencies. No
mention of any recycling or re-use of plastics bulk
packaging.

Plastics Recycling: Would stock products which
come in recycled plastic containers if they were
available but say that to take this approach with
their own-label products they would need to be
convinced on performance and safety.

Litter 'Keep Britain Tidy' symbol — or another litter message — appears on Co-op soft drinks, confectionery, milk cartons and carrier bags.

Packaging Are looking at introducing packaging materials which are biodegradable, recyclable or made from recycled materials. Are taking into account, where possible, the likely impact of space, energy efficiency and waste.

Have switched their egg packs away from any sort of plastic to recycled pulp (see page 135) which — because it is not readily available in the UK — has had to be imported.

Keen to switch from PVC to PET plastics where possible (see page 55). Also supply lightweight multi-trip glass milk bottles. Re-usable bottles are one of the most environment-friendly forms of packaging. Making them lightweight saves energy too.

Labelling: Have started using the proposed EEC symbol on plastic bottles to identify which type of plastic is used. This should help make it easier to recycle plastics.

Bags at Checkout: All the Societies have the option of stocking 100% recycled paper bags, but not all of them do. The Co-op say they are planning to increase the proportion of recycled paper bags offered. They have conducted a small-scale trial with photodegradable bags and are deciding whether to stock them in the future. Their decision will depend on technical considerations, as well as consumer response.

CFCs *Aerosols*: Claim to have been the first retailer to have removed CFCs from aerosols (in August 1987). They now use only hydrocarbon propellants.

Packaging: No CFCs used in foam-blown plastic packaging.

Refrigeration: Introducing store refrigeration systems using CFC-22 into selected new stores.

Vegetarian Range They label their products 'suitable for vegetarians' if there is a possibility of doubt. Also if a product formerly contained animal fats, or if similar products contain animal fats, they use the phrase 'contains no animal fats'.

Environmental Promotions In May 1989 the Co-op launched a major campaign, fronted by David Bellamy, called 'Co-op's Campaign for the Environment'. This involved a national exhibition visiting Co-op superstores, explaining both environmental issues and what customers can do to help. The Co-op are also setting up a trial organic farm.

They have published a *Co-op Action Guide to the Environment* — and have launched a conservation park at Stoughton, near Leicester on their farmland. It is open to the public and particularly good for school children.

Among other links: Co-op breakfast cereals environmental promotion with Royal Society for Nature Conservation. There has also been fund-raising and promotional work with RSPCA, Hydestile Wildlife Hospital and World Wildlife Fund (now World Wide Fund for Nature).

NOTE: Look out for the leaflets and write to the Co-op for them if they are not easily available.

GATEWAY FOOD MARKETS LTD ★

(Green Consumer Guide Status ★ ★)

Number of Stores: 831

Introduction Gateway have been in the spotlight for City analysts in recent months but in relation to the environment they have not been hitting the headlines. The reason is not because they have ignored the key environmental issues, but because they have not achieved any firsts. They did manage, however, to gain some publicity when they announced their move away from CFCs in their own-brand aerosols at the beginning of 1989 and in proprietary brands by the end of the year. Further than that there have been few striking developments.

Written Environmental Policy   No

Say they have guidelines on most issues.

Green Field Sites/Green Belt Areas   Do develop large sites 'on the edge of green belt land'. More positively, they also operate hundreds of supermarkets in high street, urban and village locations and helped in the regeneration of Clapham Junction and Willesden Green. About 50 of their 830 stores are situated 'out of town'.

Transport   *Public Transport Facilities*: Provide transport in some situations but not in every case.

Company Cars: All company cars less than two years old are being converted to run on unleaded fuel and all replacements will be able to use it. Of the 1,600 cars in their car fleet it is not clear what proportion are already able to run on unleaded fuel.

Rail Transport: Do not use rail transport for freight.

Energy Efficiency   In 1985 they introduced night covers on freezer units and in 1987 they started recycling the heat from refrigerators to heat domestic water in stores.

PDS Management   Are developing a series of new distribution depots and say they are aware of the need to respect environmental issues.

Waste and Recycling   *Bottle Banks*: Approximately 50 bottle banks (about 6% of stores).

Can Skips: None.

Bulk Packaging Waste: Have participated in recycling their cardboard, used for boxes, but this does not seem to be an overall policy.

Plastics Recycling: Say they would be prepared to assist in the recycling of plastics if it became economically viable. At present mixed plastics are of limited value and they are dubious about the potential for using recycled plastic containers for products.

Litter   A wide range of snack products carry the 'Keep Britain Tidy' symbol on their packs.

Packaging The survey indicated that their packaging policy is not particularly progressive.

Bags at Checkout: Recycled paper bags at the checkout are under trial. They will increase their use if the trial is successful. They re-use cardboard boxes in many of their stores and they are developing a range of biodegradable plastic bags, but are finding expert advice on this subject confusing. They will, however, expand the use of biodegradable plastic if it seems appropriate.

CFCs *Aerosols*: All own-brand aerosols were CFC-free from the beginning of 1989 and all suppliers of aerosols have been told that they must remove CFCs by the end of 1989. They feel that some of their products, like hairsprays, are less effective without CFC propellants.

Packaging: All polystyrene packaging is now CFC-free.

Refrigeration: 'Changes' have been made to the handling of the CFCs used in fridges.

Vegetarian Range Say that they have a large number of products suitable for vegetarians, but do not display them as a range — except in their superstores.

Environmental Promotions Have sponsored English Heritage and Historic Scotland initiatives. They also liaise with various other groups locally and nationally 'and are increasingly seeking advice on sensitive issues'.

ICELAND FROZEN FOODS PLC ★ ★ ★ (incorporates BEJAM)

(Green Consumer Guide Status for Bejam: No stars)

Number of Stores: 450

Introduction Iceland Frozen Foods now incorporate the **Bejam** Group. They are a specialist frozen food retailer, selling mainly frozen food and a limited range of other products.

They felt their rating in *The Green Consumer Guide* was unjustified, since they were graded alongside mainstream supermarkets or superstores.

Although we should take this into consideration, we feel it is fair to compare retailers on the basis of their overall policies and performance. Iceland seem to have taken the green issue much more seriously over the last year and have been taking significant steps to improve performance.

Written Environmental Policy   No

An internal memo has been circulated, however, to all directors requesting that they 'carefully examine every aspect of their division to ensure that staff welfare and environmental issues are addressed'.

Green Field Sites/Green Belt Areas   Although they may participate in schemes once planning has been approved, say that they 'never initiate developments on green field or green belt sites'.

They have fifty 'out of town' stores which they say are normally in industrial or retail parks, rather than standing alone.

Transport   *Public Transport Facilities*: Do not provide public transport facilities.

Company Cars: 99.5% of car fleet can run on unleaded petrol. Van fleet runs on diesel.

Rail Transport: Do not use rail transport for freight.

Energy Efficiency   An energy efficiency programme was initiated in 1981 and an Energy Manager has been appointed. Won the BETA award for energy efficiency in 1986.

PDS Management   (See under **CFCs**: *Refrigeration*)

Waste and Recycling   *Bottle Banks*: None. They say their stores have limited space.

Can Skips: None. As above.

Bulk Packaging Waste: Cardboard boxes are baled and recycled.

Plastics Recycling: All polythene products are recycled into refuse sacks or burnt off (residue gases are CO_2 and water vapour). Would be prepared to assist in recycling of plastic bottles, but have limited space. Would stock products packaged in recycled plastics if safe to use.

Litter No 'Keep Britain Tidy' labels, but have sponsored litter bins.

Packaging All suppliers have been told to review packaging and they recognise the need to select packaging that is not wasteful.

Bags at Checkout: Their chain of stores called 'Wizard Wine' offers recycled paper bags at the checkout. Plan to increase the use of recycled paper bags. Have investigated biodegradable plastic bags, but decided that they are not environmentally sound. Instead they are trying to educate people to re-use bags.

CFCs *Aerosols*: Do not stock own-brand aerosols.

Packaging: All suppliers have been told to remove CFCs from the packaging they supply. Not clear on what timescale.

Refrigeration: A programme exists to extract CFCs from refrigeration systems and to recycle them. Where possible they use ammonia or CFC-22 for commercial refrigeration. Ammonia is not ozone depleting and CFC-22 is about one twentieth as harmful as the other CFCs commonly used.

NOTE: Iceland also sell domestic fridges to the public. They were the first retailer to offer to pick up your old fridge when you buy a new one and subsequently recycle the CFCs.

Vegetarian Range Provide about 20 prepared products suitable for vegetarians, but do not have them endorsed by the Vegetarian Society.

Environmental Promotions Have supported the World Wide Fund for Nature (WWF) through a promotion on ice cream packs. They mention that their chairman is a member of Greenpeace and that they have worked closely with Friends of the Earth on the ozone layer issue.

MARKS & SPENCER PLC ★ ★ ★

(Green Consumer Guide Status ★)

Number of Stores: 280

Introduction Marks & Spencer operate under the trade name *St Michael*. They are well known and established in the UK, supplying 15% of the nation's clothes and 5% of our food, with a total of 14 million people shopping in their stores every week.

We felt that Marks & Spencer came over as complacent during our research for *The Green Consumer Guide*. The gist of their response was that consumers were happy with their quality and convenience and that Marks & Spencer would only supply environmentally-friendly products if their consumers asked for it.

Since then they have appointed an adviser on environmental issues and they have recognised that environmental concerns can be an important factor in the perceived 'quality' of a product.

Marks & Spencer are not structured like a supermarket. The majority of products covered here are found in their food department, but some of the products included will come from other departments.

Written Environmental Policy No

Have written policy statements on Food Safety, Hygiene and Quality. They say they consider that the environmental quality is an aspect of the company which they 'take very seriously'. Their 'codes of practice' are confidential documents for suppliers. There is clearly scope for improvement here. Environmental issues should perhaps be considered as a separate category rather than being incorporated into mainstream quality standards.

Green Field Sites/Green Belt Areas Have no sites on green belt land or out-of-town stores; only have three edge-of-town stores. They are very much geared to High Street or town centre locations.

Transport *Public Transport Facilities*: All stores are served by public transport, because they are predominantly in the centre of towns or cities.

Company Cars: Did not provide a figure for the percentage of company cars able to run on unleaded fuel, but say that all new company cars are able to take unleaded petrol and that people who have existing company cars that can be converted are offered this service free of charge.

Rail Transport: Do not use rail transport for freight.

Energy Efficiency Claim to have saved £50 million worth of energy since 1974, and say that this is an ongoing programme.

Have received a number of Energy Efficiency Awards: in 1976 a Churchill Fellowship for Energy Conservation; in 1980 and 1981 the Energy Management Lighting Award and in 1986 the Building Services Award for Energy in Buildings.

Some of their south coast stores have solar panels on the roof to power the lighting system.

PDS Management Do not own any production sites and their distribution is handled by third parties. Say they have made considerable improvements in reducing noise in delivery vehicles, as well as in reducing emissions. This may have been before their distribution was handled by third parties. Also have a policy to replace most vehicles every 3 years. This may allow them to keep up with technical improvements but doesn't relieve the problems caused by the existing vehicles.

Waste and Recycling *Bottle Banks*: None. Say that since most of their stores are in high street locations there is no space for bottle banks. They have, however, sponsored two bottle banks near stores in Inverness and Telford.

Can Skips: None. As above.

Bulk Packaging Waste: All cardboard in stores is compacted on site and taken away to be recycled. Most food products are delivered in re-usable trays.

Plastics Recycling: Plastic coat hangers are recycled and they have started a new trial using recycled PVC plastic for display trays.
They say they would not be prepared to assist in recycling of plastic bottles. They do not consider this a priority as they have a limited range of products in this area. They are investigating the idea of using recycled plastic for containers.

Litter   The 'Keep Britain Tidy' symbol is used on the packs of their sandwiches, drinks and juices.

Packaging   The main changes so far seem to have been in relation to removing CFCs, an area in which they have been slower than most other supermarkets that we have surveyed. Over-packaging is a key issue in assessing the environmental performance of Marks & Spencer. Part of the problem is in the 'convenience' they offer with salads, where the emphasis is on 'pre-packed', 'ready-for-eating' products.

Bags at Checkout: Used to supply recycled paper bags at the checkout but do not do so any more. Explain this by saying that these bags use a lot of energy during manufacture. They say that they do have bags made of polyethylene which is photodegradable (breaks down in sunlight) but that they are not food approved.

Labelling: Do not mention that they have labelled any of their packaging to say which type of material is used.

CFCs   *Aerosols*: All aerosols produced for Marks & Spencer have been CFC-free since the beginning of 1989. It is a little unclear as to when all the aerosols on the shelves will be totally free from CFCs. They do supply some pump sprays (which are non-aerosol).

Packaging: All their packaging supplied from within the UK is CFC-free but packaging with CFCs from continental suppliers has taken longer to phase out. They anticipated that by the date of publication even the packaging supplied from outside the UK would be CFC-free.

Refrigeration: Where possible have switched to CFC-22 in refrigeration systems.

Vegetarian Range They have developed an extensive range of vegetarian products which include main meals and snacks. They carry the St Michael Vegetarian logo.

Environmental Promotions Have a policy not to carry on-pack promotion campaigns because they 'like to keep the information on their packaging to a minimum so the customer can see and read easily the ingredients list and other important information'.

They have sponsored Groundwork, the British Wildlife Appeal and British Trust for Conservation Volunteers, as well as many local initiatives.

SAFEWAY PLC ★ ★ ★ ★ ★

(Green Consumer Guide Status ★ ★ ★ ★)

Number of Stores: 221

Introduction Safeway is part of the Argyll group, which also owns both Presto and Lo-Cost. Presto is being phased out, the larger stores to be made into Safeways and the smaller ones to be Lo-Cost.

Safeway came joint first in *The Green Consumer Guide* rating. They have used this as a promotional tool since the *Guide*'s publication and have continued to improve their range of green products. They are particularly strong on organic produce — this won them the Grocer Green Award for 'Greenest own-label Product' in June 1989.

Environmental issues seem to be important to Safeway and they are responsive to approaches from manufacturers who have 'green' products to offer.

Written Environmental Policy No

Green Field Sites/Green Belt Areas They have forty 'out-of-town' stores and say they do not make planning applications on green belt sites. This leaves it unclear whether they have any stores which are situated on green field sites.

Transport   *Public Transport Facilities*: If public transport is not available to any particular store, customers must arrive by car as they do not have a policy to provide transport.

Company Cars: At the end of March 1989, 92% of their cars were able to run on unleaded fuel. Have looked at all their cars with a view to conversion and are phasing out those such as the Volvo Turbo which at the time of the survey did not take unleaded.

Rail Transport: Do not use rail transport for freight.

Energy Efficiency   Safeway have an extensive Energy Conservation Programme. They have:
- trained personnel on eliminating waste
- revised maintenance programmes to incorporate energy efficiency
- replaced or upgraded heating equipment
- halved number of lighting tubes and replaced those left with energy-efficient lamps (Estimated savings: £360,000 per annum)
- installed Energy Management Systems which have made considerable savings (Estimated savings: £12,000 per store per annum as an average)
- managed to reduce energy consumption of existing refrigeration equipment and update equipment being installed (Estimated savings: £500,000 so far)
- helped reduce country's peak demand generating problem (Estimated savings: £45,000 per annum)
- installed warm air curtains over doors (Estimated savings: £60,000 per annum).

It is quite apparent that Safeways have been attentive to the issue of energy efficiency. The company's experience shows that energy-efficiency is both environment-friendly and profitable.

PDS Management   Safeway have made detailed specifications about the use of CFCs in refrigeration, air conditioning and building. No further details about the management of these sites was supplied.

Waste and Recycling   *Bottle Banks*: 39 stores (17%) have a total of 64 bottle banks in their car-parks.

Can Skips: Have participated in an aluminium recycling trial with British Alcan, which proved unsuccessful.

Bulk Packaging Waste: Their cardboard recycling system has been operating since the 1970s, resulting in about 35,000 tonnes of cardboard for recycling. They are now developing a new system which means that packers send produce in plastic trays which will be rented out across the whole chain of supply. These trays are re-usable and therefore cut down on waste.

Plastics Recycling: Have been carrying out trials on recycling some of their plastics but have not yet overcome some of the technical problems like identifying the different types of plastics. Say they would be prepared to stock products in recycled plastic containers and adopt a similar approach for own-brand products.

Paper Recycling: Are considering using recycled paper for head office work and said they planned to launch their own-label recycled stationery for sale in stores in the summer of 1909.

Litter   'Keep Britain Tidy' symbol is used on all appropriate packaging.

Packaging   Safeway say that environmental pressures relating to packaging are now a key point when discussing product development with suppliers.

Say they are 'moving towards' unbleached bakery bags and they have moved away from using CFCs in their packaging, in some cases replacing the board trays with recycled pulp packaging.

Labelling: As yet they do not have recycling symbols on their packaging, but do use the 'Keep Britain Tidy' logo.

Bags at Checkout: Offer recycled brown paper bags at the checkout as an alternative to plastic carrier bags. They say the supply is increasing all the time but we have noticed that in some of their stores these bags are not visible, so you have to ask specifically for one. Are considering biodegradable plastic bags.

CFCs   *Aerosols*: Claim to have been the first to remove CFCs from all own-label aerosols in February 1988, but Co-op seem to have beaten them to the post.

Packaging: No CFCs used in their packaging.

Refrigeration: New distribution depot being built with ammonia system for refrigeration and Safeway are also looking into replacing CFCs in other systems where possible.

Air Conditioning: Require manufacturers supplying air conditioning and coldrooms to drop the more damaging CFC and replace it with one that is less ozone depleting.

Building Requirements: Building specifications have now been amended to prohibit the use of materials containing CFCs in the construction of their supermarkets.

Vegetarian Range   Do not have a range of foods *specifically* designed for vegetarians, but say they have a wide range of foods suitable for vegetarians. Label these products as 'acceptable for vegetarian diet'. Do not use the Vegetarian Society symbol although they adhere to their guidelines.

Environmental Promotions   On Pack Promotions: Treesaver bags, recycled brown paper bags at checkouts; marking own-label aerosols as 'ozone-friendly'; advertising UK 2000 local contacts in all stores. Also planning to label products containing brazil nuts as 'rainforest friendly'.

Sponsorship: In July 1989 they sponsored the National Organic Wine Fair at the National Organic Garden Centre, Coventry. Also The Canals Trust Ltd, Heritage Foundation Family Tree, Habitat Scotland, UK 2000, Soil Association, Green Consumer Week launch event and various local organisations.

SAINSBURY'S ★ ★ ★

(Green Consumer Guide Status ★ ★ ★ ★)

Number of Stores: 285

Introduction Sainsbury's said in answer to our questionnaire:

'The essence of our marketing strategy is to offer a range of high quality merchandise at very competitive prices. Naturally we research very carefully what our customers want in terms of range and as the demand for environmentally friendly products grows, so we will seek to adapt our range to meet this demand. In addition we recognise a responsibility as leaders in our trade to take positive action on environmental issues.'

Given that Sainsbury's sell one eighth of all food retailed in Britain, they have enormous potential power as a Green Purchaser.

They came joint first in *The Green Consumer Guide* and have since promoted themselves on this basis, pointing out what they have done to 'go green'. They have appointed a committee, to review their products on the basis of their environmental performance and they are even planning to transform one shop into a completely green store.

In 1989 they won the Grocer Green Award for 'the retailer with the greatest commitment to the environment'.

Written Environmental Policy No

Any environmental policy statements are, at present, for internal use only.

Green Field Sites/Green Belt Areas Over half of Sainsbury's new supermarkets built in the last four years have used derelict or rundown urban sites. Other sites used are on land unsuited for other development because of its proximity to motorways or railways. If they build in rural areas they give land for nature conservation and take care to retain local wildlife and its habitat. They have 48 out-of-town or edge-of-town stores.

More than a quarter of Sainsbury's selling space has been open for less than three years. They are expanding rapidly and are opening more and more stores, which will certainly be putting pressure on the environment.

Transport   *Public Transport Facilities*: Do not make free buses available to the public but do discuss with local bus companies the routeing of services to stores.

Company Cars: Sainsbury's company car fleet is currently being converted to take unleaded petrol. Have not indicated on what time-scale they are planning to achieve conversion but have committed themselves to all new company cars being able to run on unleaded. Lorry fleet is exclusively diesel.

Rail Transport: Do not use rail transport for freight.

Energy Efficiency   They have a strong commitment to energy saving. Today's stores use only 60% of the energy consumed by similar stores built 10 years ago. Won the Beta award in 1989 for energy efficiency and the Gas Energy Management 1988 award for energy management. All new Sainsbury's stores since 1976 use heat extracted by refrigeration to heat the shopping areas.

PDS Management   Sainsbury's sent us a long list of rules they follow in the management of production and distribution sites.

This includes:
• environmental consideration taken into account when selecting branch sites
• back yards enclosed to reduce noise levels and debris spread
• activities at Depots/Branches scheduled to minimise noise effect on local residents at unsocial times of day
• vehicles waiting to be unloaded switch off engines to reduce noise and exhaust emissions
• route planning takes into consideration the avoidance of highly populated or sensitive areas
• air brake silencers fitted to vehicles
• waste oil disposal or recycling

● a switch to air suspension for trailers resulting in less noise and vibration.

Waste and Recycling   *Bottle Banks*: Bottle banks at 27 stores, with a further 37 planned by the end of 1989. Updated information sent prior to publication saying that 52 sites had by then been identified for the introduction of bottle banks, representing 18% of stores.

Can Skips: 4 aluminium can banks.

Bulk Packaging Waste: Cardboard and polythene are baled for collection and recycling in many stores.

Plastics Recycling: They say that if they were asked to assist in recycling of plastic bottles they would examine the practicality and effectiveness likely in relation to energy savings and environmental impact.

If a branded manufacturer proposed a product packaged in recycled plastic they would thoroughly investigate the technical suitability of the packaging, but would consider the idea sympathetically. The same considerations, as well as cost factors, would apply to their own brand development in this area.

Paper Collection: Two newspaper collection points are being installed and one is under negotiation.

Litter   'Keep Britain Tidy' symbol appears on their crisps and snacks, bags of confectionery, canned soft drinks, most bottled soft drinks and most canned beers. The bottled soft drinks and canned beers are being amended so that all carry the litter symbol.

Packaging   Have added environmental issues to the list of factors they consider when deciding on a particular piece of packaging. Have removed trays from the outer packaging of certain bottled soft drinks which now have only shrink wrapping on for travel and no supporting trays.

Bags at Checkout: They have recently changed to a different type of polythene for carry-out bags which has meant an approximate 45% saving on materials used. In a small number of stores where the off-licence has a separate checkout they use recycled paper bags, but they are not planning to increase the use of paper bags. They are currently conducting trials to check the viability of the many types of biodegradable plastic.

Labelling: Do not operate a scheme labelling packaging with the type of material used.

CFCs   *Aerosols*: Their aerosols have been CFC-free since October 1988. They withdrew an aerosol oven-cleaner altogether when they concluded that an alternative propellant was unacceptable.

Packaging: Have removed the most harmful CFCs from all their foam-blown packaging but some of their packaging still uses CFC-22 (which is one-twentieth as ozone depleting as the CFC-11 or -12 which was used before.)

Refrigeration: All cold store depots already use CFC-22 and from September 1989 all new supermarkets and those due for refurbishment will use CFC-22 as the sole refrigerant. Are holding technical discussions with chemical manufacturers on the development of a CFC-free refrigerant and they have a member of staff serving on international committees debating the future development of CFCs in refrigeration.

Vegetarian Range   Offer an extensive vegetarian range endorsed by the Vegetarian Society. They were the first supermarket to develop a range of dishes using mycoprotein (see page 147) as the main ingredient. Provide a free list of products suitable for vegetarians and vegans.

Environmental Promotions   They do not like to carry on-pack promotions with their own-brand products, but are happy to accept these from branded manufacturers. They have worked with Friends of the Earth and have sponsored a wide range of environmental activities.

SPAR ★ ★

(Green Consumer Guide Status: No stars)

Number of Stores: 2,450

Introduction Spar has a central office for the Spar Organisation, which is a voluntary group of independent wholesalers serving 2,450 independent retailers. They expect Spar retailers to support and promote Spar policies, but can only make recommendations.

Say that environmental pressures will have a strong influence on product development, because they attempt to respond as quickly as possible to perceived consumer demand.

Spar were not happy with their no-star rating in *The Green Consumer Guide* and have been trying to improve, although the independent retail sector always tends to lag behind the supermarkets. They have, however, come out with their own environmental labelling logo — 'Future Friendly'.

Written Environmental Policy No

Green Field Sites/Green Belt Areas Do not have a policy. They say it is not relevant because the majority of Spar shops are owned by retailers and not by the Spar Organisation. 955 of their shops are in neighbourhood precincts, parades or villages.

Transport *Public Transport Facilities*: Do not provide transport. The size of most Spar shops would not warrant this.

Company Cars: At the central office, 90% of the cars are able to run on unleaded petrol. Are changing over to unleaded for all the other cars.

Rail Transport: Do not use rail transport for freight.

Energy Efficiency Spar retailers have been encouraged to change to sodium-filled tubes for lighting, which is more energy efficient. Are also encouraged to put timers on their refrigeration and lighting so that they are not on when not needed.

PDS Management   Do not have their own production sites. Responsibility for the management of the wholesale depots rests with the individual wholesalers who own them.

Waste and Recycling   *Bottle Banks*: Say that they do not know how many exist because they have so many stores. We have therefore no information available to suggest they have a positive approach to this issue or that they actively encourage their licensees to be concerned.

Can Skips: As above.

Bulk Packaging Waste: Individual shops make their own arrangements for this. If you have a local Spar shop, it is worth asking them what they do and suggesting that they join a collection scheme.

Plastics Recycling: They would be prepared to stock, and to use themselves, products packaged in recycled plastic containers if it were commercially viable to do so.

Litter   Spar have worked with the Keep Britain Tidy Group and use their symbol on certain own-brand packs — bottled soft drinks, crisps, snacks, nuts and canned lager.

Packaging   The first users of non-detachable ring-pulls on carbonated soft drinks cans. This helps cut litter.

Bags at Checkout: Some Spar checkout bags are made of recycled paper — Tree Saver bags. Also the Spar Kraft counter bags which are white and brown contain a large percentage of recycled paper. Spar say they may well increase their use if practicable. They have two sorts of bio-degradable plastic carriers at the checkout and were the first users of this in the 1970s.

Labelling: They have identified the type of can on carbonated drinks to facilitate recycling.

CFCs   *Aerosols*: All own-brand aerosols have been CFC-free since mid-1988.

Packaging: None of the plastics for Spar brands contain CFCs. Some of the individual Spar retailers could stock other brands which may not be CFC-free as yet.

Refrigeration: Details of a recovery service for CFCs in refrigerators have been sent to all Spar retailers so that they can be recycled.

Vegetarian Range Have not sought endorsement by the Vegetarian Society, but do have a number of products suitable for vegetarians, including Spar frozen and canned vegetables range. Also several Spar soups and the vast majority of Spar biscuits do not contain animal fats. Unnecessary animal fats are being removed where possible.

Environmental Promotions They have run two competitions — 'Improve Your Area' and 'Cash for the Community'. The winners were those with the best ideas for improving the area. They have no on-pack promotions with environmental themes as yet.

TESCO ★ ★ ★ ★

(Green Consumer Guide Status ★ ★ ★)

Number of Stores: 380

Introduction Since Tesco's rating of three stars in *The Green Consumer Guide* they have been competing heavily with Safeway and Sainsbury's for the top slot.

Tesco launched its 'Tesco Cares' campaign in January 1989. This campaign included publishing a booklet on environmental issues (they were the first supermarket to do this); labelling their range of more environment-friendly products; labelling packaging with symbols identifying the material to facilitate recycling; improving their recycling facilities and looking at many of their activities in relation to how they affect the environment. They reaped their reward, receiving a substantial amount of publicity and followed this up with a major press advertising campaign under the strapline 'Tesco. The Greener Grocer'. To give an idea of how rapidly the competition has been moving, Sainsbury's quickly hit back with their campaign — 'Sainsbury. The Greenest Grocer'!

Tesco may have come out with a wide range of innovations, but it took a while to get the campaign operational in all their stores and they *do* have a conflict in that they have a rapid expansion programme which is bound to increase their land-take.

Written Environmental Policy No

No written environmental policy at the time of our survey but said that one was being formulated.

Green Field Sites/Green Belt Areas Do not have a specific policy on the use of green field sites or green belt areas. Approximately 150 stores are situated 'out of town'. They have moved wild-flower meadows in response to the concerns of conservationists. Will not sell wild bulbs or corms, which can be linked with species loss or habitat destruction in the source countries.

Transport *Public Transport Facilities*: Provide free buses as a supplement to public transport, when considered necessary.

Company Cars: About 51% of their 1,600 cars have been converted to unleaded fuel. No new cars will be bought unless they can run on unleaded fuel.

Rail Transport: Do not use rail transport for freight.

Energy Efficiency Have received a number of awards for saving energy in their stores. Specify that their lights and revolving doors should be energy saving. Heat from their refrigeration is recycled into the store.

DPS Management Six full-time environmental consultants are employed by the Technical Services Department.

Waste and Recycling *Bottle Banks*: 64

Can Skips: 10

Bulk Packaging Waste: They compact the cardboard and polythene which is returned to a contractor who uses it to make new boxes. The polythene goes into making bin liners.

Plastics Recycling: Use 'PET Recyclable' logos to identify PET bottles, which they hope will encourage the plastics industry to develop a workable scheme to recycle PET plastic. Would be prepared to stock products in recycled plastic, provided they were safe.

Paper Recycling: Are involved in customer paper recycling schemes at 5 of their stores. The head office stationery is due to switch to recycled paper.

Litter The 'Keep Britain Tidy' symbol is used on cans, bottles, cartons, carrier bags, crisps and confectionery.

Packaging Use recycled material wherever possible and avoid excessive packaging. Have introduced recycled paper and cartons, non-CFC aerosols and CFC-free foam trays because of environmental pressures.

Bags at Checkout: Do not offer recycled paper bags at checkout and are not planning to introduce any. They are investigating the issue of biodegradable plastics but have not yet replaced their plastic bags at checkout with anything more degradable.

Labelling: Use logos to identify packaging on their products to encourage recycling of all materials.

CFCs *Aerosols*: All own-brand aerosols were CFC-free by September 1988. They do stock pump sprays (which are non-aerosol).

Packaging: Had not yet fully implemented their policy on all foam packaging being CFC-free at the time of our survey but were in the process of sorting it out.

Refrigeration: All new stores will use CFC-22 instead of CFC-11 or -12. Old stores will continue to use the CFCs -11 and -12 but they say they will ensure that there are no leaks and that the CFCs are recycled when appropriate. They are waiting until tests on the improved coolant have been completed and show that it is a feasible technical replacement.

Vegetarian Have developed a vegetarian range which
Range includes burgers, steaklets and pâtés.

Environmental They have worked with Friends of the Earth local
Promotions groups, the Civic Trust, the Nature Conservancy
Council, Groundwork and the Green Alliance and
have supported some other organisations —
CLEAR, Wastewatch, Gas Energy Management,
BETA Awards, Civic Trust and Watch.

WAITROSE

Waitrose was the only supermarket group which we approached that refused to participate in our Green Supermarket Survey. The company noted that, as part of the John Lewis Group, 'we do not take part in market research surveys of this kind'. Waitrose did respond in general terms, however, noting that:

'. . . we already have CFC-free aerosols, meat, poultry and egg trays. We stock PVC-free clingfilm and toilet tissue and disposable nappies made of non-chlorine bleached paper pulp. We are soon to introduce phosphate-free detergents and cleaners.

'We do not carry out any product tests on animals, nor are any of our own-label products tested on animals in the course of their development.

'We recycle our cardboard, are changing some plastic packaging to a more easily recycled form and we have had substantial success in conserving energy.

'We sell organic fruit and vegetables in most of our branches which conform to the standards established by the International Federation of Organic Agricultural Movements (IFOAM). We also sell the following vegetarian foods: cheeses, delicatessen counter produce, pâtés, ready-to-eat meals, soups and stock cubes. The range of organic foods includes cheeses, bakery products and snacks.

'We sell free-range eggs and poultry. All Waitrose meat is produced free of hormones, unnecessary feed additives and antibiotics except where specifically prescribed by a vet and we routinely test for pesticide residues in our fruit and vegetables.'

Like the other supermarkets, Waitrose plans to continue to bring forward more environment-friendly products, 'provided they appeal sufficiently to our customers and satisfy our quality and value standards.'

Fresh Fruit and Vegetables

In some parts of the country, seagulls no longer follow the plough because there are no longer any worms or insects to gobble. Such soil, as *The Times* put it, is little more than 'plasticine to prop up crops fed on chemicals'.

Chemical farming has become so sophisticated that farmers can grow the same crop in the same spot year after year, with the help of artificial fertilisers, growth regulators and pesticides. This very sophistication masks some of the underlying trends in the health of Britain's agricultural soils. Soil erosion problems are growing all the time, fuelled by a combination of the chemical diet we feed to our farmland and the stripping away of thousands of miles of hedgerows every year — which enables the wind and rain to eat away at already weakened soils.

Modern agriculture is also highly energy-intensive. On the typical farm, the energy originally needed to make the fertilisers and pesticides used is at least equal to — and generally more than — that used to power the tractors, pesticide-spraying vehicles and harvesters.

Modern farming methods have indisputably helped to ensure that there are plentiful supplies of vegetables and other foods available — to the extent that all over Europe we are building up 'food mountains' and 'wine lakes'.

So what sort of vegetable mountain do we eat our way through each year? Some 5.89 million tonnes of fresh vegetables were sold in Britain in 1988, with 1989 sales expected to be well over 6 million tonnes. To get some sense of what these figures mean, we weighed a Webb's lettuce (1 lb or 453 g) and a Cos (14 oz or 396 g). Round lettuces are much lighter. So six million tonnes of lettuce would represent at least 13 *billion* lettuces!

The key trend, meanwhile, is the move to low- or no-chemical farming methods. At the moment, however, if you ask for 'organic' (or 'no-chemical') produce, you will generally find that it is more expensive — often much more so. For example, at the time of writing, for 69p in one supermarket you got two organically grown grapefruit, while for just 3p more you got four 'ordinary' ones. In some stores, chemical-free potatoes were almost three times more expensive than normal ones. So far, organic production only accounts for around one per cent of vegetable sales in Britain, although the Soil Association has ambitions to increase the proportion to between 10 and 20 per cent (see Organic produce, below).

This is very much a trend in the making. As Prince Charles put it: 'It is increasingly felt by members of the public that large-scale soil erosion, the destruction of wildlife habitat and the excessive use of chemicals and unnatural substances are unacceptable and cannot continue unabated without ruining the countryside for future generations and causing long-term health hazards'. In 1989 he also became a patron of the pioneering Henry Doubleday Research Association (HDRA), which runs the National Centre for Organic Gardening. The supermarkets have a key role to play in ensuring that the organic food revolution is not held back. Unfortunately, they insist on uniformity in the produce they sell. Because carrots, for example, need to look as though they have been injection-moulded in plastic, with every vegetable the same size, shape and colour, millions of tonnes of vegetables are thrown away and left to rot each year. The more perfect produce the supermarkets stock, the more we become accustomed to it. Until we ask for something different, the supermarkets can continue to say they are responding to consumer demand.

Often, because of the high quality standards imposed, only a third of a crop of vegetables is suitable for sale to a supermarket. At the same time, the supermarkets may play off one supplier against another to drive prices down, which generally means that growers are unwilling or unable to invest in improving the long-term productivity of their land.

Exotic produce

As people have travelled abroad more often, and have gone further afield, there has been growing interest in exotic fruit and vegetables. In the early 1970s, avocados, capsicums, mangoes, guavas, coconuts and artichokes were among the new varieties that started to appear on supermarket shelves. Many of these fruit are brought long distances, involving the burning of a great deal of fuel. But even some fairly ordinary fruits come from further afield than we might imagine.

Eating food out of season either means that it has to be flown in to Britain from countries with a suitable climate, or that it is grown in a glasshouse environment — which involves the use of a great deal of energy. Many of the strawberries we eat during Wimbledon week, for example, are imported from countries like Spain. This means that the 'energy content' of our diet, in terms of the energy used to get our food to our plate, is much higher than it was. No one suggests that we go back to a diet composed exclusively of potatoes and leeks, but our developing taste for exotic foods does clearly have important implications. In the Greenhouse world of the future, we may need to ask whether it makes sense to bring so much of our food from so far afield.

Greenhouse crops

One way to avoid the transport costs involved in importing fruit and vegetables from overseas is to grow them here, which generally means growing them in greenhouses. One West Sussex nurseryman is even growing kiwifruit, normally imported from New Zealand. But steep rises in gas prices in

1989 underscored the dependence of much of the glasshouse crops sector on high energy inputs.

Many growers said that they were threatened with ruin, while the customer could be faced with higher prices for such salad crops as tomatoes, lettuce and cress. Heating is one of the three greatest costs of producing glasshouse crops, accounting for around a third of the total. The two other areas of major expenditure are labour and packaging.

Until recently, growers benefited from cheaper gas in exchange for agreeing to power cuts if demand from domestic and other users surged beyond the capacity of the gas system. From the autumn of 1989, however, gas prices will be fixed, which growers say will increase their energy costs by at least 100 per cent. The growers protest that their main option, where they can afford it, will be to rip out their gas-burning equipment and replace it with boilers fired with (more polluting) heavy oil.

Lemons

Many lemons are waxed — and thereby preserved — immediately after harvest. Early in 1989, **Safeway** introduced wax-free lemons to its supermarket shelves. This development was welcomed by consumers who use lemon rind in food and drinks, but it is worth noting that the lemons are now preserved in a polypropylene wrapping!

In a number of other countries, such fruit are labelled to say whether or not they have been wax-coated. We should have a similar system here. In the meantime, if you are using lemon zest or rind in your cooking or when making drinks, think about buying the organic variety — or buy the uncoated variety at your nearest Safeway.

Pesticides and Other Agrochemicals

Each year, chemicals worth around £350 million are used to grow food in Britain. Four hundred pesticides were cleared for use here in 1985 by the Ministry of Agriculture, Fisheries and Food (MAFF). But, as a result, 43 per cent of the vegetables sold in Britain contain pesticide residues, according to a MAFF survey.

There have been a number of scares about pesticide residues in our fruit and vegetables. One of the most recent was the controversy about the use of the chemical daminozide, known as Alar, and sprayed on apple trees to help the apples set. The main concern was that in some animal tests the chemical turned out to be a potential carcinogen, or cancer-causing agent. One problem is that such chemicals cannot simply be washed off the skin of fruit — they can be found in the flesh itself.

Alar has been used on between 5 and 10 per cent of Britain's apples and on a smaller number of pear trees. It is used to make apples redder, firmer and more resistant to rotting during storage. The difference between the UK and US regulatory approaches in this area was underscored by the fact that while Alar was banned in the States, in Britain it was given the all clear by the Government's Advisory Committee on Pesticides. In the summer of 1989, Parents for Safe Food, a pressure group set up by Pamela Stephenson and other celebrities, commissioned a study of Alar levels in apples and apple juice. This involved taking a random sample of products from supermarket shelves. Trace levels of Alar were measured in milligrams per kilogram (mg/kg). The limits of detection were 0.1 mg/kg, so that results below that level meant either that the product was Alar-free, or that only infinitesimally small traces were present.

The highest levels were found in **Del Monte** apple juice (1.4 mg/kg) and *Fresh English Apple Juice* from **Safeway** (1.0 mg/kg). Lower levels were found in **Sainsbury's** apple juice (0.8 mg/kg), **Safeway**'s *Apple Juice* and **Waitrose**'s *English Apple Juice* (0.4 mg/kg). On the other hand, **Tesco**'s *English Apple Juice* seemed to be effectively Alar-free (0.1 mg/kg).

Half of the fresh apples bought and both brands of apple baby food (**Heinz** *Pure Fruit Baby Food* and **Cow & Gate** *Apple Dessert*) were also found to contain traces of Alar. If you want to make sure that your fruit is Alar-free, shop in the organic section at your local supermarket.

Complacency has prevailed for so long in MAFF that government safety inspectors visit the average farm about once every 30 years! If members of the public — or the land worked by organic growers — are affected by pesticide spray drift, the chances of their getting redress in the courts are vanishingly small. And almost no work is being done to look at any interactions between the different chemicals we eat — the so-called 'cocktail effect'.

According to *Which?*, although the way in which pesticides are used has been controlled since 1985, there has been no limit on the amount of residues left in the food we eat. When the Consumers' Association tested lettuce, tomatoes and cucumbers, it found pesticide residues in all of them, although none exceeded international safety standards. The magazine recommends that anyone who buys non-organic fruit and vegetables should wash or scrub them before eating and remove the outer leaves of leafy produce. 90 per cent of lettuces are sprayed and the pesticide residues tend to be concentrated on — or in — the outer leaves.

Early in 1989, Friends of the Earth found excessive levels of tecnazene, a pesticide used on stored potatoes to slow down sprouting, on potatoes bought at branches of three supermarkets, Sainsbury, Gateway and Budgen. The levels reported were double those permitted under standards set by the World Health Organisation. Tecnazene is also now thought to be posing a threat to drinking water supplies and to fish, because so much of the chemical is flushed into rivers from potato washing plants. Water authorities were ordered to begin monitoring the problem by the Department of the Environment.

We asked the supermarkets whether they tested their produce for pesticide residues. Both **Safeway** and **Tesco** said that round lettuces were most likely to contain high residues, although **Tesco** also mentioned potatoes. Safeway say they are working closely with their suppliers to achieve the total elimination of tecnazene.

Most of the supermarkets had not withdrawn any products because of pesticide contamination, although **Sainsbury's** said they had ceased importing cherries from certain suppliers in 1988 because of high residues of copper sulphate. **Asda** have stopped selling Turkish dried apricots, having found that they contained too much sulphur dioxide — the chemical used to preserve them.

Organic produce

You can now find a growing range of organic produce in the supermarkets. **Safeway** was the first major chain to introduce organic fruit and vegetables, as long ago as 1981. **Sainsbury's** followed suit in 1986 and **Gateway** in 1987. **Tesco** came in during 1988 and **Marks & Spencer** announced that it would begin stocking some organic produce in 1989. The state of play at the time of our survey is shown in the Table on pages 109 – 10.

So what is 'organic' produce? According to the Soil Association, which has pioneered in this area, organic farming is based on:

- the use of plant and animal composts for soil nutrients, instead of artificial fertilisers

- the use of crop rotation, to reduce the build-up of crop-specific pests and the development of soil nutrient imbalances

- the control of pests by the use of:

    – physical barriers (e.g. tar papers on trees or mulches against weeds)

    – carefully chosen cultivation methods, including intercropping (with different types of plants planted close together, to confuse pests)

    – the deliberate introduction of pest predator species

    – flame treatment to eliminate weeds

    – selected, plant-based pesticides.

Organic farmers stress that they are not returning to the past. Indeed, modern organic farming is a new system of food production, relying on recent advances in understanding of ecology, plant physiology and biochemistry. It continues to develop rapidly — and would do so even faster if it were to be government-aided at the level enjoyed by conventional farming.

The Soil Association's 'Living Earth' campaign is designed to provide a spur for:

- consumers, to buy more organically grown food
- retailers, to stock more organic produce and food products
- producers, to convert to organic farming systems, so increasing the area farmed organically
- policy makers, to provide the financial support, research and advice so desperately needed to ensure the continuing development of organic farming systems. (There are no government grants to help farmers to convert from conventional growing to organic, an expensive process since land has to lie fallow for at least two years to obtain a Soil Association certificate. Nor are there government grants to help organic farmers to develop new plant strains or cultivation methods.)

The organic movement believes that organically grown food brings a number of benefits for the consumer and the environment. These include:

- much lower pesticide residues than found in conventional foods
- lower levels of nitrate
- lower water content, so the foods should have more flavour
- no artificial additives
- less processing than is the case with conventional foods
- no artificial hormones in meat or dairy products.

And there are a number of wider benefits, including the following:

- a major contribution to countryside conservation, including a renewed emphasis on small-scale production systems — which helped to create many of the rural landscapes we now value

SUPERMARKET POLICIES FOR STOCKING ORGANIC PRODUCE

Supermarket	Stock organic produce?	In how many stores?	Standards followed	Plan to stock more?	Why?††
Asda	Yes	50 (about)	Soil Association; IFOAM*; Conservation Grade; Asda's own standards	Yes	To promote healthier eating, to offer customer best choice and to respond to growing customer needs
Co-op	Yes	'Where there is a demand'	Soil Association	Yes	Response to growing healthy eating trend and to offer customers a wider range. Opened trial organic farm in Spring 1989
Gateway	Yes	84 stores	Soil Association	Yes	Steady increase in customer demand
Iceland	No	N/A	N/A	N/A	Want urgently to sell organic produce, but having trouble finding sufficient supply for 450 stores
M & S	Yes (launch May '89)	To be decided	To be confirmed	Yes	To offer the customer a choice

Continued overleaf

SUPERMARKET POLICIES FOR STOCKING ORGANIC PRODUCE continued

Supermarket	Stock organic produce?	In how many stores?	Standards followed	Plan to stock more?	Why?†
Safeway	Yes	All stores	Soil Association; IFOAM*; Biotop; Bio Dynamic; Nature et Progrès	Yes	Beneficial to the environment and consumer long term
Sainsbury's	Yes	70 stores	Soil Association	Yes	Growing interest
Spar	No	N/A	N/A	N/A	They would like to stock organic produce in line with consumer demand
Tesco	Yes	57 stores	Soil Association	Yes	To meet growing demand from customers – after a very slow start

* International Federation of the Organic Agriculture Movement
† These comments are based directly on the replies in the supermarket questionnaires.

- much lower environmental pollution

- reduced food surpluses

- increased rural employment.

But the organic farming industry still has a long way to go if it wants to become a credible, reliable supplier to the supermarket sector. (And it is worth pointing out here that there are many organic growers who believe that they should only supply local outlets rather than national supermarket chains.)

Those growers and farmers who do want to move in this direction will need to improve their quality assurance and presentation. It is certainly ironic that around 60 per cent of the organic produce sold in this country has to be imported. In part this is because we can't grow products like grapefruit or avocados in our climate, but there are weaknesses in the organic sector itself which are partly to blame for this situation.

In 1989, for example, **Sainsbury's** berated organic producers for supplying products that are 'an insult to the consumer'. The company accused organic growers of believing they have 'a divine right to sell the fruits (and vegetables) of their labours, regardless of quality'. Many of the supermarkets responding to our survey stressed the problems they had been having in sourcing adequate supplies of organic produce, both in terms of quantity and quality.

Such transitional pains are inevitable, although they are aggravated by the fact that there have been a number of competing labelling schemes for organic farming and produce. This situation may be improved by the introduction of the UK Register of Organic Food Standards (UKROFS) in 1989. Consumers must be assured that organic food is really organic, which implies that a unified labelling system is necessary.

The organic sector is quick to dismiss the arguments advanced by the supermarkets. Organic suppliers retort that the supermarkets are using the wrong standards to assess their produce. **Gateway**, for example, says that it wants organic produce to meet EEC Grade 1 quality standards. This, as the Organic Growers' Association has pointed out, means that apples should not have leaf mould, cucumbers should be straight and potatoes must be free of a silvery must. 'None of these qualities has anything to do with the taste or the safety of the product,' said one exasperated grower.

Supermarkets are difficult customers to deal with at the best of times, whether you are an organic grower or not. They reject around 60 per cent of the produce offered to them, which means that the grower loses a good deal of money. It seems that there could be a major opportunity for Body Shop-style retail outlets buying and selling organic produce in a suitable way. Indeed, a number of entrepreneurs are already working towards this goal.

One of the ironies of organic production is that organic produce needs to be clearly identified and separated from other products, to ensure that what you buy meets the appropriate standards. As a result, you will generally find that organic produce is heavily packaged — whereas many consumers might prefer to buy it loose — or indeed in bulk.

Genetic engineering

A new non-mushy tomato, produced by means of genetic engineering, is under development by ICI and is being grown in commercial greenhouses. But because of safety guidelines governing the release into the environment of genetically engineered plants and organisms, the ICI scientists involved in the work will not be allowed to eat the tomatoes. 'If people swallowed the tomato seeds,' an ICI spokesman explained, 'the plants could end up growing in a sewage farm somewhere and this would be an unauthorised release of a genetically engineered organism!'

The idea is to produce tomatoes which do not become soft within a week or so of picking. Normally, growers have to pick tomatoes when they are still green, so that they do not become pulpy by the time they reach the supermarket shelf. These green tomatoes are artificially ripened with ethylene gas and are not as tasty as the naturally ripened variety. ICI's wrinkle-free tomato can be picked red and does not need to be artificially ripened. In the United States, tomatoes worth about £2 billion are sold each year, but over 10 per cent are thrown away because they are too mushy.

Many genetic engineers believe that their work will enable farmers to grow crops without the need for high inputs of agrochemicals. The plants, they say, will fight off pests without needing to be sprayed with pesticides — and will produce their own nitrogen fertiliser from the air. These are seductive promises, but we should remember that the nuclear and chemical industries made similarly seductive claims. Genetic engineering has an important future in food production, but we should keep a very close eye on what genetic engineers get up to!

CONTACTS

Henry Doubleday Research Association, National Centre for Organic Gardening, Ryton-on-Dunsmore, Coventry CV8 3LG or on 0203 303517.

Land and Food Company, 1 Junipor Cottage, Wick Street, Stroud, Glos GL9 7QR (Plans to open a chain of green supermarkets based on organically run farms.)

Soil Association, 88 Colston Street, Bristol BS1 5BB or on 0272 290661.

UK Register of Organic Food Standards, via Food from Britain, 301 – 344 Market Towers, New Covent Garden Market, London SW8 5NQ or on 01-720 2144.

Meat, Poultry and Fish

Initially, the Green Consumer has two main options with meat, poultry or fish: to eat or not to eat. Vegetarianism and, to a lesser extent, veganism, are growing trends. However, given that most Britons still eat a considerable quantity of meat, this is the first food we shall discuss here.

THE MEAT COUNTER

Each week, Britain slaughters some 65,000 cattle, 300,000 sheep and 280,000 pigs. Many of these animals are reared — and slaughtered — in appalling conditions. The meat consumption of the average adult Briton is 135 lb (61 kg) of meat per year, about 42 lb (19 kg) of which are accounted for by beef and veal.

Supermarket meat departments have begun to throttle traditional butchers' shops in the same way that they squeezed independent grocers. Between 1986 and 1989 the supermarkets' share of beef sales rose from 28 per cent to almost 33 per cent, with similar gains in lamb sales. In the pork market, the butchers' share has contracted from nearly 46 per cent in 1986 to under 39 per cent, while the multiples have expanded from just over 30 per cent to 38 per cent.

Leaving aside their impact on the diversity of our High Streets, there is a wide range of issues related to the production and quality of the meat and meat products which the supermarkets have to address. These include:

- contamination (by antibiotics, hormones, other growth promoters, and pesticides)

- animal welfare, particularly in intensive rearing systems

- pollution (slurry and silage) from intensive livestock units — and their visual impact on the countryside

- energy- and resource-efficiency

- the harvesting of wild meat

- tropical deforestation.

Antibiotics and hormones

Increasing reliance on intensive livestock production methods has fuelled the growing use of antibiotics and pesticides in meat production. Drugs originally used to treat individual animals are now used continuously to treat entire herds. From the farmer's point of view, the advantage is that livestock can be kept in unnatural conditions with epidemic diseases kept at bay by medication. Antibiotics are likely to have been used both to improve feed conversion and to stimulate growth.

The supermarkets and meat companies all say that they permit antibiotics to be used, but they insist on a period of grace before slaughter to ensure that the meat contains no residues. Many supermarkets now have written policy statements on contamination (see Table).

While antibiotics can be used legally in meat production, most hormones are now banned. Whereas antibiotics are used to protect animals against disease, including those caused by

SUPERMARKET MEAT QUALITY STANDARDS

Supermarket	Lay down their own written standards?	Comments
Asda	Yes	Have written standards with permitted levels of growth hormones to ensure that all the meat is free from antibiotics and that pesticide residues are below recommended EEC and UK requirements
Co-op	Yes	Have an extensive document outlining specifications for meat suppliers. Ban any suppliers of fresh or processed meat from using growth promoters such as hormones and anabolic steroids, but not from using antibiotics. For lamb and pork they specify: 'No carcase should contain residues of an agricultural or veterinary nature. Such preparation as may be used for animal health purposes must be observed prior to consignment for slaughter'
Gateway	No	Conform to all legal UK standards
Iceland	No	Have no written standards but they say requirements are understood by suppliers
M & S	Yes*	The standards are part of their manufacturing specifications, but they are confidential. Say they have policies on permitted levels of hormones, antibiotics and other growth promoters as well as rearing of meat animals which apply to all suppliers
Safeway	Yes (for beef only)	No written policy for pork or lamb. They do not ban antibiotics in meat production because they say this would mean no products would be available. Looking closely at this issue for meat suppliers from outside the UK for the future. As far as beef is concerned: 'It is the supplier's responsibility to ensure that cattle destined for our stores are free from Hormone Implants or Antibiotic Residues'
Sainsbury's	Yes	Specific requirements which adhere to standards laid down by government and 'ensure that no residues are left in the meat' They have standards relating to rearing of animals, transport and handling of animals, slaughtering and abattoir procedures and testing for residues. Will not accept animals which have been ritually slaughtered

SUPERMARKET MEAT QUALITY
STANDARDS Continued

Supermarket	Lay down their own written standards?	Comments
Spar	No	No fresh meat supplied centrally by Spar. All their meat conforms to UK regulations
Tesco	No	Specifications they have are confidential to the company. Regular testing of products is conducted by independent laboratories. They say that any offenders would be de-listed but none yet found

* Some written and some verbal, but not enclosed because considered confidential.

intensive farming conditions, hormones are solely used to boost animal weight — or milk production. European concerns about hormones in meat date back at least to the early 1980s, when the synthetic hormone diethylstilbestrol (DES) was discovered in baby foods made with veal. In some parts of the world, the result of the use of DES was premature puberty in young children. Girls of just five or six began to develop breasts and started menstruating, while some boys began to develop breast tissue. DES is now banned in many countries, but continuous vigilance will be needed to make sure that it is not imported in meat products. A Belgian consumer magazine alleged that a survey of butchers' shops in the country showed that a quarter of the samples tested contained DES or other illegal chemicals.

When various synthetic hormones were banned by a number of European countries, the implications for US meat producers were particularly grave. More than half of the 35 million US cattle sent to market each year receive at least a small amount of hormones, so the European Community ruling blocking US imports of beef, worth $140 million a year, was a severe blow.

Most traditional growth promoters have now been banned, but new types of hormone are beginning to come into use.

These include bovine somatotropin (BST), likely to be used to boost milk production, and porcine somatotropin (PST), designed to boost the growth of pigs. BST can also be used to boost the ratio of lean meat to fat in cattle, sheep and pigs. Companies like Monsanto are hoping to commercialise BST. If BST is licensed for wide use, other new hormones will follow on to the market. Tests are also underway with drugs called beta-antagonists, claimed to boost animal growth and help produce low-fat meats.

Companies like **Birds Eye** argue that since the use of hormones and other growth promoters is illegal, all UK meat is 'real' meat. But the campaigners for 'Real Meat' would disagree. They have also stressed the importance of a number of other issues, including pesticide residues and animal welfare (see Box page 126 – 7).

It is worrying that the EEC Federation of Veterinarians recently singled out Britain for criticism when describing Community meat hygiene as disgraceful. In England and Wales, only 8 per cent of slaughterhouses came up to EEC export standards.

Pollution

Intensive livestock operations are significant sources of both water and air pollution. Britain's eight million pigs, for example, produce around 4 kg (8.8 lb) of slurry per head per day. Overall, farm animals produce up to 200 million tonnes of excreta a year. This material is typically three times as polluting as the sewage produced by people, so in addition to direct poisoning of rivers it strips the oxygen out of the water — suffocating fish and other organisms. As explained in Chapter 3, the number of water pollution incidents caused by farm slurries and silage has grown rapidly in recent years, but very few farmers have been taken to court — and those who have been have got away with derisory fines. The pressure must be increased.

Animal Welfare

The demand for beef of a consistent quality, particularly for supermarkets, has led to a rapid increase in intensive beef rearing. Calves are separated from mothers within a week of birth, transported to a rearing unit, usually via a cattle market, and then reared on substitute milk, often medicated. They may spend some time at pasture, but increasingly are kept indoors. If they are weak, they will be slaughtered to produce pet food — and rennet, an enzyme used in most cheese production.

Britain slaughters some 15 million pigs a year. The vast majority of pork and bacon pigs are reared intensively. Sows are kept in permanent restraint in stalls, or are tethered with a chain around their neck. Young pigs' tails are cut off, the males are castrated without anaesthetic. Intensively farmed pigs are raised in overcrowded conditions. Deprived of space to play and straw to exercise their rooting instinct, many become frustrated and listless.

Late in 1986, the Government announced that it would ban the use of veal crates. At the time, 10,000 calves were still being reared in this way. By keeping the animals confined in the dark, the idea was to produce delicate white meat. The cost was that calves were anaemic and lived out their brief life in intolerable conditions.

Animal welfare groups are also now challenging the slaughter of deer in abattoirs. Deer are highly strung animals and unused to human management, so shooting them in the open by a licensed marksman is almost certainly a more humane method of slaughter than that afforded by the ordinary abattoir.

Beef

A recent issue to emerge has been the possible contamination of small quantities of beef following outbreaks of 'mad cow disease', or bovine spongiform encephalitis (BSE). The cattle were thought to have caught the disease when given feed containing ground-up sheep which had been infected with a similar disease, scrapie. The Government announced in May

1989 that the use of beef brains in meat pies and other foods would be banned, to prevent the spread of BSE. Milk from infected cows was banned in December 1988, while the use of beef offal in baby foods was banned three months later.

Beefburger

Unlike some fast-food beefburgers, it seems that the beefburger products on offer in Britain's supermarkets need not concern the Green Consumer in terms of rainforest destruction. (See page 18.) The bulk of the meat comes from Europe.

Canned meat

As the London Food Commission points out, Britain produces some 200 million cans of meat each year. We also import large quantities of canned meat from countries as diverse as Denmark and Brazil, Yugoslavia and Botswana. Some even comes from Ethiopia, where millions of people have been starving (see Corned beef). In total, we buy over 300 million pounds by weight of canned meat, ranging from luncheon meat to meatballs, from chicken casserole to corned lamb.

However, these products potentially provide a means of disguising the origin and nature of a range of meat products, so the Green Consumer would be well advised to check for the country of origin before purchase. The main concern is about meat imported from Brazil, where there is currently no strong policy of preventing rainforest clearance for cattle ranching. (See also Corned beef.)

Among the companies that use some Brazilian meat in their products are **Brooke Bond Foods**, **Campbell's** and **John West Foods**. Brooke Bond, the £400 million-a-year company formed from Brooke Bond Oxo and Batchelors Foods, stresses that 'none of the meat we use comes from cattle born, bred or raised in areas which have been deforested'. Their brands include *Fray Bentos*, *Batchelors*, *Vesta*, *Microchef* and some *Walls* canned meat.

BEEF AND COUNTRY OF ORIGIN

SUPERMARKET OWN BRANDS

Supermarket and beef type	Product	Country of origin
Asda	Beef	UK
Co-op Canned	Minced Beef & Onion	Ireland
	Steak Chunks	Eastern Europe
	Frozen Burgers	UK
	Corned Beef	Brazil
Co-op Chilled	Beef Sausages	UK or EEC
	Pork & Beef Sausages	UK or EEC
	Steak Pies	UK or EEC
	Steak & Kidney Pies	UK or EEC
	Minced Beef & Onion	UK or EEC
	Roast Beef	UK or EEC
Co-op Fresh Meat	Fresh Beef	UK
Gateway	Fresh Beef	UK and Eire
	Tinned Beef	Yugoslavia, Rumania, Holland, Denmark, Brazil and Argentina
Iceland Frozen Meat	Beef	UK and Eire
M & S	Tinned Beef	UK and Brazil*
	Fresh Beef	UK
Safeway	Beef products	UK or Eire
Sainsbury's	Frozen Beef	UK
	Fresh Beef	UK and Eire
	Tinned Beef	not stated
Spar	Corned Beef	Brazil
	Stewed Steak, Minced Beef	UK
	Chilli con carne	UK
	Irish Stew & Beefburgers	UK
Tesco	Fresh Meat	UK or Eire
	Corned Beef	Uruguay†
	Frozen Beef Strips	France

MANUFACTURERS' BRANDS

Company	Product	Country of origin
John West	Beef products	Brazil, Uruguay†, Argentina, Yugoslavia and France
Farquhar North & Co	Beef products	Mainly home produced Australia and South America

Campbell's	Beef products	USA, South America
Brooke Bond (*Fray Bentos, Walls, Batchelors, Vesta*)	Beef products	Brazil, Yugoslavia, Argentina, West Germany, Holland and some African countries

* M & S have not stated which products come from Brazil.
† Beef that comes from Uruguay is unlikely to be implicated in recent tropical deforestation although it is from South America.

Corned beef

60 per cent of the corned beef eaten in the UK comes from Brazil, 30 per cent from Argentina and the rest from several countries, including Zimbabwe. There have even been shipments to Europe from starvation-racked Ethiopia.

Sold on the Continent under the trade name *Leenox* and *Jo*, sometimes with the country of origin hidden, this Ethiopian meat has led to considerable controversy. **Tesco** refused to stock it, for example. Bob Geldof, however, has suggested that we should have no qualms about buying the meat. Like Oxfam, he believes that the trade is beneficial to Ethiopia, bringing much-needed foreign currency.

On the other hand, until Brazil controls its cattle ranching effectively — which on present evidence may not happen until it is too late for the threatened rainforests of Amazonia — the Green Consumer may want to think long and hard about buying corned and canned beef products from Brazil. Our table shows some of the brands which use Brazilian beef.

Marks & Spencer say that they sent a member of their staff to check with the sources of their Brazilian beef and have been assured that it has not contributed to rainforest destruction because the cattle are reared in areas of Brazil which were not originally rainforest. Another company which seems to be innocent in this respect is **Brooke Bond Foods** (see Canned meat).

Veal

Any Green Consumer who still eats veal should avoid it when eating abroad. It is not even clear that veal calves are being raised in acceptable conditions in the UK, let alone in countries where animal welfare is a much lower priority. In West Germany, concern about illegal 'meat factories', using banned hormones to produce veal, recently triggered a wave of concern — which helped create the conditions for a US – EEC trade war. Meat sales plummeted and took some time to recover.

Pork, Ham and Bacon

The Dutch Meat Board has been working with **Asda**, **Marks & Spencer** and **Sainsbury's** on a more 'naturally reared pig', although this is still very much in the development stage and the resulting bacon, ham and other products will inevitably be more expensive.

Ask your supermarket what it is doing to check for antibiotic or growth promoter residues in bacon, ham and pork. **Marks & Spencer**, which operates to guidelines set by the Ministry of Agriculture, Fisheries and Food, says it permits low levels of antibiotics in feedstuffs for 'bacon' pork.

Sausages

Apart from the contamination, pollution and animal welfare issues already covered, there is the question of whether sausages are good value for money. When you consider the fat, generally high salt levels and various preservatives, colourings and emulsifying agents that they contain, they appear to be poor value for health, too.

The **Pure Meat Company**, on the other hand, stresses quality — and will make 'real meat' sausages to your own recipe! Custom-made sausages are becoming increasingly popular.

Game

Legally or illegally, game has formed part of the British diet for centuries. In these days of intensively reared animals, it provides the most obvious source of free-range meat and poultry. Game animals and birds are also highly prized because they are much more likely to be free of hormones and other additives, although — because they feed on crops that have often been treated with agrochemicals — the consumer should note that they are not guaranteed free of pesticide residues!

Neither fresh nor frozen game can be sold more than 10 days after the close of the season, unless it is imported dead into the country. Avoid French foods based on wild birds like thrushes. Up to ten million song thrushes are shot as they fly south over the continent each winter. Some British birds are protected at all times — including the Common Scoter, Long-tailed duck, Scaup duck, Velvet Scoter and Whimbrel. It is also illegal to sell wild geese.

Venison

If you are buying venison, check whether or not it comes from farmed deer. If it does, ask whether the supplier operates to the standards laid down by the British Deer Farmers' Association. And contact the RSPCA to see whether the supplier has a good reputation in terms of animal welfare.

In areas where deer have become a pest species, culling offers a number of ecological advantages. It is worth noting that the low intensity farming of deer in the Highlands is an excellent way of harnessing the resources of Scotland's poorer lands in an environmentally acceptable way. But deer farmers have found that their animals do much better on dairy and arable land (from which we originally drove them), so expect to see more deer farming in the lowlands.

Some supermarkets are selling venison from farmed deer slaughtered in abattoirs. The meat is processed into 'veniburgers', pâtés or sausages. Venison is taking off because it offers low fat and high protein, coupled with a fine taste and texture. UK production rose by around 100 tonnes in 1988 to 250–300 tonnes. British deer farmers, via the British Deer Farmers' Association, are linking up with Food from Britain to work on a venison quality standard mark to bring consistency to this fast-expanding market. The proposed standards would cover absence of hormones and growth promoters, hygiene levels, and carcase age.

THE 'REAL MEAT' TREND

If you are a meat-eater who wants to buy additive-free meat from organically grown animals reared in conditions tailored to their welfare (as set out below), you will find that you still can't get what you want in the supermarkets.

The pioneers in this area include the **Real Meat Company**, founded 1986, and the **Pure Meat Company**. The Real Meat Company, which supplies sausages, burgers, minces and pies containing no colouring, preservatives or chemical additives, has adopted a code of practice which includes the following points:

- Pigs cannot be kept in intensive systems. No tethering or constant-crating of sows. No tail cutting or castration of piglets. All pigs are straw-bedded for comfort and to allow 'rooting'.

- Calves are reared by natural suckling and kept outdoors, except in hard weather. No market trading of young calves is allowed.

- Lambs are reared by natural suckling. Particular attention is paid to winter housing and lambing procedure.

- Abattoirs are carefully monitored and any unable to meet the company's standards are dropped.

The Pure Meat Company has been negotiating to sell 'Conservation Grade' meat to the supermarkets. The company does not permit the sale of additive-free meat alongside conventionally produced meat unless it is pre-packaged, to ensure consumer protection and help guarantee the product's authenticity. In order to help boost supplies, the Pure Meat Company joined forces with Phillimore Farms to produce a Conservation Grade animal feed.

One problem in this area has been that there have been so many competing standards and labels. The launch of the UK Register of Organic Standards (UKROFS) in 1989 should help the consumer by simplifying the task of finding organically produced meat. Among the key points stressed by UKROFS are the housing and welfare of animals; livestock diets; the use of chemicals (no chemical treatments are allowed); straw and stubble burning (UKROFS is against burning); and the operation of silage silos and slurries, both of which can cause water pollution.

But what about the poultry and fish counters? As far as poultry goes, the Real Meat Company also produces chickens, ducks and turkeys. Antibiotics are used, but for site-specific treatment only. And, in the wake of the Campaign for Real Ale and Campaign for Real Bread, there has even been talk of a Campaign for Real Fish. Farmed fish, says Egon Ronay, 'has a distinctly muddy taste, whereas wild salmon really tastes like salmon. It is much the same as comparing frozen chickens with fresh chicken'. Wild fish tend to be much leaner than farmed fish which generally have much higher levels of fat.

THE POULTRY COUNTER

Each week, some nine million poultry birds are slaughtered in Britain. The demand for fresh poultry has doubled over the past 20 years, as consumers have switched away from red meat. Each year, the average Briton eats 13 kg (28 lb) of poultry meat, including some 9.5 kg (21 lb) of chicken and 3 kg (6 lb 8 oz) of turkey. Unfortunately, most of the poultry eaten in Britain now comes from battery units.

You do not have to be a member of Chickens' Lib to accept that the conditions found in many battery units are inadequate. Chickens and turkeys are the most intensively reared animals in Britain. They are subjected to artificially extended daylight, debeaking in the case of turkeys (and some hens), drastic overcrowding and inadequate dry bedding, often leading to blisters on their legs.

Free-range poultry

Some supermarkets are beginning to stock free-range poultry (see Table). These should be tastier, but in most cases there is no guarantee that their food has not contained antibiotics or growth promoters. As yet, the demand seems to be uneven, with only **Sainsbury's** and **Tesco** seeming happy with the position. A number, including **Co-op**'s Leo stores, **Gateway** and **Safeway**, stock free-range chickens from Moy Park, which has developed its own Free Range Charter. This requires that birds should:

- have 24-hour access to open fields, fenced to protect the birds against predators and not treated with chemicals

- be stocked at a maximum density of 4,000 birds per acre

- be provided with houses on site for shelter

- be fed on wheat, soya, vegetable oil, vitamins and minerals

- be on a free range farm for a minimum of 28 days.

AVAILABILITY OF FREE-RANGE POULTRY

Supermarket	Stock free-range chickens (own brand)?	Stock free-range turkeys (own brand)?	Good demand?	Feed and residues standards	Comments
Asda	Yes	Not stated	No	They do not set standards but supplier specification is approved by technical department	Only stock fresh free-range chickens
Co-op	Yes	Only in a few large stores	No	Moy Park standards (Co-op Leo)	No national stocking policy for free-range poultry – depends on demand. Co-op Leos stock Moy Park
Gateway	Yes	Not stated	No	Moy Park standards	Stock Moy Park, both whole chickens and portions, but only in limited number of stores
Iceland	Yes	No, but may consider this for Christmas	No	Have not set standards for either feed or residues	Stocking Iceland free-range chickens from April/May 1989

Continued overleaf

AVAILABILITY OF FREE-RANGE POULTRY (continued)

Supermarket	Stock free-range chickens (own brand)?	Stock free-range turkeys (own brand)?	Good demand?	Feed and residues standards	Comments
M & S	Yes	Yes	No	They require 'nil extraneous residue'	Reviewing idea of extending range
Safeway	Yes	No, but may consider this for Christmas	Yes	They do not yet set standards for feed but are planning to get involved	Stock Moy Park
Sainsbury's	Yes	Yes	Yes	Conform to government legislation but have own specifications on welfare and husbandry	Also sell free-range goose and duck and planning to extend free-range selection. All their game is free-range by its nature, but not labelled
Spar	No	No	N/A	They do not have their own standards, operate under UK regulations and Industry code of practice	
Tesco	Yes	No	No, but increasing	Set standards on bacterial contamination	Stock Moy Park

Salmonella and Listeria

The main recent concern has been about salmonella poisoning. The evidence suggests that if you buy chicken meat in the high street, be it frozen or fresh, in eight cases out of ten it will be infected with *Salmonella enteridis* — and the problem has caused even more controversy in the eggs market.

The fact that the poultry you buy is contaminated does not automatically mean that you will be infected, although the number of salmonella poisonings has increased very substantially in recent years. Reported cases of salmonella poisoning increased from 1,101 cases in England and Wales in 1982 to over 6,800 in 1987 — and more than 10,000 by November 1988. The problem affects free-range flocks, too, although it seems to be aggravated by poultry industry methods of recycling animal by-products (including both manure and slaughterhouse wastes) as feed-stuffs, and by the way in which chickens are slaughtered and packed. According to the Institute of Environmental Health Officers, in fact, the number of salmonella-related food poisoning cases could be in excess of two million a year in Britain.

Listeria monocytogenes is another pathogen found in pre-cooked chicken and in foods like runny cheeses. It can cause potentially lethal listeriosis. Deaths caused by this disease increased from 38 in 1983 to 59 in 1987. For the moment, the best thing to do is to cook all poultry products thoroughly. But ask your supermarket what it is doing to tackle these problems.

Pâté de foie gras

This is pâté made from the livers of force-fed geese. The process, which the French call *gavage*, involves forcing up to 2.5 kg (6 lb) of salted fatty maize down the goose's throat every day. In a trial in France, with 100 geese force-fed and 100 left to feed themselves, the force-fed geese produced more foie gras, but of a significantly lower quality. Challenged on the subject, the French Agriculture Ministry retorted that foie gras was not a matter for environmentalists. You could switch to vegetarian pâtés (see page 148).

Eggs

Every one of us, we are told, eats an average of 222 eggs a year. Despite the best efforts of the egg marketing people, however, the egg was undergoing a long-term decline in popularity even before the salmonella scare erupted. Among the issues that you face every time you crack the top of a boiled egg are: is it salmonella-free? is it free-range?

Salmonella

Although the chance of any given egg being contaminated with salmonella was very low, and the risk of infection generally confined to sensitive groups like young children and the elderly, the salmonella-in-eggs controversy shook the poultry industry to its roots. Egg sales fell by more than 20 per cent. The Government was forced to step in with an initial £19 million emergency rescue package. The fact remained, however, that with 200 million eggs eaten each week, a serious public health problem had been identified.

It was feared that egg producers who promptly began labelling their eggs as 'salmonella-free' might be deceiving the public, because there is no way of guaranteeing the quality of an individual egg without breaking it open. But the British Egg Industry Council recognised that a great deal could be done to ensure that eggs from particular farms were as safe as could be. It launched its SAFE slogan, made up as follows:

S for selected farms
A for assured chicks from salmonella-free breeders
F for feed similarly guaranteed
E for eggs regularly tested for salmonella.

The table summarises some of the steps the major supermarket groups have taken to ensure, as far as possible, that their eggs are salmonella-free.

Animal Welfare

The next thing to think about when buying eggs is whether they have been produced by one of Britain's 37 million battery hens. One of the reasons that so many of our hens are infected with

SUPERMARKET POLICIES ON SALMONELLA IN EGGS

Asda 'All packing stations supplying Asda submit samples once per month and conform to DHSS standards.'

Co-op 'All our packers must adhere to relevant Government legislation and codes of practice and must carry out continuously specified tests. The Co-op Leo requirements from its suppliers far exceed the current MAFF codes of practice for egg production and packaging.'

Gateway 'All suppliers contacted and all flocks have been tested and found free. All feed checked and found free. All chicks tested and found free. All the above is ongoing.'

Iceland They say that stringent checks are made by all their suppliers.

M & S 'Together with our suppliers we have established the highest standards of safety and hygiene for all our food products, including fresh eggs. These are produced and packed to detailed specifications and codes of practice which have been agreed between qualified technical experts employed by Marks & Spencer and their suppliers.' M & S go on to list a number of points which emphasise the care they have taken in relation to the potential threat of salmonella in eggs.

Safeway 'All suppliers who deliver to us are being tested on a weekly basis at our depots. In addition, we are ensuring all egg suppliers adhere to MAFF code of practice for the control of Salmonella in commercial laying flocks. Suppliers also have to make sure that both feed, mills and hatcheries are meeting the codes of practice which apply to them. No positive results have been found.'

Sainsbury's Suppliers follow the relevant MAFF and British Egg Industry Council codes for poultry producers and packers of eggs. They have detailed these and they include checking flocks regularly for salmonella.

Spar The production unit is inspected by Spar quality control analyst and the supplier has rigorously high standards including testing of feed stocks. Egg and environmental results have so far shown freedom from salmonella.

Tesco 'No poultry by-products allowed in feed. The feed is tested microbiologically and specs demand compliance with code of practice. Suppliers perform rigorous monthly checks for salmonella using Tesco methods. Own laboratories conducting routine tests.'

salmonella is that some live in extraordinarily contaminated circumstances and are fed — in part — on chicken processing wastes and offal.

The standard battery cage measures 18 in × 20 in (45 cm × 50 cm) and has five hens squeezed into it. Two million battery hens die in their cages every year and vets talk of diseases of intensification, including egg peritonitis, infectious bronchitis, cage layer fatigue and tumours.

The battery hen's natural laying life is three to four years, against a natural span of five or six. Once a bird stops laying, however, it is generally spent, almost featherless and diseased. It is whisked off to a processing plant to be rendered down into soups, stock cubes or even baby foods.

The increasing availability of free-range eggs has encouraged growing numbers of consumers to try them out. The real problem here has been that there are a number of different definitions which can be used. The EEC has four standards:

- **Free range**: Under this system birds must have continuous daytime access to open-air runs mainly covered with vegetation and with a maximum stocking rate of 1,000 hens per hectare (405 hens per acre). Hen house conditions must comply with those for deep-litter systems (see below). So long as these requirements are met, however, poultry farmers can pack almost as many hens into their poultry houses as they like.

- **Semi-intensive**: Birds must have continuous daytime access to open-air runs mainly covered with vegetation and with a maximum density of 4,000 hens per hectare (1,619 per acre). Hen house conditions must comply with those for deep-litter systems (see below).

- **Deep-litter**: Birds are kept in hen houses with a maximum stocking density of 7 birds per square metre of floor space. At least a third of the floor space should be solid, covered with straw, wood

EGGS

Supermarket	Sell free-range eggs?	Free-range stocked in same sizes as other eggs?	Other eggs stocked	Type of egg in paper pulp packaging	Type of packaging	Comments on packaging
Asda	Yes	No	97% semi-intensive 3% perchery	Some eggs	75% paper pulp	Packaging will be 100% paper pulp by Autumn 1989.
Co-op	Yes	No	100% semi-intensive	All eggs	90% paper pulp 10% pulp base with clear top shrink-wrap	The pulp they use is 90–100% recycled. They say they have switched to alleviate waste problems with plastics. Seem to be rather good in this area.
Gateway	Yes	No	95% semi-intensive 5% deep litter	All eggs	70% paper pulp 30% EPS plastic	Gradual change throughout 1988 following awareness over green issues. EPS packaging now without CFCs.
Iceland	No	N/A	100% intensive	Some eggs	50% paper pulp 50% EPS plastic	All packaging for egg-boxes is CFC-free and they are considering switching to a higher proportion of paper pulp.

Continued overleaf

EGGS (continued)

Supermarket	Sell free-range eggs?	Free-range stocked in same sizes?	Other eggs stocked	Type of egg in paper pulp packaging	Type of packaging	Comments on packaging
M & S	Yes	Yes	Not stated	Free-range & eggs laid on the same day	66% paper pulp 34% clear plastic	They have been selling some eggs in paper pulp for years but have recently launched an even fresher egg, laid and packed on the same day. This is in paper pulp packaging.
Safeway	Yes	Yes	Not stated	Free-range	25% paper pulp 58% clear plastic 17% fibre based with clear top shrink-wrap	Some of the barn eggs have been packaged in paper pulp but they are switching to the sort of boxes that have a shrink-wrapped top and a fibre base.
Sainsbury's	Yes	No	Not stated	Free-range	7% paper pulp 33% clear plastic 60% fibre base with clear top shrink-wrap	
Spar	Yes	No	100% perchery (barn)	Free-range	10% paper pulp 90% clear plastic	
Tesco	Yes	No	90% deep litter	Free-range and 18/24 battery	10% paper pulp 90% clear plastic	Moved to ozone-friendly boxes in 1988

shavings, sand or turf. And at least a quarter of the floor area should be used for the collection of droppings.

- **Perchery (barn)**: Eggs produced in this way, a variation of the deep-litter system, are called 'barn' eggs. It uses a series of perches and feeders at different levels to enable the farmer to cram in more birds — up to 25 hens per square metre.

Wherever possible, buy free-range eggs — but avoid the rather misleadingly labelled 'barn' eggs if you can.

Packaging

Eggs — arguably the most elegantly packaged objects in creation — are further packed in a range of man-made materials.

Worst were the spongey foam plastics, most of which were blown with ozone-damaging CFCs. This picture is now changing, as manufacturers move away from CFCs — but if you buy eggs in this sort of packaging, ask your supermarket to guarantee that it is CFC-free. Also avoid clear plastics, unless you are able to re-use or recycle them. They may give you a good view of the product, but they are wasteful and do not biodegrade. The best choice by far is cardboard egg-boxes, which are not only biodegradable, but are made from recycled paper. Almost all free-range eggs come in this form of packaging. As the Table shows, the **Co-op** comes out head and shoulders above its competitors in terms of its use of paper pulp packaging.

THE FISH COUNTER

With meat's popularity waning, fish has been enjoying a come-back. Fish eaters face some of the same issues as meat eaters, including the growing use of hormones. But from a natural resources point of view, fish offer a much better way of converting feed into animal protein than do farm animals. Fish is also highly nutritious and contains many oils which are important for our health.

If we are to eat fish, it has to come from somewhere. The world's seas are in growing danger of being overfished. Take the North Sea. Far too many boats are chasing too few fish. 'The sea's exhausted,' one fish merchant told the *Independent*. 'It badly needs a rest. As a result, it is thought that the European Community's total fishing fleet will need to be cut by at least 20 per cent.

Scotland's fishing industry is in crisis. A thousand jobs or more could be lost over the next couple of years because of the over-fishing of haddock, the industry's mainstay. Cod, the second most important whitefish, has also been over-fished. Unfortunately, the decline in the fisheries has often been masked by dramatic improvements in the efficiency of the fishing fleet. The new boats are larger, more powerful and better equipped. With sonar and echo sounders, the 'luck' factor in fishing has gone out of the window.

In 1988, Britain's fishermen were able to catch only 70 per cent of the UK's haddock quota and 90 per cent of the cod quota, because there were simply not enough of the two species to go around. Government scientists say that up to 30 per cent of the fish caught may be thrown back dead into the sea, because they are undersized. Most of the supermarkets report that they have had difficulty tracking down adequate supplies of cod and haddock.

As the marine fisheries become increasingly over-stretched, so we will need to turn to fish farming. Unfortunately, however, farmed fish are also associated with a number of environmental problems including pollution and the weakening of wild fish populations (see Fish Farming).

The supermarket fish counter is not the place to vote for better management of our fish stocks. Supermarkets are not in business to promote fisheries conservation: they simply switch to alternative sources of supply. The best way of voting is to help keep up the general environmental pressure on governments — which, in the end, are responsible for controlling fish-catch quotas and other aspects of fisheries management.

Fish farming

There are now well over 400 fish farms in the UK, a high proportion of which are engaged in salmon production. Indeed, less than 5 per cent of the salmon we eat is caught in the wild (see Salmon). Longer term, new fish species will be farmed, including halibut.

Although fish farming is a sensible way both of relieving harvesting pressure on wild fish stocks and of converting feed into animal protein at higher efficiencies than those achieved by intensive livestock units, fish farms can cause a variety of environmental problems. These include:

- local pollution
- the introduction of disease into wild fish populations
- the release of highly bred 'escapees', which may interbreed with and weaken wild fish
- pressure on predators — particularly herons (in the case of trout farms) and seals (in the case of salmon farms).

The pollution results from the food and faeces that fall through the bottom of the fish cages or nets and from the use of a wide range of chemicals. For every 10 tonnes of feed, 1 tonne of solid waste falls to the bottom of the sea beneath the fish cages and a further half tonne of soluble nitrogenous compounds enters the water column. The Clyde Purification Board estimates that one tonne of fish produces the same amount of sewage as 300 people. An average 25 tonne farm produces the same as over 7,000 people. The microbes breaking down these wastes need more oxygen, triggering algal blooms that can be toxic both to farmed and wild fish. These problems can be particularly severe in the sheltered, shallow waters of Scottish lochs, where the natural flushing effect of the tides is weak.

As far as chemicals are concerned, salmon farmers routinely use toxic Nuvan 500, formaldehyde, malachite green and a number of antibiotics. Among the many recent controversies

FARMED FISH

Supermarket	Proportion of fresh fish from fish farms	Types of fish from fish farms	Test for hormones or growth promoter residues?	Some own-brand processed products made with farmed fish
Asda	10%	Salmon, trout	No	Salmon fishcakes
Co-op	20%	Salmon, trout	No	None
Gateway	8%	Rainbow trout, salmon	No	Salmon and shrimp pâtés, no tinned products
Iceland	Very little	Salmon, trout (frozen only)	No	N/A
M & S	Small proportion	Salmon, trout, warm water prawns, mussels	No (but do specify feed)	Salmon: en croûte, à la crème, steaks with herb butter, tagliarini, fish cakes, pâté, filled with herb butter in crumb, poached salmon terrine Mussels: marinière, bonne femme, garlic Prawns: prawns in cream sauce, prawn tikka masal with rice, butterfly garlic prawns in crumb Other: seafood paella prawn
Safeway	15%	Salmon, trout, mussels	No	Not sure about how much farmed fish is used in fish products but 'bound to be increasing' in products like: pâtés, en croûte, recipe dishes, fish cakes and battered Anges
Sainsbury's	22%	Salmon, trout	Yes	None of their processed products come from farmed fish
Spar	N/A	N/A	N/A	N/A
Tesco	Less than 5%	Salmon, trout	No	Smoked salmon roulade and smoked trout pâté

that have revolved around the industry, one of the most potentially serious was the row between trawlermen harvesting shellfish off the west coast of Scotland and salmon farmers over the effects of Nuvan 500. This is a highly toxic chemical used by salmon farmers to control pests such as sea lice. One of the by-products produced as the chemical breaks down in the sea is dichlorvos, listed by the 1987 North Sea Convention as one of the 26 most dangerous chemicals. Scientists at Aberdeen University have argued that the chemical may be to blame for the fact that growing numbers of wild salmon are going blind.

The spread of disease is a proven problem, whereas the possibility that escaped farmed fish might interbreed with — and weaken — wild fish is still unproven. What is beyond dispute is that fish are escaping. Early in 1989, for example, 7,000 farmed salmon escaped into Loch Aline in Argyllshire after the propellor of a boat towing nets of young salmon out to sea cut into one of the nets. A recent survey of 54 Norwegian rivers found that 15 – 20% of the fish examined were escapees.

As far as the pressure on predators is concerned, herons and seals can certainly cause damage to farmed fish. A single seal destroyed 13,000 salmon, worth around £20 apiece. As a result of such damage, according to the Marine Conservation Society, salmon farmers are killing 1,000 seals, 200 herons and 2,000 cormorants and shags a year.

Considerable problems, clearly, but not beyond the wit of man to solve. If we are to feed our growing numbers, we must learn to harvest the seas in a sustainable manner, and fish farming will be a key industry of the future. The problem at the moment is that it is still at the pioneering stage — and is struggling to reach an accommodation with the environment. To date, the environment has been getting the worst of it. For the Green Consumer, the advice must be to welcome fish farming but to keep a close eye on the way that the industry behaves. If it misbehaves, we can vote for better behaviour in the supermarket!

The proportion of farmed fish stocked by supermarkets is not enormous, as the Table shows, but it is significant — and is certain to grow. **Safeway** says that it cannot tell how much farmed fish is used to make canned products, but that the proportion is bound to be growing.

Of the supermarkets that responded to our survey, **Sainsbury's** seems to be the only one that is testing farmed fish for residues. One of the areas where we should expect supermarkets to help is by putting pressure on fish farming companies to ensure that their operations are environmentally acceptable.

Caviar

Made from the roe of the sturgeon (especially the beluga) and other large fish obtained from the lakes and rivers of Eastern Europe, caviar production has caused the over-fishing of sturgeon populations in the Caspian Sea. Its scarcity makes it enormously expensive — and increases the pressure on the slow-breeding fish. Most supermarkets offer lumpfish roe, which may be an ecologically preferable substitute because it comes from species which are not under such hunting pressure.

Fish fingers

Due to a Greenpeace campaign designed to persuade consumers to boycott fish fingers containing Icelandic fish, as a protest against Iceland's continued whaling operations, there is a common misperception that these fish fingers are made from whale-meat. Not so. They generally contain cod.

In July 1989 Greenpeace stopped their campaign because Iceland ceased its whaling operations.

Salmon

The 240,000 barrels of crude oil spilled from the *Exxon Valdez* in Alaska early in 1989 caused an ecological disaster. Six-month-old salmon leaving river inlets for the open sea faced being wiped out by the oil. Normally, they would spend up to 18 months in the Pacific before returning to Prince William Sound as fully grown pink salmon. Industry analysts predicted that catches in the 1990 season could be decimated. Pink salmon are generally canned and Prince William Sound was expected to supply 45 per cent of 1989's pink salmon catch.

The tremendous fishing pressure on wild salmon populations is fuelling the interest in salmon farming. The salmon farming industry has climbed from infancy in two decades to become a £100 million-a-year business, with production expected to soar from 1989 levels of about 20,000 tonnes to 50–70,000 tonnes. (For associated problems, see Fish Farming.)

Smoked fish

Smoking fish and fish products used to be an excellent way of extending their life, since fish is a highly perishable commodity. The dramatic increase in the availability of smoked salmon products is just one indication of the growth in the supply of farmed fish. It is worth remembering, however, that smoked fish can contain high levels of sodium or salt, and is often artificially coloured. Go for quality.

Trout

This is the most extensively farmed fish in Britain — with the expanding number of trout farms (over 300 throughout the UK) implicated in water pollution and pressure on local heronries.

Anglers on the River Avon in Hampshire claim that the scores of trout farms there extract up to 70 per cent of the river's flow, passing it through crowded trout tanks, and then tip it back into the river along with fish droppings, which can carry diseases to which wild fish may have little resistance.

At the same time there is evidence that our native brown trout is under threat from pollution, from East Anglia to the River Tweed in Scotland. Scientists blame a mix of acid rain and agricultural pollution.

Properly handled, however, trout are an excellent way of producing protein from feed. 1.5 tonnes of feed can produce 1 tonne of fish.

Tuna

The main concern about tuna, until recently, was its mercury content. Some of this was thought to come from industrial discharges into rivers and oceans, but a fair amount also stems from natural sources, including submarine volcanoes. The supermarkets say that either they or their suppliers check all tuna for mercury.

The latest concern links tuna fish sandwiches and those smiling intelligences of the sea, the dolphins. The sad fact is that millions of dolphins have been killed by tuna fishermen. Some species of tuna are more likely than others to be accompanied by schools of dolphin, which makes it important to know what sort of tuna you are buying — and where it has come from.

The conservation organisation Care for the Wild has investigated this issue in some depth. It concludes that the only tuna that causes particular concern is Yellowfin tuna — and the only place where the problem arises is in the Eastern Tropical Pacific. Europe imports large amounts of this tuna and the Table shows the supermarkets that stock Yellowfin.

There have been horrific tales of a veritable dolphin holocaust perpetrated by the tuna-fishing fleets of the Eastern Tropical Pacific. The tuna fishermen catch $1 billion of tuna a year by hunting the dolphins, spreading their purse-seine nets to catch both. Unfortunately for the dolphins, they and the tuna swim together, the schools of dolphins on the surface, the Yellowfin tuna a few feet below them.

'I saw dolphins being drowned, mutilated and butchered,' American environmentalist Sam La Budde told a US Senate sub-committee last year. 'Many were caught in the net and hoisted out of the water. Some fell back into the sea as their flippers and beaks were broken or ripped out of their bodies. I saw 500 dolphins shrieking in panic as they fought against the net and gasped for air. I saw crew members toss a baby dolphin back and forth like a football or stand by helplessly as living dolphins were dragged aloft, thrashing and flailing in terror before being literally crushed to death in the power blocks.'

Budde, who posed as a ship's cook, filmed the holocaust in

TUNA

SUPERMARKET OWN BRANDS

Supermarket	Types of tuna	From which countries?
Asda	Yellowfin	Spain, Florida
Co-op	Skipjack	Japan, Fiji, Solomon Islands, Thailand
Gateway	Skipjack Yellowfin Bonito	Thailand, Fiji, Mauritius Senegal, Ivory Coast, Indonesia, Philippines, Seychelles
Iceland	N/A (but stock John West)	N/A
M & S	Skipjack	Philippines
Safeway	Skipjack	Thailand, Maldives, Philippines, Mauritius
Sainsbury's	Skipjack, Yellowfin	Fiji, Solomon Islands
Spar	Skipjack	Thailand
Tesco	No own brand	N/A

MANUFACTURERS' BRANDS

Company	Types of tuna	From which countries?
John West	Skipjack Yellowfin	Thailand, Mauritius, Fiji, Ivory Coast, Maldives, Philippines
Farquhar	Skipjack	Thailand, Bali, Indonesia

Note: All the supermarkets in our survey said that they or their suppliers tested for mercury.

progress on a Panamanian vessel, the SS *Maria Luisa*. Six million dolphins are estimated to have been killed over the past 30 years. At least 300 are still being killed every day.

All skipjack, albacore, bonito and white meat tuna are thought to be acceptable. **Sainsbury's** does sell Yellowfin tuna (see Table) under the name of *South Seas Tuna*, but it has been confirmed that this is imported from Fiji, and caught on a line rather than in nets, and that dolphin deaths are not involved.

Marks & Spencer sent experts to the Philippines to see how its tuna are caught. It now guarantees that no dolphins are slaughtered in the process.

If you buy fresh tuna, it will not be Yellowfin. **Gateway** sells filleted fresh European tuna. If you are buying Yellowfin tuna anywhere else, the countries to be wary of are the United States, Mexico, Panama, Spain, El Salvador, Costa Rica, Vanuatu and the Cayman Islands. Other countries act as handling agents and are equally suspect, including Thailand (by the far the largest), Indonesia, Japan, Taiwan and the Philippines.

THE VEGETARIAN OPTION

According to a Gallup Poll survey in 1988, 3 per cent of the adult population are vegetarians, while many more have switched to low-meat diets. Around 9 per cent of children are said by their parents to be vegetarian or beginning to avoid red meat.

Among the reasons given for switching away from meat are general concerns about health and, more specifically, worries about the contamination of meat and meat products, about animal welfare and the resource-efficiency of meat production. It can take roughly 10 kilos of animal feed to produce a kilo of meat. At a time when the world's population is soaring and the pressure on farm land is intensifying on every continent, a no-meat or low-meat diet makes increasingly good sense to Green Consumers.

Some supermarkets have been taking this trend very seriously indeed, stocking an expanding range of products tailored to vegetarian dietary requirements, including straightforward vegetarian dishes and meat substitutes such as tofu and Quorn (see Box). Among the vegetarian alternatives to meat are **Realeat's** vegetarian sausages, the *Vegeburger* and *Vegebanger*. These are now stocked by some supermarkets and can be found in most health food stores. They are also sold frozen or as mixes.

Among the supermarkets saying they stock some products for vegetarians were: **Iceland** (soya-based mince), the **Co-op** (**Birds Eye** *Vegeburgers, Dale Park Grills*), **Gateway** (*Vegeburgers*, and

QUORN: FEASTING ON FUNGUS

Quorn is a revolutionary new food based on a fungus originally found in a field near High Wycombe. Developed by **Rank Hovis McDougall (RHM)**, best known for brands like *Hovis* and *Mother's Pride*, the fungus — when in its raw state — is virtually odourless and tasteless.

It contains about 45 per cent protein and 13 per cent fat, a composition which brings it into the same class as grilled beef — and, to RHM's delight in these diet-conscious days, it proved to have a lower fat content than raw beef and to be high in dietary fibre.

But perhaps the most extraordinary thing about this versatile fungus (which belongs to the same family as mushrooms and truffles) is the way in which it can be turned into a complete spectrum of foods, from soups and fortified drinks through biscuits to convincing replicas of chicken, ham and veal.

Grown in fermenters filled with glucose syrup, the fungus produces long strands that can be, in effect, woven to produce meat substitutes and other foods for those on low-meat or vegetarian diets. The fungus turns out to be much more efficient at converting carbohydrate into high quality protein than are traditional farm animals like chickens, cattle or pigs.

Quorn is now becoming more widely available in the form of prepared 'ready meals'. Look in the chilled and freezer cabinets in your supermarket. Among the supermarkets now stocking Quorn-based products are: **Sainsbury's** (*Chicken Style Savoury Pie, Beef Style Savoury Pie, Potato Topped Savoury Pie, Sweet and Sour Flan* and *Tomato Masala Flan*), **Tesco** (*Chasseur Provencal, Kashmiri Korma, Mushroom and Onion Quorn Harvest Pie, Onion and Quorn Harvest Pie*) and **Waitrose** (*Quorn, Salad, Savoury Casserole, Sweet and Sour Casserole*).

The product is not yet available separately as an ingredient for home cooking, but this is very much part of RHM's plans for the future. Further details from the Quorn Information Service, Freepost, London SW1P 1YZ.

are looking at *Quorn*), **Marks & Spencer** (a wide range of vegetable cutlets and crispbakes), **Safeway** (*Quorn*) and **Sainsbury's** (*Vegeburgers* and *Quorn*-based *Savoury Pie*).

Many Green Consumers will want to avoid pâté de foie gras. Instead, try some of the vegetable pâtés available under the **Living Foods** and **Euvita** labels. **Vessen** offers vegetarian pâté snacks, including herb, mushroom and sweet pepper flavours, while **La Terrinerie** offers a range of vegetarian pâtés and terrines.

CONTACTS

Pure Meat Company, Coombe Court Farm, Moretonhampstead, Devon TQ13 8QD. Tel: 0647 40944

Real Meat Company Ltd, East Hill Farm, Heytesbury, Warminster, Wiltshire BA12 0HR. Tel: 0985 40436

The Dairy Counter

There's nothing more natural — and rural — than a herd of dairy cows grazing on lush green grass. Unfortunately, the modern dairy industry is anything but natural. It raises a number of issues both in relation to milk and milk products — including cream, yoghurt, butter and cheese.

Milk

There are a number of issues in relation to our daily Pinta. For example:

- what's in our milk?
- how has it been treated?
- what's it packed in?
- is there such a thing as organic milk?

One of the main trends is that the milk market has seen a great deal of emphasis on what is *not* in the product. In a health- and diet-conscious society we have been turning our backs on normal full-fat milk and switching to low-fat and skimmed milks. The consumption of low-fat milks, which was negligible at the beginning of the 1980s, now accounts for around a quarter of milk sales. One result has been that more cream products are now available (see Cream).

But there has also been concern about possible contamination of milk, whether by radiation, pesticides or hormones. In West Germany recently, the concern was about radioactivity from the Chernobyl disaster. In Britain, meanwhile, the main controversy has been about the proposed use of a hormone, bovine somatotropin (BST), to boost milk production in dairy cows. The BST issue is briefly described in the Box. The policies of the major supermarkets are spotlighted in the Table.

SUPERMARKET POLICIES ON BST IN MILK

Asda	They would like to give the consumer the choice between BST or BST-free and would like suppliers to give them this information.
Co-op	They are opposed to the use of BST for increasing the milk yield of cows.
Gateway	'We do not knowingly approve of its use.'
Iceland	They say 'BST is now banned as a hormone to promote milk production.' The fact is that BST is not banned — it has not been cleared for use.
Marks & Spencer	Concerned with the secrecy surrounding trials. They have made a representation to the Ministry about this. They have a policy to disclose relevant information to customers about products particularly in relation to additives.
Safeway	They say they are bound by the 1968 Medicines Act as are all producers and sellers.
Sainsbury's	They say that milk from trial farms is incorporated into the normal milk supply, so it is possible that small quantities of milk from these trial farms are included in the milk they sell. Sainsbury's are unhappy about the secrecy but say they have been assured by both MAFF and the Milk Marketing Board that there is no risk to the public.
Spar	No policy
Tesco	They say that it is not permitted except in government-sponsored secret trials over which supermarkets have no control or choice. Tesco say they resent this.

MILKING THE SUPER-COW

Throughout Europe, consumers and farmers are worried about the potential impact of bovine somatotropin (BST). BST is a naturally occurring protein. All cows secrete it and those which produce the most milk also produce the most BST. By using the hormone, farmers can boost the yield of milk per kilo of feed. So, for those consumers worried solely about the efficiency with which animals convert their feed into milk, meat and other products, BST could be seen as a welcome development.

To start with, BST was extracted from the pituitary glands of cows, but it can now be produced in great quantities by genetically engineered bacteria. It is thought to be safe, because it has been found to have no effect on people. Indeed, all cow's milk naturally contains trace elements of BST, generally at the level of less than two parts per billion.

The main issue in relation to BST is lack of consumer choice. Trials are being carried out with various dairy herds and the milk is coming on to the market, but neither retailers nor consumers can select milk on the basis of whether or not it contains synthetic BST. Many see this as worrying, whether or not BST has any effect on our health.

Once injected into a cow, BST boosts milk yields by 10 – 15 per cent and feed efficiency by 5 – 15 per cent. Unfortunately for BST producers, however, the demand for milk has levelled off in Europe, while production has continued to grow. The result has been a sizable 'milk lake'. The European Commission has already been forced to introduce tough milk production quotas, which have forced many small dairy farmers out of the business.

Against this background, the introduction of BST looks likely to lead to further concentration of dairy production on the largest, most intensive farms, the collapse of more small farms and widespread job losses. One US study suggested that America would need 25 per cent fewer cows, while the number of dairy farmers would be cut by a third.

Another controversy raged around the pasteurisation of milk when the Government announced its intention to ban the sale of untreated or 'green top' milk following concern about the contamination of raw milk with salmonella and other microbes. The supporters of green top milk, which accounts for 2 – 3 per cent of milk sales in England and Wales (but is not sold by supermarkets), said that there was no danger from such diseases as tuberculosis or brucellosis: all dairy herds are now tested for these diseases as part of a national programme. The campaign for raw milk, or perhaps one could call it 'Real Milk', has been led by the Association of Unpasteurised Milk Producers and Consumers. In June 1989 the Government decided to allow the continued sale of green top milk.

As far as the packaging of milk is concerned, there has been a steady switch away from returnable glass milk bottles as the supermarkets have sold ever-growing quantities of milk in paper cartons. The Table shows that only the **Co-op** still sells a (tiny) proportion of its milk in glass bottles, with the bulk sold either in cartons (the favourite) or plastic bottles. Wherever possible, buy milk in returnable glass bottles — and return them. In the supermarket, buy paper packs rather than plastic ones.

The Milk Marketing Board has moved even further away from environment-friendliness by working on a Milk Can product. The milk will come in a ring-pull can, that awful icon of throwaway packaging technology.

MILK PACKAGING

Supermarket	% of milk in glass bottles	% of milk in cartons	% of milk in plastic bottles
Asda	Nil	80%	20%
Co-op	1.3%	70.4%	28.3%
Gateway	Nil	60%	40%
Iceland	Nil	90%	10%
M & S	?	'Most'	?
Safeway	Nil	62%	38%
Sainsbury's	Nil	60%	40%
Spar	Nil	90%	10%
Tesco	Nil	65%	35%

Interestingly, organic milk is now on its way. **Unigate Dairies** has been test-marketing its *Pastures Pure Organic Milk*. Carrying the Soil Association's organic label, the 500 ml cartons contain semi-skimmed, pasteurised milk produced on organic farmland in the Channel Islands. The company believes that demand will quickly outstrip supply, since there are only a small number of existing organic milk producers — and new entrants have to spend at least two years 'cleansing' their land and herds according to the Soil Association's standards.

Soy milks are used as a substitute for cow's milk and are favoured by vegetarians and vegans. However, they came under fire in 1989. Doctors claimed that they contained about 100 times as much aluminium as human milk — and 10 times as much as cow's milk. Aluminium can accumulate in the growing bones and brains of babies and, in rare cases, have a poisonous effect. Soy milk is also low in zinc, which normally competes with aluminium for absorption into the body, so increasing the body's aluminium intake even further. Mothers feeding their babies on soy milk should take medical advice. Organic brands are beginning to come on to the market, meanwhile.

Cream

The growing demand for low fat and skimmed milks has boosted the quantities of cream available. As a result, the price has been falling, in relative terms at least, and sales have been growing. In 1988, for example, sales rose by 7 per cent, producing a market worth £325 million.

It is worth thinking about the packaging issue here. Most cream is sold in plastic tubs, topped by a foil lid; some have a re-sealable plastic lid as well, so can be re-used. Cream is also available in Tetra-Pak cartons and cans.

Butter and margarine

In a large supermarket you can count more than 50 brands of products which are known in the trade as 'yellow fats'. They include butter, sunflower margarine, low fat spreads, dairy spreads and standard margarine.

Butter consumption fell by 50 per cent during the 1980s, with much of the running in recent years being made by margarine producers such as **Van de Bergh** (which makes *Flora, Stork, Blue Band, Krona, Echo, Summer County* and *Delight*) and **Dairy Crest**. They have benefited from the growing interest in healthier foods, particularly those with a lower fat content. Some products based on sunflower oil are high in polyunsaturates and low in saturated fats and cholesterol. By 1992, companies like **St Ivel** believe, low-fat spread and health products will account for 60 per cent of the yellow fats market.

Butter and margarine are wrapped in a variety of foils and papers. It seems likely that the metallised foils will take much longer to break down in the environment than paper-based packaging. Some products come in plastic containers. Again, ask yourself: Can the container be re-used? Avoid products that are individually wrapped (e.g. butter portions) as these are highly intensive to produce and create a lot of waste.

One interesting issue is whether butter imported from New Zealand consumes more energy to produce and distribute, because it needs to be transported over long distances, than British or European butter. We don't know the answer, although shipping is generally more energy-efficient than road transport. What may tip the balance is the fact that butter travels in refrigerated ships. Apart from the energy-efficiency considerations, are CFCs used in the refrigeration systems?

Cheese

Much of what looks like cheese isn't. Many pizza manufacturers, for example, use cheaper substitutes — like vegetable fats — because they can save up to £400 a tonne by doing so. The real issues, however, concern what is in ordinary cheeses.

Environmentally, the main issue is probably that the small cheese producers who, in a minor way, help to keep Britain's rural landscapes small-scale, are threatened not only by competition from the big cheese-makers but also by EEC agricultural changes and health questions.

There is no doubt that listeria bacteria found in some cheeses can cause ill-health, even death.

The impact of the listeria scare on the international cheese industry was profound. Supermarkets like **Marks & Spencer** and **Tesco** de-listed unpasteurised cheeses, withdrawing cheeses such as Danish Blue, Swiss Emmenthal and Gruyère, Parmesan and Canadian Cheddar. To counter the trend, French Premier Jacques Chirac munched a morsel of the Vacherin Mont d'Or soft cheese that was reported to have killed at least 25 people in Switzerland. The French cheese-makers insisted that their cheeses were safe, because they are made in a different way from the Swiss cheeses.

Many of the small cheese-makers who were hit by the controversy, and the ensuing bans on unpasteurised products, felt that the large dairy companies had encouraged the ban — because they were worried about the inroads that the smaller operations were making on their market share.

Many vegetarians eat cheese, although it raises a number of tricky issues. Rennet-free cheeses are felt to be less worrying for vegetarians, and the Table lists a range of suitable cheeses now available from the supermarkets. Many use a vegetable 'rennet', which is the scientific successor to the traditional use of plants like lady's bedstraw, nettles, butterwort, fig tree juice or holy thistle in cheese-making. A number of **Co-op** branded foods also contain vegetarian cheeses, including their *Cheese and Onion Pasty*, *Deep Filled Mixed Vegetable Pizza*, *Cheese and Vegetable Snack*, and *Wholemeal Provençal Quiche*.

VEGETARIAN CHEESES

Asda   Asda Brand Cheddar
Asda Brand Cheshire
The following cheeses are not sold specifically under 'vegetarian' headings but are made with vegetarian rennet:
Bleu d'Auvergne
Capricorn
Caws Caron
Cornish Yarg
Cornish Cream Cheese
Duddleswell
Galway Bay Cheeses
Pant-ys-gawn
Ribchester
Ribblesdale

	Sage Lancashire
	Tasty Lancashire
	Westmorland
Co-op	Co-op Brand Vegetarian Cheddar
Gateway	St Ivel Vegetarian Cheddar
	Gateway French Le Roulé (3 varieties)
	Gateway Italian Dolce Latte
	Polenghi Italian fresh Mozzarella
	Polenghi Italian Ricotta
	Pencarreg
	Acorn Ewes Milk Cheese
	Polenghi Italian Mascarpone
	some of the French Brie
Iceland	none
M & S	Strong Mature Cheddar
Safeway	Safeway Vegetarian Cheddar
	Dairy Crest Vegetarian Cheddar
	Cottage Cheese — assorted
	Trimrite Cottage Cheeses
	Cream Cheese
	Curd Cheese
	Goats Cheese — assorted
	Exquisa — assorted
	Fraisy and Horseradish
	Miree — assorted
	Safeway full fat soft cheese — assorted
	Roulé — assorted
	Brie — assorted
Sainsbury's	Danish Blue
	Vegetarian Cheddar
	Cream Cheese — assorted
	Curd Cheese
	Skimmed Milk Soft Cheese
	Half Fat Cottage Cheese — assorted
	Full Fat Soft Cheese with Garlic and Parsley
	Cottage Cheese — assorted
	Creamery Full Fat Soft Cheese
	Half Fat Creamery Cheese
	Bavarian Soft Cheese Whipped
	Mozzarella Cheese
	Welsh Goats cheese — assorted
Tesco	Vegetarian Cheddar

Organic cheeses are beginning to come on to the market, too. Among the supermarkets stocking them are **Asda** (*Pencarreg and Cardigan* organic cheese), **Co-op Leos** (*Pencarreg and Cardigan*), **Safeway** (*Pencarreg*) and **Sainsbury's** (*Pencarreg*).

Among recent product introductions is **St Hubert**'s *Biobree*, an organic French brie. The land used to graze the cows is guaranteed free of pesticides and other toxic residues.

A number of non-dairy cheeses are also available, including *tofu* and a rennet-free soya cheese from Sweden, distributed by **Kallo Foods**.

Eggs   (see Poultry, page 132)

Yoghurt

There has been enormous growth in the consumption of yoghurt and similar products, which are generally healthy and nutritious. This is an intensively competitive area, with considerable pressure on **Express Foods**, who relaunched the UK's oldest and biggest yoghurt brand, *Ski*, in 1989. Yoghurt has always had a healthy image, but there is now growing interest in organic products. We asked the supermarkets whether they stocked organic yoghurts, and a surprising number said they now do.

Those that did were **Asda** (*Bio Best*), the **Co-op** (*Onken Biogert*, which contains organic fruit and is stocked by the Co-op Leos), **Gateway** (*Onken Soog*), **Safeway** (*Baileys Bio Best Yoghurt, Busses Farm Organic Yoghurt, Onken Bio Yoghurt*) and **Sainsbury's** (*Busses Farm Organic Yoghurt*).

Onken Dairy, a German company, has also launched *Bio Fruit Dessert*, claimed to be the first organic fromage frais to be sold in the UK. Additionally, the company offers *Bioghurt Pot*, a set yoghurt. The four fruit varieties include organically grown fruit and wholegrain. Interestingly, Onken has introduced the concept of re-usable packaging to its range, including the re-sealable Bioghurt Pot container which is dishwasher-proof and can be used in your freezer. The larger the pack you buy, clearly, the less packaging you are using per litre of product. **Country Care** yoghurt suggests that you use their pots as storage jars — you send off for cork stoppers and labels.

Many organic yoghurt products never appear in the supermarket, however. **Rachel's Dairy** Organic Products, for example, are produced on a farm that has been organic since 1943. Apart from eight flavours of Very Low Fat and Wholemilk Natural Yoghurt, Rachel's Dairy also supplies rennet-free Cottage Cheese, Clotted and Guernsey Cream, Butter and Buttermilk.

CONTACTS

Association of Unpasteurised Milk Producers and Consumers, Path Hill Farm Cottage, Goring Heath, Reading, Berkshire RG8 7RE.

Rachel's Dairy, Brynllys Farm, Borth, Dyfed.

Convenience Foods, Snacks and Nuts

Look along the shelves — or in the freezer compartments — at your local supermarket, and you will be struck by the range of convenience foods now on offer. From baked beans to new foods based on exotic ingredients like Quorn (see page 147), it is worth thinking about the environmental implications of the convenience you buy. The snack-food trend, covered below, also has implications for the quality of our urban and natural environments.

As the number of single-person and smaller households grows, and the value put on time increases, so the demand for convenience foods — and for microwave ovens — will continue to soar. The way in which convenience foods are processed, with much of the work already done for the consumer, has major implications for waste disposal.

The supermarkets are offering quite a variety of ready-made meals aimed at the Green Consumer. **Asda** offers a vegetarian range of meals, but some contain cheese manufactured with animal rennet. **Iceland** has 20 prepared products suitable for vegetarians. The **Co-op** has no national stocking policy in this area, but most large Co-op superstores will sell Vegetarian Ready-Made meals. **Gateway** offers the *Goodlife* range of vegetarian cutlets. A growing range of vegetarian meals can also now be found in **Marks & Spencer**, **Safeway**, **Sainsbury's** and **Tesco** stores. **Spar** is considering stocking products in this area.

Apart from the packaging issue, perhaps the key issues in relation to convenience foods relate to the way in which they are treated to ensure a long shelf-life. (See pages 166 – 9.)

Baby foods

In the face of mounting concern about the contamination of foods by pesticides, baby food companies are making efforts to ensure that their products are free of pesticide residues. In the States, **Heinz** took the lead, by banning the use of a number of pesticides on crops used to make baby foods. In the UK, the company says, 'we take great care to follow the Ministry of Agriculture, Fisheries and Food statutory safeguards concerning pesticide usage. All our raw materials meet a demanding specification which lays down that only permitted pesticides may be used in an approved way. Recognising the increased sensitivity of babies, we undertake rigorous analytical testing of products as part of our stringent controls.'

Another issue here is the deliberate contamination of baby food products, in what has been called 'supermarket terrorism'. It is clearly important that this risk be tackled with increasingly tamper-proof packaging, but this, in turn, adds to the packaging problem and — because a number of different materials tend to be used — may complicate recycling.

Baked beans

We asked the supermarkets if they tested their baked beans for pesticide residues. **Asda**, the **Co-op**, **Gateway**, **Safeway**,

Sainsbury's, **Spar** and **Tesco** do not test for pesticide residues, while **Iceland** and **Marks & Spencer** do not sell baked beans. **Heinz** replied, 'We test the raw material — the ingredients — before they go to make the finished product. We have found no detectable levels. We use specific suppliers and impose stringent controls.'

On the labelling front, **Tesco's** baked bean cans are labelled 'Steel Recyclable'. The **Co-op** and **Spar** said that they would be prepared to label their cans in this way, while **Gateway** and **Sainsbury's** seemed a good deal less enthusiastic about the idea.

Ice cream

Ice cream sales have also been growing rapidly, jumping by 9 per cent in 1988 alone. In terms of quality, British ice cream is often extremely disappointing. The Milk Marketing Board has criticised the main ice cream manufacturers for keeping to the lowest allowable standards, with a great deal of air and vegetable fat in many leading brands. 'Try to sell our soft ice cream in France and Germany,' says the London Food Commission, 'and you would go to court.' About half of the volume of a typical ice cream is made up of air, while in soft-scoop ice cream the air content can reach 65 per cent.

According to the London Food Commission, many commercial brands of ice cream contain a number of additives whose other uses raise a number of question-marks over their healthiness:

- piperohal, used as a vanilla flavouring, but also commonly used as an ingredient in lice killers

- diethylene glycol, used in anti-freeze and paint stripper, which is employed in ice cream as a cheaper binding agent than eggs

- amyl acetate, also used to clean leather and textiles, instead of real banana flavouring

- ethyl acetate, a known skin irritant, used to simulate the taste of pineapple

- butyraldehyde, used instead of expensive nut flavours, and commonly found in rubber cement.

By contrast, the success of speciality ice cream producers like **Denbigh Farm Ices**, the **Neal's Yard Creamery**, **Thornton**'s and **Real Dairy Ice Cream** (which produces the Loseley brand), suggests that there is a market for ice cream high in dairy cream and real fruit flavours. Unfortunately, with the exception of Loseley, such products are not widely available in supermarkets. More positively, **Ben & Jerry**, an American company, plans to launch a range of ices using ingredients sourced from the rainforest, in an attempt to create a value for the rainforest standing rather than the rainforest fallen, as logs.

The main environmental issues here are the use of energy and CFCs in refrigeration and plastic packaging. Heavy ice cream eaters have probably run out of things to do with empty ice cream tubs, so plastics recycling is the logical next step.

Nuts

Supermarket sales of nuts and nut-based snacks have been increasing steadily, with the main growth at the premium end of the market. Sales of pistachios, cashews and macademias have all been on the rise. The biggest manufacturer here is **KP**, a subsidiary of **United Biscuits**.

We asked **UB Brands**, the overall holding company, whether it thought environmental issues were important in relation to other issues with which it has to deal. It replied that they are of 'low importance'. But it then went on to say that it planned to give 'more serious consideration' to environmental issues in future. And one of the main areas where it expected pressures to build as Britain moves deeper into Europe is on the environmental acceptability of packaging.

The main environmental issue in this category in 1989 related to brazil nuts. The assassination of Francisco Mendes Filho, who led the fight by Brazil's rubber-tappers to protect large areas of Amazonia's rainforests, underscored the dangers facing those who stand up against rainforest destruction. But, surprisingly, the brazil nut may provide a certain amount of leverage.

'Chico' Mendes was campaigning for the establishment of 'extractive reserves', believed by many to be the best hope for the future of the Brazilian rainforests. He argued that people would fight to keep the trees standing if they were seen as a source of important commodities like rubber and brazil nuts. Research has shown that rubber-tappers, most of whom also collect brazil nuts, get more income out of the rainforest, while leaving it standing, than do cattle-ranchers, who fell and burn the trees. Interestingly, because brazil nut trees are found only in the wild rather than in plantations, brazil nuts are both a product and a symbol of a healthy rainforest.

Sucden Products, part of France's **Sucres Denrees** group and probably the largest importers of brazil nuts in Europe, have been helping to lobby the Brazilian government to introduce higher prices for brazil nuts — to encourage their collection and export. 'We are not so naive as to believe that eating a few more brazil nuts in Europe is going to save the Amazon rainforests,' explained Jeremy Holt of Sucden, 'but there is no doubt that a more positive approach could have an effect.'

Sucden has been approaching British supermarkets to see if they would be interested in a new 'rainforest-friendly' labelling scheme for brazil nuts. They found the response 'fairly cool', but we pushed the supermarkets on the subject. The **Co-op**, **Gateway** and **Marks & Spencer** said they would not consider it, but **Asda**, **Sainsbury's**, **Spar** and **Tesco** said they would. **Safeway** will start labelling in Autumn '89.

Peanuts and peanut butter

We also asked the supermarkets whether they had looked into the impact of peanut cultivation on soil erosion. They all said they hadn't, although **Sainsbury's** said that its peanuts come from farms that guard against soil erosion, using crop rotation and hedgerow planting to protect the soil against the wind.

Gateway said that it was collaborating with the US Peanut Council and the Georgia Peanut Council to ensure soil conservation, although subsequent cross-checking with the company suggested that this collaboration involved little more than standard industry contacts. **Sainsbury's** checked with its own supplier, which confirmed that the peanuts used for its peanut butter are grown on a rotational basis in areas not thought to be suffering from soil erosion.

As an interesting aside, **Whole Earth**, who have been making natural peanut butter since 1972, have backed badger watching groups by supplying free peanut butter. Badgers adore peanut butter, apparently. Whole Earth say they try to source organic peanuts 'wherever possible' — for human consumption! At the time of writing, they had contracts for 200 tonnes of organic peanuts.

Rice and pasta

We asked the supermarkets whether they stocked organic rice. Only **Gateway** (*Witte Wonder Organic Brown Rice*) and **Safeway** (*White Organic Rice*) said they did. On the pasta front, **Sainsbury's** said they had stopped stocking imported Italian pasta in 1988, because they believed there was a problem with pesticide residues. One organic pasta product which may be available in some supermarkets is made by **Whole Earth Foods**. Founded in 1967, the company has developed a range of vegetarian foods, including *Pasta Pots* — a line embracing 'Napoli', made with dried tomato, oregano, garlic and onions; and 'Pesto', which contains dried tofu, basil, parsley and garlic.

Snacks

Snacking, or 'grazing' as the Americans call the habit of eating frequently while on the move, is now an established feature of British eating habits. The snack urge, according to industry figures, hits the average Briton at least five times a day! As a result, we consumed five billion packets of crisps in 1988 alone. Bagged snacks have been showing steady growth, with crinkle-cut, thick-cut and jacket potato crisps, or adult-oriented corn snacks in exotic flavours. Nuts, meanwhile, may be honey-roasted, yoghurt-coated or chicory-smoked (see Nuts).

A great deal of packaging is used in this sector and new types of packaging are constantly being launched. Most have more to do with salesmanship than with environment-friendliness. Products aiming at the up-market end of the snack market have been launched or re-launched in metallised film — like **Derwent Valley**'s *Phileas Fogg* range. Typically, the metallised films are based on polypropylene. Interestingly, too, one of the reasons they are increasingly being used is that crisps and other products can become rancid when exposed to ultraviolet radiation from supermarket lighting. Metallised and pearlised films overcome this problem, although it is not clear if they are more energy-intensive or less biodegradable. We are also seeing more 'multipacks', as in **Golden Wonder**'s *Crisp and Snack Ten Pack Mix* and many others. This is a notable example of double-packaging: convenient for the consumer, but wasteful of raw materials.

As far as organic snacks go, the main product is made by **Hedgehog Foods** of Powys. Hedgehog Crisps are based on organic potatoes and the company has a promotional campaign, based on clip-out coupons on each bag, to help the British Hedgehog Preservation Society. The crisps are available in three flavours: lightly sea-salted, cheese (vegetarian, of course) and tomato, and sea salt and cider vinegar.

Asked how important environmental issues were in helping Hedgehog Foods stand out from the commercial crowd, the firm replied: 'crucial'. Interestingly, too, the company says it tried to use biodegradable plastic films to pack its crisps, but the product spoiled. Hedgehog Crisps are stocked by **Asda**, **Safeway** and **Sainsbury's**.

Soups

Packaging, energy efficiency and vegetarianism are all considerations when buying soup. They are highly convenient and often highly nutritious, with dried and concentrated products clearly using less packaging — although we are not sure whether the energy used to dry or concentrate products outweighs the energy content of the packaging materials that would otherwise have been used.

Many of the soups stocked by the supermarkets are suitable for vegetarians, although very few are labelled to say so. **Safeway** is one store which has labelled its products clearly, however. One vegetarian brand of soup which you can find in a number of supermarkets is *Baxters*.

Tinned, Bottled, Frozen or Irradiated?

As supermarket shopping accounts for a growing proportion of our average shopping expenditure, so the number of times we go to the supermarket has fallen and the amount we buy on each visit has increased. As a result, there has been a considerable impetus behind the drive to make products last longer. From an environmental point of view it is clearly desirable that the food and drink that farmers and manufacturers produce does not go to waste, but the methods used to preserve food raise a number of important issues.

Traditional methods: These include bottling, canning, drying and pickling. Bottling is probably better than canning, if you re-use the bottles, but for fast-moving supermarket products canning makes a good deal of sense. The key next step here, though, will be to boost can recycling nationwide.

One of the companies that has changed its canning technology in response to health concerns about the lead used in the solders employed to make the cans, is **Heinz**. 'We converted our can making technology from soldering to welding to remove lead solder,' the company explains. 'This cost about £12 million. Cans are now made of tin-free steel.

We asked the supermarkets what proportion of their preserved fruit came in cans and bottles. Cans won hands down, with over 97 per cent of the market. **Iceland**, the **Co-op** and **Spar** said that all their preserved fruits were in cans. **Marks & Spencer** said that most of its 'contained fruit' comes in PET plastic containers.

Chemical preservatives: As far as the use of preservative chemicals goes, this began a long time ago, with the addition of salt and vinegar, for example, but an extraordinary range of chemicals are now used for this purpose. Preservatives and other food chemicals do make food last longer. The average six-day life of bread is cut by a quarter if preservatives are left out. Some soft spreading cheeses may last only two weeks instead of six without their chemicals. Preservatives also make us last longer! When we die, our bodies apparently now last four days longer than they used to, because of the preservatives we have consumed in our food.

In the wake of a major consumer campaign and the success of books like *E for Additives*, manufacturers and retailers have been cutting back on additives in a wide range of products. Initially the concern was about the potential of some food and drink additives to cause cancer, but the campaign soon expanded to tackle additives — like tartrazine — that can cause allergic reactions in sensitive children. As always, there will be trade-offs: taking additives out will lead to shorter shelf-lives and possibly also to an increased incidence of food poisoning.

Unfortunately, although the presence of some harmful food spoilage organisms is obvious from mould or smell, some of the rarest and deadliest — like those responsible for listeriosis and botulism — are odourless and do not change the appearance of the food.

Freezing and vacuum packs: A more energy-intensive way of preserving food is freezing. Eighty-two per cent of British households now have a freezer. But if you look inside the average freezer, you find that almost a quarter of its capacity is occupied by bulky frozen chips and other potato products. Obviously, it would be more energy-efficient to use fresh potatoes, although for consumers who do use frozen products, we look forward to the day when frozen organic potato chips and other foods become available. (Remember, too, that a full freezer is more energy-efficient.)

Frozen vegetable sales were expected to grow from 585,000 tonnes in 1988 to over 600,000 tonnes in 1989. Canned vegetables, representing a traditional form of vacuum-packed food, are a declining market for all products, except baked beans and tomatoes. Sales in this sector in 1988 amounted to 632,000 tonnes, forecast to fall to 544,000 tonnes in 1989. Sales of baked beans accounted for an astounding 50 per cent of the canned vegetable market in 1988!

Among the high-tech methods, vacuum-packing is perhaps the most intelligent application of science to preservation needs — although it tends to involve the use of plastics.

Irradiation: The most controversial of the modern food preservation techniques is irradiation — which is now legal in Britain. The **Co-op** has already said it will not use irradiation, even though it is legalised and it will be interesting to see how other supermarkets respond to the issue.

Exposure to gamma radiation kills off many (but not all) of the bacteria and other organisms which cause food to spoil, rot or go mouldy. It can also delay the ripening of some fruit and vegetables, although — confusingly — critics say it can accelerate the ripening of others.

Clearly, the longer shelf-life afforded by irradiation would mean higher profits for manufacturers and retailers. However, more than half the people questioned in a recent *Which?* survey said they would not buy irradiated foods even if they were cheaper. About half said they would rather buy food preserved with conventional additives than food preserved by irradiation.

It is important to note that irradiated foods may not be totally sterile. Foods are given a dose of radiation which would kill a human, but will only reduce the population of salmonella bacteria — and may leave deadly *Clostridium botulinum*, responsible for botulism, unaffected.

And there are other problems. Irradiation can affect the flavour of some foods. For example: oily fish, fatty meats and cocoa beans end up tasting musty; milk tastes chalky; many fruits and vegetables ripen faster. Worryingly, too, even if irradiation kills the bacteria in a particular food, it won't deal with the toxins they may have left behind. There has been concern that irradiation would be used to cover up failure in food manufacturing, rather than as a way of cleaning up the food production chain, which would make this toxin problem particularly acute.

The Consumers' Association has argued that we 'need to know more about the effects of irradiation on the chemical structure of food additives, pesticide residues and the material in which foods are packaged, as well as on the degree of vitamin loss caused. We are not opposed in principle to irradiation, but want more evidence on its effects.' If food irradiation ever becomes a widely used preservation method in Britain, it will be essential to label all irradiated foods prominently — to make sure that consumers have a real choice.

Condiments

As our diet becomes more international in character, so we use more condiments, from herbs and spices to soy sauce. Here are a few products which have come to our attention, with some of the issues associated with their production or use.

Gelatine

Made by rendering down many of the inedible parts of animals, gelatine is found in a considerable number of supermarket products. Among the products that may contain gelatine are jellies, mousses and fools, some yoghurts and some glazed products. Clearly, it is not favoured by vegetarians. We asked the supermarkets if they provided a vegetarian equivalent of gelatine such as the seaweed extract agar agar. None did.

Honey

Since bees collect pollen and nectar from plants that may have been sprayed with agrochemicals such as insecticides, it is important that honey be checked for pesticide residues. In fact, pesticide contamination of honey is currently under investigation by the Honey Importers and Packers Association (HIPA), with a view to defining acceptable standards.

The supermarkets say that they do not test their honeys for pesticide contamination. **Safeway** said that it stocks organic honey, although apparently the label stresses that while the producers try to encourage the bees towards organically grown plants, they cannot guarantee that that is where they end up!

In South and Central America, however, another problem has hit the bee population. In 1956, hardy South African bees were introduced into Brazil in the hope that they would interbreed with and invigorate the much less productive domesticated European bees which were the backbone of the industry at that point.

Unfortunately, the African bees are much harder to tame and can go on the rampage, with potentially fatal results for anyone caught in their path. Following the escape of some African swarms, over 70 per cent of the European bees were displaced in an area of Brazil as large as Britain — and the African bees have been spreading northwards ever since. Expected to reach the United States in 1990 or 1991, they are now thought to pose a serious threat to the US beekeeping industry.

Jams

Since pesticides are used to protect many of the fruits used in jam-making, the organic option is proving increasingly attractive. **Duerr**'s organic orange fine cut and thick cut Seville marmalades were launched in 1989. The fruit comes from orange groves on the Isla de Cartuja, where the fruit is grown in the traditional way — without the use of chemical insecticides and fertilisers. Vida Sana, a leading Spanish organic agriculture association, has certified that the fruit conforms to standards set by the international federation of organic agriculture movements. In Britain, **Whole Earth**'s plum jam is made with organically grown English fruit. The plums are guaranteed by Organic Farmers and Growers. If your supermarket does not yet stock such products, suggest that they try them out.

To meet organic standards, jams must not only contain organic fruit but also must avoid using colourants, antioxidants, preservatives and artificial flavourings. As far as sweeteners are concerned, natural beet syrup and unrefined sugars are preferred.

Remember that even jam makers can be polluters. In 1988, for example, the American company **Ocean Spray** was fined $400,000 because one of its plants had been releasing acidic effluents into the sewage system, the river and nearby marshes. The authorities had fined the company repeatedly since 1980 and as a result, Ocean Spray is now spending $3.2 million on upgrading its plant, including $100,000 on new sewage treatment equipment for the town of Middleboro, Massachusetts.

Oils

There has been growing demand for healthier cooking and salad oils, ranging from grapeseed and safflower to walnut. However, avoid unbranded oils when abroad, unless you know exactly where they have come from. In Europe a number of serious mass-poisoning incidents have been caused by contaminated oils. In Spain, for example, adulterated rape seed oil illegally sold as olive oil eventually killed over 600 people and damaged the health of nearly 25,000 others, many for life.

The boom in production of oil seed rape has been turning many areas of Britain yellow. There are several main strains of oil seed rape. The most common, and the one which we see in the UK, produces an oil that is used in cooking oils, margarine (although it is not particularly suitable for this application, so has to be hydrogenated), biscuits, chocolate, crisps and confectionery. Another strain produces a non-edible oil that is used in such applications as photographic development and plastic clingfilm, but is apparently not grown in Britain.

The area sown to oil seed rape increased from 64,000 hectares in 1978 to 348,000 hectares by 1988. The main issues revolve around the crop's impact on the countryside, pests and hay fever sufferers.

Initially the main concern was that landscape quality was suffering as the crop 'erupted' in the midst of traditional landscapes, although there were always those who felt that the blaze of yellow added as much as it took away — as long as the landscapes involved were not in the midst of Areas of Outstanding Natural Beauty. Increasingly, however, the concern has widened to embrace the possibility both that new pests may develop in the rape crop for which, since the plant is an imported one, there will be no natural controls, and that pollen from the crop is aggravating hay fever problems.

Doctors blamed a wave of 'flu-like hay fever symptoms in the late spring of 1989 on pollen from oil seed rape. The crop may be causing allergies in other ways: volatile vapours given off by the strong-smelling crop may also be implicated; plus the crop attracts a mould known to be linked to asthma. Oil seed rape pollen is not just a rural problem: pollen traps on the roof of St Mary's Hospital, Paddington, have caught oil seed rape pollen in the heart of London — and at least 15 miles from the nearest rape field.

Products that contain rape seed oil include **Asda** *Vegetable Oil*, **Iceland**'s *Vegetable Oil*, **Co-op** *Vegetable Cooking Oil*, **Gateway** *Encore Vegetable Oil*, **Safeway** *Blended Vegetable Oil* and *Low Fat Spreads*, **Sainsbury's** *Blended Vegetable Oil*, **Spar** *Vegetable Oil Blend*, **Tesco** *Vegetable Oil*, **Spry** *Crisp'n'Dry*, **Golden Fields** *Rapeseed Oil* and **Trex** *Oil*. **Marks & Spencer** say that no *St Michael* brands contain rape seed oil. Most producers are moving towards using rape seed for their oils because it is cheaper.

Pepper

There has been concern that the cultivation of pepper vines has accelerated tropical deforestation, although where forest clearance is already taking place pepper cultivation has been proposed as a way of persuading the loggers to leave at least some trees standing! The vines can then be grown up supports strung between the surviving trees, with the trees also providing shade which the pepper vines need.

Among the supermarkets, **Co-op**, **Gateway**, **Safeway** and **Sainsbury's** have not visited the areas in which their pepper is grown, whereas **Tesco** says it has. Tesco also noted that white pepper cultivation in Indonesia and black pepper cultivation in

India and Brazil tend to be a small cottage industry carried out in 'barren areas' and that Tesco pepper products have not led to forest clearance. Whether or not the pepper industry caused the forest destruction, it's interesting to ponder what grew on those barren areas before.

Salt

Environmentally, rock salt (which has to be mined deep underground) takes more energy to produce than sea salt (much of which is evaporated in shallow coastal ponds using solar energy).

The medical evidence suggests that we would do well to cut down on the amount of salt we eat, wherever it comes from. Among the alternatives for those who can't cut down: **Boots'** low sodium table salt, **Kinge**'s *LoSalt* and **Prewett**'s new formula low sodium salt substitute.

Stock cubes

A useful ingredient in many areas of cooking, but generally out-of-bounds for vegetarians and vegans. The **Co-op**, **Gateway** and **Spar** do not offer vegetarian stock cubes. **Iceland** and **Marks & Spencer** do not sell stock cubes at all. Supermarkets that do sell vegetarian stock cubes are **Asda** (**Bovril** *Vegetable Stock Cubes*, **Friggs** *Stock Cubes*, **Knorr** *Vegetable Stock Cubes*), **Safeway** (own-label), **Sainsbury's** (own-label, **Friggs** and **Knorr** brands) and **Tesco** (**Knorr** *Vegetable Stock Cubes*).

Sugar

Despite a reduction in the amount of sugar the average Briton eats, we still consume a sugar mountain worth £390 million a year. Sugar is added to a wide range of food and drink products, including soups. Granulated sugar still accounts for around 85 per cent of the market, which is dominated by **British Sugar** (which produces *Silver Spoon* and uses European sugar beet) and **Tate & Lyle** (which produces *Lyles* and *Fowlers* and uses cane sugar).

A key issue with Third World sugar production has been that this cash crop has hit many local forms of food production. Sugar production can also cause environmental problems, both in the growing areas and during processing. Thallium sulphate used to control cane rats in Guyana sugar-cane plantations has caused a considerable number of human poisonings in that country, for example, while in this country **British Sugar** spilled concentrated sugar syrup into the River Lark in Suffolk in 1987, killing almost 12,000 fish. This, it should be noted, was something of a 'freak' occurrence — but then many pollution incidents are.

Europe now produces far too much sugar. Every year, some 3 million surplus tonnes of beet sugar are produced at a cost to the European taxpayer of around £1.25 billion. The sugar industry is now looking around for markets in the Third World. The average Chinese, for example. eats 'only' 10 lb (4.5 kg) of sugar a year, compared to about 80 lb (36.5 kg) per head in Britain. The health and environmental implications of moving the rest of the world over to a high-sugar diet need to be looked at very carefully indeed.

Vinegar

We don't know of an organic malt vinegar, although if you are simply using the vinegar to clean your loo, perhaps it doesn't matter!

If you buy organic cider vinegar, it has been produced from fresh, organically grown apples and fermented naturally. Organic producers are banned from using colourants, dried or pulped apples treated with sulphur dioxide, antioxidants, preservatives, artificial flavourings, and unnaturally produced or added acetic acid.

Bakery Products

This is another area in which the supermarkets have been expanding their range and, in the process, knocking many of the smaller bakers out of the High Street. Thankfully, however, many speciality bakers have managed to survive — indeed thrive. Their success has encouraged the multiples to diversify even further into increasingly exotic bakery products and products baked on the premises.

The key issues here are:

- brown bread versus white

- the wheat monocultures used to produce our daily bread

- the pesticide residues sometimes found in flour and the products made from it

- the availability of organically grown products.

The organic products are important because they are produced by methods which both reduce the prevalence of agriculture monocultures (based on a single crop, and much more vulnerable to pests), and eliminate the use of most agrochemicals.

Flour

There are three basic types of wheat flour used in British baking:

- wholemeal or wholewheat (which contains the whole of the wheat grain, with nothing added or taken away)

- brown (usually contains 85 per cent of the grain)

- white (usually contains about 75 per cent of the grain, although even lower extraction flours can be produced).

Another flour, for which there is growing demand, is 81 per cent extraction, which bridges the brown-versus-white divide.

Because most of the vitamins and minerals in wheat are removed to varying degrees in lower extraction flours, iron and B vitamins are restored — by law — to the level found in 80 per cent extraction flour. However, you will still find that wholemeal flours produce a more nutritious result.

The **Co-op** says that its Leo stores stock **Doves Farm** organically grown flour. Doves Farm was the first winner of The Green Grocer Awards, launched in 1989, in the Food Products category. The company was founded in 1978 by Michael and Claire Marriage, who produce a comprehensive range of organic flours on traditional stone mills. Organic wholemeal and organic white varieties of strong, plain and self-raising flours are available.

Bread

Nine out of ten Britons eat bread every day, giving a national daily consumption of some 10 million loaves. White bread sales continue to decline, falling from 68 per cent of the market in 1983 to 52 per cent by 1987. Meanwhile, wholemeal and wheatmeal 'brown' breads have broadened their appeal, with sales rising from 19 per cent to 27 per cent over the same period. Speciality breads, such as rye, pitta, French and Indian varieties, are doing well both at the supermarket checkout and in smaller bakers.

Unfortunately for those who like their dietary fibre, bran-based products are likely to contain higher levels of pesticide residues than wholegrain products. This is because pesticide residues tend to be found mainly in the outer skins of grains, fruit and vegetables, and bran is part of the husk of the grain. So what are the supermarkets doing to screen their raw materials and products for pesticide residues?

Asda says it tests bread in its own laboratories and has demanded from suppliers that bread and cereal products conform to the Food and Environmental Protection Act, 1985. **Iceland** also said it had contacted suppliers, but did not give the results of the exercise. The **Co-op**, which has the largest farming interests in Britain and therefore has enormous potential power to encourage the push towards more environment-friendly forms of agriculture, announced its first organic farm in the late spring of 1989. **Gateway**, **Marks & Spencer**, **Safeway**, **Sainsbury's** and **Spar** all said that they did not do the testing themselves, but that their suppliers did. **Tesco** do test for pesticide residues, but not regularly.

As far as organic breads are concerned, the **Co-op** now stocks **Doves Farm** *Organic Loaf* and the **Barleycorn Bakery** *Organic Batch Loaf*. **Marks & Spencer** said it planned to introduce a new range of loaves based on organic flour in the autumn of 1989. **Sainsbury's** reported that two of its loaves were produced from organically grown Canadian wheat, *Nature's Choice White Bread* and *Nature's Choice Wholemeal Bread*, but said that it could not guarantee that the other ingredients used were organic. **Tesco** said it did not sell organic bakery products. And, just as we went to press, **Hovis** announced that it planned to bring out a stoneground wholemeal loaf made from organic flour. The new loaf will be the same size as traditional Hovis loaves, but cost more.

Among the speciality breads widely available are Indian naan, pain de campagne and brown and white garlic baguettes (try **Marks & Spencer**). **Sainsbury's** uses frozen French dough for in-store proving and baking of pain de campagne, baguettes and fluted French breads. **Waitrose** sells Greek-style wholemeal, Italian rye, German-style coarse grain rye, naan, chapatis and malted wheat sesame bread.

Cereals

A small but growing range of organic cereal products are being stocked by some supermarket chains. **Asda**, for example, stocks *Mornflake Organic Oats* and *Porridge Oats*, while the **Co-op** is developing its own brand of cereals with organic ingredients. **Waitrose**, the only supermarket chain we approached which did not answer our questionnaire, stocks the **Jordan**'s range of cereals — which includes *Organic Grade Pure English Porridge Oats*. The Jordan's range — also stocked by **Sainsbury's** — is predominantly based on 'Conservation Grade' cereals, which are grown using agrochemicals, but only those that do not leave residues in the soil.

Biscuits

The average Briton eats 18 lb (8 kg) of biscuits every year, and — given that old people tend to eat more biscuits — the ageing of the population means that this figure will almost certainly rise in the coming years. By 1992, it is estimated, Britain will consume an annual biscuit mountain weighing 486,000 tonnes. Fast-growing sectors include chocolate, speciality, hand-made and continental biscuits, but the biggest growth is likely to come from 'healthy image' products as demand grows for low-sugar, additive-free and preservative-free products.

Sales of cereal bars, introduced in 1981, more than doubled between 1985 and 1987. Research carried out by the London Food Commission and published in 1989 suggested that most cereal bars, which one would expect to be high in dietary fibre and low in sugar, contained relatively high levels of sugar and fat and were 'surprisingly low in fibre'. Manufacturers, the Commission concluded, 'appear to be giving misleading information on their products'. In terms of fibre content, the various *Crunchy* and *Chewy* products offered by **Jordan**'s came out well, although they also had a fairly high fat content.

Interestingly, the **Co-op** say they are developing biscuits with organically grown ingredients. One range of biscuits already on the market is **Doves Farm**'s biscuits, which includes *Wholemeal Digestive*, *Carob-coated Digestives*, *Wholemeal Gingernuts* and *Wholemeal Bourbon*.

Packaging is a key consideration in this sector. Some vulnerable products are heavily protected by plastic trays to make sure they reach you undamaged. Some biscuits come single-wrapped, some double-wrapped and some, like certain brands of brandy-snaps, triple-wrapped. Probably the worst cases of overpackaging, though, are to be found among imported Continental biscuits — at the 'wealthy' rather than 'healthy' end of the biscuit spectrum.

Puddings and suets

We asked the supermarkets whether they stocked suet-free puddings suitable for vegetarians. Those that didn't were **Iceland**, the **Co-op**, **Gateway** (although it does sell *Copperfields* vegetarian 'suet'), **Sainsbury's** and **Spar**. Those that did were **Asda** (*Asda Sponge Pudding* and *Homepride Microbake*), **Marks & Spencer** (sponge puddings of various flavours), **Safeway** and **Tesco** (*Tesco Bread and Butter Pudding* and *Homepride Microbake*).

CONTACT

Doves Farm, Salisbury Road, Hungerford, Berkshire RG17 0RF.

Beverages

The healthier eating trend has been paralleled by a healthier drinking trend. Bottled waters and fruit juices are all benefiting considerably from this trend. On a daily basis, 81 per cent of Britons drink tea, compared with 58 per cent drinking coffee and 49 per cent soft drinks.

We have already stressed the importance of packaging, which is a key issue in the beverages sector too. One trend we are seeing is the labelling of mineral water and other soft drink products packaged in PET as 'recyclable'. True, as far it goes, but not yet recycled! Our congratulations, meanwhile, to **A. G. Barr plc**, which has not only put the 'Keep Britain Tidy' symbol on all its products, but also continues to operate probably the largest returnable bottle operation in Britain outside the milk industry. Its branded products include *Tizer*, *St Clements* and *Jusoda*.

As demand for soft drinks continues to grow, there will be more pressure on the industry to help provide recycling facilities. It is already involved in the Sheffield 'Recycling City' project, but there must now be a concerted move to set up a nationwide network of recycling facilities. Even the Wine and Spirit Association has gone on record calling for bottle banks to 'become as common as pillar boxes'.

SOFT DRINKS

Bottled waters

Amazingly, when pigs were brought to London for the mammoth British Food and Farming Festival in Hyde Park in May 1989, they turned up their snouts at London water! Vets said that the animals were visibly wilting, but were used to 'fresh, clean spring water' and were determined that they were not going to be fobbed off with anything less. In the end, like many resident Londoners, they found they had little option.

Industry has enthusiastically leaped aboard the clean water bandwagon, however, determined to offer a choice — to people, if not to pigs. Sales of water filters — which promise to filter out toxic substances like lead, chlorine, copper, insecticides and, sometimes, nitrates — have been booming. Groups like **Friends of the Earth** are concerned that people may worry less about water quality if they have bought such a product, so have refused to endorse any water filters, no matter how well they do their job.

Mineral water sales have been climbing faster than any other sector of the UK soft drinks market. Total sales of bottled water in 1988 were up by 30 per cent on 1987, with more than 175 million litres of bottled water drunk in 1988.

The market had grown by an astonishing 145 per cent in the three years from 1985 to 1988, although UK consumption still lags behind that of most other EEC countries. France heads the league tables with 83 litres a year per head, compared to 2.5 litres a head here. The UK market is dominated by **Perrier**, **Evian** and supermarket own-label brands, together accounting for over 70 per cent of sales.

'The concerns about the quality of tap water, the leaching of nitrates and other chemicals, and the trend towards better health' are among the factors driving this growth, according to Richard Foulsham, managing director of Evian Agencies. In fact, pollution concerns have been helping to drive mineral water sales here since the late 1960s.

The UK challenge to the big French suppliers — and to more exotic brands like *Ramlosa*, the Royal Swedish mineral water —

has been building for a number of years, led by *Highland Spring*, *Malvern*, *Ashbourne* and **Wells** *Cwm Dale*. One of the latest entrants is **Hildon House**, which is promoting its *Gently Carbonated* and *Delightfully Still* products as the first in what it calls a range of 'healthy and environmentally sensitive' lines. It's not totally clear what they mean by 'environmentally sensitive', but the company, which will be operating a door-to-door delivery service in the south-west and Greater London, is using glass bottles — which can be recycled.

When the Consumers' Association tested bottled waters recently, it reported that its 'best buys' were *Ashbourne*'s product and **Sainsbury's** *Scottish Spring*. *Perrier* and *Ramlosa* also got top ratings, although *Perrier* was found to have a higher nitrate level. (But all the mineral waters tested turned out to have less than half the nitrate that you would find in tap water in some parts of East Anglia.) *Ramlosa* was found to contain a higher level of sodium (implicated in heart disease). While you should be aware of these facts, the levels of contamination found are very low. Recommended still waters were *Chiltern Hills*, *Evian*, *Glendale Spring*, **Safeway**'s *Braeuisge Spring* and *Volvic*. Bottled waters, incidentally, cost around 600 times more than tap water!

One of the most environmentally active bottlers appears to be **Spadel**, whose brands include *Brecon St Davids* and *Brecon Carreg*. In Belgium and The Netherlands, the company is involved in kerbside PET collection schemes, while in Britain it has switched from PVC bottles to PET bottles, with a view to boosting PET recycling here. Spadel has also played up the environmental purity of the Brecon Beacons National Park, from which it draws its water, in its advertising. The company has bought land around its springs and given the National Park Committee control over it.

In response to our questionnaire, **Spar** said that it was concerned about the long-term impact on mineral water quality if the greenhouse effect caused climate change. Both **Asda** and **Tesco** said that they do not permit the use of agrochemicals near the springs from which their mineral waters are taken. Tesco also said that it was continuing to test water for radioactivity in the wake of the Chernobyl disaster, although most suppliers said that they had been unaffected by the fallout from the damaged Soviet reactor.

Are the bottlers taking care not to extract the water too fast, by pumping too hard? **Asda**, **Co-op**, **Safeway**, **Sainsbury's**, **Spar** and **Tesco** all said that they had checked and were reassured. Only **Marks & Spencer** and **Gateway** were not doing anything to protect the water catchment area used, although Gateway say they are currently launching a new development in this area.

Energy efficiency eyebrows must be raised, however, by the news that we are now importing mineral water — *NZ Natural* — from as far afield as New Zealand!

OWN-BRAND BOTTLED WATERS

Supermarket	Checked supply to see if taking water at a sustainable rate?	Measures taken to help protect catchment area?	Considered environmental acceptability of packaging?
Asda	Yes	Yes	Currently reviewing this issue
Co-op (have one supplier)	Yes	No	Will be featuring recycling symbol
Gateway	No*	No	No
M & S	No	Yes (but have not specified what)	No, but are introducing plastic containers which they claim will be easier for the customer
Safeway	Yes	Yes	Constantly looking at alternative methods of packaging
Sainsbury's	Yes	Yes	A general review of environmental acceptability of packaging
Spar	Yes	Yes	Researching into possibility of using biodegradable bottles
Tesco	Yes	Yes	Use PET 'recyclable' logos

* But new development currently being launched.

Fruit juices

The total UK fruit juice and fruit drinks market is worth nearly £700 million a year, representing around 1 billion litres, and is growing at a rate of about 10 per cent a year. Pure fruit juices account for two-thirds of the market, with orange juice commanding a 70 per cent share of the fruit juice sector. Many products are packaged in clay-coated board or in Tetra-Paks. As the Table shows, only **Asda** and **Safeway** seem to stock any organic fruit or vegetable juices, although this must be a growth area in the 1990s.

Growing fruit juice consumption is not automatically A Good Thing, however, particularly if growers select only a limited number of fruit species and protect them with heavy applications of herbicides and pesticides. Substantial areas of forest have also been cleared in some Third World countries to make way for fruit crop plantations. Interestingly, **Coca-Cola** shelved plans for a major citrus plantation in Belize at the end of 1987, following international pressure from groups like Friends of the Earth.

OWN-BRAND FRUIT JUICES

Supermarket	Considered environmental acceptability of packaging?	Recycling symbols on packaging?	'Keep Britain Tidy' symbol on packaging?	Stock organic fruit or vegetable juices?
Asda	Yes	No	Yes (some)	Yes
Co-op	Under review	Introducing them	Introducing them	No
Gateway	No	No	No	No
Iceland	Yes	No	No	No
M & S	Yes	No	Yes	No
Safeway	Yes (nothing done)	No	No	Yes
Sainsbury's	Yes	No	No	No
Spar	Yes	No	Yes	No (not under Spar brand)
Tesco	Yes	No	No	Not stated

Soft drinks

No one walking through the litter drifts that pile up in our cities, towns and countryside would be surprised to hear that we consume a great deal of soft drinks: the environment is overflowing with the resulting cans, bottles and cartons. The fact that manufacturers like **RHM** (who handle *One Cal*, *Capri Sun* and *De L'Ora* soft drink brands) puts 'Keep Britain Tidy' symbols on all its packs is obviously to be welcomed, but such initiatives only scratch at the surface of the problem.

As our Table shows, most of the supermarkets have not yet put recycling information on their soft drinks packaging, although the 'Keep Britain Tidy' symbol seems to have achieved reasonable penetration.

OWN-BRAND SOFT DRINKS

Supermarket	Packaging	Recycling symbol?	'Keep Britain Tidy' symbol?
Asda	PET (and cans)	No	Yes
Co-op – soft drinks	PET	Introducing one	Yes
Gateway	PET	No	No
Gateway – mixers	Glass	No	No
Iceland	PET (recycled)	No	No
M & S	Plastic	No	Yes
Safeway	PET	No	No
Sainsbury's	PET/PVC/cans	No	Yes
Spar	PET (and cans)	Yes (but only on cans)	Yes
Tesco	PET	Yes	Yes

See page 46 for a table comparing the environmental performance of different types of packaging.

We drank an astounding 7 billion litres of soft drinks in 1988, worth around £3.5 billion, and the market is growing at 5 – 8 per cent a year. Fizzy drinks accounted for 50 per cent of the market, followed by squashes (32 per cent), fruit juices and drinks (14 per cent), bottled water (3 per cent) and still drinks (1 per cent).

The average Briton consumes 61 litres of fizzy drinks each year, but has still some way to go before — God forbid — he or she catches up with the average American, who downs 163 litres! This sector of the market is dominated by **Coca-Cola & Schweppes Beverages**, which is investing £50 million in a new Wakefield soft drinks production plant claimed to be Europe's largest.

Soft drinks now account for 12 per cent of adult beverage consumption and the leading suppliers see massive potential for future growth. If so, they are going to have to spend a great deal more time, effort and money on recycling schemes. Perhaps Coca-Cola's endorsement of the proposed European Recycling Association is a first step in this direction? Given the high proportion of soft drinks now packaged in PET (see Table), PET recycling must be a top priority.

HOT BEVERAGES

Cocoa and drinking chocolate

We asked the supermarkets whether they had visited the countries where their cocoa was grown — or whether they had any information on the impact of cocoa production of deforestation. The main areas of cocoa production are in West Africa, Brazil and Malaysia. **Gateway**, **Marks & Spencer** and **Safeway** said that they had sent people out to these regions, but none of the supermarkets knew whether or not their cocoa suppliers had contributed to deforestation.

Only **Marks & Spencer** said it tested its cocoa for pesticide residues, and also said that there had never been a problem.

We asked the same questions of chocolate manufacturers. **Rowntree Mackintosh**, for example, noted that 'users of raw cocoa in the UK maintain close and frequent contact with their suppliers. For many years the UK chocolate manufacturing industry, working through its trade association, has been in close contact with the authorities in the former British colonial territories producing cocoa in their efforts to combat pests and diseases affecting the crop. Through a long-standing arrangement, approval for the use of specific pesticides, fungicides and fumigants on cocoa will only be given by those countries after trial samples have been examined by the industry and confirmation given that no detectable harmful effect is present.'

The company also noted that, while cocoa trees might not be as effective a source of oxygen as a 300 year old forest, 'cocoa is an environmentally useful crop which maintains moisture, nutrients and organic matter in the soil'. But have cocoa plantations led to the destruction of tropical forests? 'It is not correct to say that cocoa cultivation has led to widespread forest destruction,' Rowntree Mackintosh replied, 'but cocoa cultivation can provide a beneficial use for the land when the forest has been destroyed'.

Cadbury went further in its questionnaire. It said that it did not believe that 'cocoa cultivation is now, or ever has been, a *cause* of widespread forest clearance. The primary forest is initially cleared for timber extraction. This clearance will leave total devastation unless a useful crop is planted. Cocoa is one such crop'. Interestingly, too, the majority of the world's cocoa crop is grown under forest shade trees, which have been left after the more financially valuable timber has been felled.

Cadbury was also involved in a recent initiative, extending over eight years, to collect threatened wild cocoa tree genes from the Amazon Basin and establish a gene-bank. 'The urgency of further constructive efforts of this kind before these genetic resources are destroyed forever cannot be over-emphasised,' the company said, 'and Cadbury Limited are taking a further initiative in another area of the Amazon Basin at the present time.' It would be good to see such companies supporting the protection of tropical forests in situ, in addition to funding such salvage operations. (See also pages 18 – 19.)

Coffee, ground and instant

Twenty years ago, we drank six cups of tea for every cup of coffee. Tea, as the marketing people liked to put it, had 'a giant share of throat'. But today the gap has narrowed to two cups of tea for every one of coffee, and in the under-40s age-group the balance is even. By the time this new generation takes over, coffee will probably have toppled tea from its perch.

In the last ten years, consumption of coffee, in terms of tonnage, has risen by 31 per cent, while tea has declined by 20 per cent. The leading firm here is **Nestlé**, whose brands include *Nescafé* and *Gold Blend*, with a 45 per cent market share. Second comes **General Foods**, with its stable of brands led by *Maxwell House* and accounting for 25 per cent of the market. Powdered coffee sales are falling, in favour of higher quality granule and freeze-dried products, and of real coffee. It's worth noting that some fairly extraordinary chemicals are used in processing coffee, including some used in dry-cleaning, although the chances are that these are less of a health problem than coffee itself!

Interestingly, more money is spent per £1 of retail sales on advertising coffee than on any other food. While chocolate makers spend three- per cent of sales on advertising, for example, coffee makers spend six per cent. This makes it an expensive market to break into, with **Brooke Bond** apparently having already spent £20 million on building up its *Red Mountain* brand to around six per cent.

Lyons Tetley said it did test its coffee for pesticide residues, but had never found any problems. **Gateway**, **Marks & Spencer** and **Spar** said their suppliers tested for pesticide residues, while **Tesco** had looked at pollution caused by the Brazilian coffee industry and **Safeway** said that it also planned to visit its coffee suppliers. Our Table summarises the replies we received. The picture is patchy, particularly in areas like pollution and tropical deforestation, but the Green Supermarket questionnaire has helped stimulate considerable activity among the leading supermarkets.

Asda said it bought its coffee ready-blended, so did not consider deforestation and other environmental issues. Some of the other supermarkets do buy coffee from countries which are losing their forests at a rapid rate, although the linkages between coffee production and deforestation are not yet clear enough to recommend cutting down on brands from particular countries.

OWN-BRAND COFFEE (Ground and instant)

Supermarket	Test for residues?	Looked at pollution issues?	Vetted supplies?	Could they supply information on tropical deforestation?	Supported local environmental development initiatives?	Countries of import
Asda	No	No	No	No	No	Buys coffee blended and therefore does not consider issues relating to production
Co-op	No	No	No	No	No	Brazil
Gateway	Yes	No	No	No	No	Central & South America, Africa
M & S	Yes	No	No	No	No	Brazil, Colombia, Costa Rica, Honduras, Ivory Coast, Mexico, Sierra Leone
Safeway	No	No	No	No	No	Brazil, Colombia, Costa Rica, India, Indonesia, Kenya, Uganda
Sainsbury's	No	No	No	No	No	Principally from Africa and South America. Buy from UK suppliers
Spar	Yes*	No	Yes	No	No	Africa, Central and South America
Tesco	No	Yes	Yes	Yes†	No	Brazil, Kenya, Colombia, Central America, East Africa, Uganda

* The supplier tests for pesticide residues.
† Information only for one plantation in Brazil.

The problems are most likely to occur in Brazil, Central America and West Africa. (See also pages 18 – 19.)

A final point on coffee: if you are pregnant, cut down on your consumption — or, if you can, cut it out altogether. There is evidence that coffee can depress fertility in women who drink a good deal of it and may also help cause miscarriages early in pregnancy.

Coffee filters

The main problem here is the use of chlorine bleaching in the production of the paper used in the filters (see page 202). **Lyons Tetley** said that chlorine bleaching is used for its coffee filters and noted that 'we are actively looking at the use of alternative, unbleached products'.

Manufacturers like **Melitta** started out offering consumers a choice between bleached and unbleached filters in Scandinavia, with Melitta introducing its unbleached filters into Britain early in 1989. They should now be available through most supermarkets. If your local supermarket does not stock them, ask it to get some unbleached filters in. Or switch to a coffee-making machine which uses a metallic filter instead.

Tea

On average, according to the Tea Council, every Briton — including children of 10 and over — drinks 3.65 cups a tea per day, or some 70 billion cups of tea a year for Britain as a whole! Generally it has no artificial additives such as colourings or preservatives and, unless milk or sugar are added, is calorie-free.

Gateway, **Marks & Spencer** and **Tesco** say they test for pesticide residues, although Tesco said they had done so only once. As far as pollution was concerned, **Lyons Tetley** told us: 'We are not aware of any potential pollution created by the plucking, crushing, fermentation or drying of tea leaves.'

'Most suppliers must be aware that originally forests were cleared for tea planting,' **Brooke Bond Foods** noted. 'However, forest canopy is replaced by dense tea bush canopy, so rainfall and erosion are not affected. We also actively promote packaging alternatives to the tea chest, including sacks, which would minimise deforestation caused by the production of plywood.' This was an aspect of the deforestation issue that had not even occurred to us! Lyons Tetley also reported that 'our factories in the UK are currently being modified to process a 100 per cent intake of sacks.'

Brooke Bond commented: 'There has been a groundswell of opinion in Brooke Bond Foods to support environmental issues for some time. We perceive them to be ever more important issues.'

Teabags

We asked manufacturers whether their teabags were wholly or in part based on recycled paper. 'The level of recycled fibre is determined by the teabag tissue manufacturer,' said **Brooke Bond Foods**, noting that such information was 'confidential'. Chlorine bleaching is used in producing the mixed natural and synthetic fibres used in teabags, although manufacturers said they were sure there was no health problem. Brooke Bond said it was 'currently investigating the implications of using paper without chlorine bleached wood fibre'.

BEERS, WINES AND SPIRITS

Beers

The Germans always had the right idea. Beer brewing is a serious business in West Germany, where the relevant 'purity law' (or *Reinheitsgebot*) dates back five centuries. The law lays down that beer may only contain hops, barley malt, water and yeast. There is a good deal of confusion in this field. For example, Asda told us that they stocked organic beer, assuming that the German purity laws denoted 'organic' production. They do not.

We think that **Waitrose** may stock an organic beer, but they did not answer the questionnaire. As our Table shows, none of the other supermarkets stocked organic beers at the time of our questionnaire, although **Gateway**, **Safeway**, **Sainsbury's**, **Spar** and **Tesco** all said they were considering doing so.

One of the most important recent trends in this sector has been the growth in the market for alcohol-free or alcohol-reduced beers. None, to our knowledge, is yet organic.

On the packaging front, most supermarkets reported that their beer shelves were mainly stocked with canned products, although **Marks & Spencer** stood out from the crowd with 100 per cent of its beers stocked in bottles!

BEER

Supermarket	Stock organic beer?	Considering organic beer?	% of beer sold in cans	% of beer sold in bottles
Asda	No	Not stated	80%	20%
Co-op	No	No	85%	15%
Gateway	No	Yes	80.2%	19.8%
Iceland	No	No	'Majority'	
M & S	No	No	Nil	100%
Safeway	No	Yes	98%	2%
Sainsbury's	No	Yes	83%	17%
Spar	No	Yes	80%	20%
Tesco	No	Yes	Not stated	Not stated

Ciders

Anyone who thinks that old-style alcoholic drinks were safe should take a look at what has been happening in the West Country — where the hung-over can find that a 'blinding headache' means exactly what it says. A neurologist at the Bristol Eye Hospital has warned anyone drinking rough 'scrumpy' cider that they risk going blind, because apple pips in the brew can break down into cyanide, damaging the optic nerve. And just in case you thought this was a theoretical problem, the hospital had been treating more than 20 patients, some of whom did indeed go blind.

The commercial cider market, meanwhile, is becoming much more sophisticated, indeed **Taunton Cider** has even launched a 'blush' version of its *Diamond White* cider. The company, which also handles brands such as *Autumn Gold* and *Piermont*, has been launching products aimed at young, image-conscious drinkers. Perhaps the next stage will see the supermarkets stocking a growing range of organic ciders?

If you are looking for an honest pint of organic cider, track down a copy of *The Good Cider Guide*, published by CAMRA. It has around 2,500 entries. One good candidate is **Aspall**'s *Cyder*, whose products sport the Soil Association's logo. Unfortunately, you still can't buy most of the products listed in *The Good Cider Guide* in your local supermarket.

Wines

We have woken up to wine in a big way. Indeed, the British now drink more exported French wine and spirits than any other country in the world. At the same time, the interest in organic wines, grown without artificial pesticides or fertilisers, is booming.

Organic wines are now stocked by everyone from specialist, upper-crust firms like **Berry Brothers & Rudd** of St James's through to a growing number of the major multiples. Supermarkets active in this area include **Asda**, the **Co-op**, **Gateway**, **Safeway**, **Sainsbury's** and **Tesco**. **Iceland** and **Marks & Spencer** both said they were actively investigating this area.

Safeway helped organise the 1989 National Organic Wine Fair at the National Centre for Organic Gardening. 'There is no proof,' said Jackie Gear, who helped found the Centre, 'but I strongly believe that organic alcohol does not leave you with that terrible morning-after feeling'. Sounds like a suitable problem for a controlled experiment!

The trend has been fuelled by a number of major European wine scandals. In Italy in 1985, for example, methanol-contaminated wine killed 23 people. And Austria ended up using millions of litres of wine as an anti-freeze additive, after revelations that many dealers had been sweetening and smoothing their wines with diethylene glycol, a component of some anti-freeze products.

Even when done properly, however, conventional wine-making uses enzymes, sorbic acid to slow the yeasts down, diammonium phosphate to feed them, kaolin and bentonite to 'fine' the wine, citric acid to stabilise it, and tartaric acid and carbonates to alter the acid balance.

Among the phrases you should look for on French organic wines and champagnes are *culture biologique, sans produits chimiques, sans engrais chimique, ni herbicide, ni insecticide de synthèse* or simply *made from unsprayed grapes*, together with a certifying symbol. Among the organic viticulture organisations in France are: *Nature et Progrès, Terre et Vie* and *Lemaire Boucher* (which uses the *Terre et Océan* logo). On German wines, look for the symbols of *Naturland, Bioland, Demeter, Oinos, Biokreis* and *Bundesverband Okologischer Weinbau (BOW)*. Spain relies on *Vida Sana*, Italy on *Suole e Salute* and England on the Soil Association.

Instead of using synthetic fertilisers and spraying chemical herbicides and pesticides, organic growers generally use copper sulphate, a naturally occurring mineral salt, or powdered sulphur to control pests. The vineyard soils are fed with compost, animal or green manure, bonemeal, mineral fertilisers (including rock phosphate, seaweed, wood ash, limestone and chalk). And weeds are controlled by the cultivation of plants like alfalfa and clover, barley, trefoil or grass, or by the use of black plastic sheeting as a mulch. Pheromones, or insect sex hormones, are used to attract and trap some pests, while baited jam jars and wild birds account for others.

Organic wine-growing is more labour-intensive and less productive than chemical-intensive viticulture, but many experts say the wine tastes better, the burden on the environment is certainly less and Europe, which is up to the gunnels in wine lakes, can presumably afford to cut back on quantity in favour of quality production.

Many organic wines are not identified as such on the label, however, partly because the wine producers are unaware that it might be a marketing advantage. An excellent source of information is *The Organic Wine Guide* (Mainstream Publishing, 1987), by Charlotte Mitchell.

Cosmetics and Toiletries

We spend around £2 billion a year on cosmetics and toiletries. The cosmetics industry is very much part of the fashion business and will therefore be very difficult to 'green', since some people will do almost anything to look younger, healthier or more sultry. But we can do a great deal to curb the industry's excesses.

Prince Charles struck a blow for the ozone layer when he banned aerosol hairsprays from the Palace, helping to trigger enormous press and consumer interest in the ozone issue. He may not have been aware that some aerosols were already CFC-free, but his action helped to spur on the rethinking process within the aerosols industry. Meanwhile, the 'cruelty-free' sector has grown from very small beginnings to a business worth over £40 million a year, with the **Body Shop** proving to be one of the fastest growing businesses in the country.

Companies in the cosmetics and toiletries business are certainly now watching the Green Consumer trend very carefully. They are aware of at least five major issues:

- use of CFCs as aerosol propellants
- the dioxins-in-paper-products controversy
- use of recycled paper in products

- animal testing
- over-packaging.

Let's look at each of these in turn, before focusing on some of the specific products that you are likely to buy in the supermarket.

Aerosols and CFCs

Following intense pressure during 1988 and 1989 from environmentalists, consumers and supermarkets, Britain's aerosol makers began to switch away from CFC propellants. The rate at which some cosmetics companies came out of CFC propellants took their slower competitors totally by surprise. Firms like **Mennen**, **Clairol** and **Alberto-Culver** were quick to exploit the 'ozone-friendliness' of their products in major advertising campaigns.

Many manufacturers have switched from CFC propellants to hydrocarbons, although some have moved to non-aerosol forms of packaging such as pump-action sprays. By the end of 1989, the whole of the cosmetics and toiletries sector is due to have switched away from CFCs.

However, groups like Friends of the Earth will not rest satisfied with their success in getting CFCs out of aerosols. The next challenge will be to aerosol cans themselves, which most environmentalists still see as a highly undesirable form of packaging. This is because the cans are not recyclable and, where hydrocarbon propellants are used, they take up a third of the space in the aerosol and, when released to the atmosphere, can contribute to photochemical smog and the Greenhouse Effect.

Paper Products — Dioxins and Recycling

We use an ever-increasing volume of paper products. Apart from the sheer quantity of trees needed to satisfy our demands (250 trees every five minutes), there is the question of the energy used — and pollution generated — during the processing of the trees into pulp, the bleaching of the pulp and the production of finished products.

Paper production can be a dirty process, particularly when the trees are broken down by mechanical or chemical means to separate the cellulose wood fibres used to make paper. The process can create very smelly air pollution, and consumes up to 300,000 litres of water for every tonne of paper made. The resulting discharges into water can be highly polluting. For example, up to 7 kilograms of toxic organochlorines (such as chlorinated benzenes, phenols and chloroform) are produced as by-products for every tonne of paper produced. At the same time, a range of chemicals are used to dye, whiten or strengthen paper.

This is a market which has been shaken up considerably in the last year. When, early in 1988, we asked leading paper product manufacturers whether they felt using recycled paper might help their sales, their answer was unequivocal. Consumers, they implied, weren't sufficiently interested in the environment. 'We would not use the fact that some of our products contain recycled paper as a selling factor,' **Kimberly-Clark** told us.

Although concerns about inferior quality and hygiene would be misplaced, the company, like many of its competitors, was convinced that advertising any recycled content of its products would actually hurt sales. Even today, many paper companies will tell you that the recycled paper content of their products is confidential. **British Tissues** says it uses 40,000 tonnes each year, yet refuses to say how much goes into particular products. The signs are that this attitude could soon change, however. The launch of **Fort Sterling**'s *Nouvelle* (see under 'Loo paper') suggests that the recycled content of some products is becoming an important selling feature.

Most of the paper and paper products we use are white (loo rolls, tissues, nappies). The pulp from which they are made has to be bleached, since its natural colour is closer to that of cardboard. The bleaching issue surfaced early in 1989 with the publication of *The Sanitary Protection Scandal* by the Women's Environmental Network (WEN). As a result, the use of chlorine bleaching in many consumer products sold in Britain became a considerable media controversy.

The initial concern was that products like disposable nappies (see under Nappies), based on chlorine-bleached pulps, might include harmful levels of potentially cancer-causing dioxins.

Although companies like **Peaudouce** and **Procter & Gamble** insist their chlorine-bleached disposable nappies were safe, they have been switching to different bleaching processes that do not produce dioxin contamination. Procter & Gamble have switched to 'active oxygen bleaching', which uses oxygen and a chlorine compound. Chlorine, which produces the dioxin, is no longer used and the company says that it is legitimate to call pulp bleached in this way 'non-chlorine-bleached'.

The controversy soon spread to a wide range of bleached paper products, from milk cartons, coffee filters and tea-bags to paper doilies, cups, plates and napkins. A number of manufacturers are now following the lead of disposable nappy manufacturers like **Peaudouce** and **Procter & Gamble**, and stressing the 'natural creamy' colour of their non-chlorine-bleached products, rather than the 'snowy-white-brightness' of the products they are replacing.

A government inquiry subsequently gave paper products the all-clear, concluding that the dioxin-cancer scare was 'nothing to worry about', but the paper industry and manufacturers of sanitary products were asked to consider marketing unbleached alternatives, to give the consumer a choice. They are beginning to do so.

However, the reason why chlorine-free products are desirable has more to do with environmental pollution than with health. The levels of dioxin detected in pulp and paper in North America and Europe are very low indeed. Usually they are in the region of 10 parts or less per trillion. Even though dioxin is a highly toxic material, these are vanishingly small amounts: for comparison, 1 part per trillion is equivalent to 1 second in 32,000 years. Where detectable, the levels found in paper products were lower still. **Procter & Gamble** tested conventional disposable nappies and found no dioxins, even at a detection limit of 1 – 2 parts per trillion.

But worries about effluents from chlorine-bleaching plants in the countries which supply us with paper pulp have helped to trigger a switch by a growing number of supermarkets to oxygen-bleached or to unbleached products.

Where unbleached or non-chlorine-bleached products are available, we recommend that you buy them, for the environmental impact you will have rather than for any health benefits you will enjoy. But we have a long way to go before we catch up with a number of other countries. In Sweden, for example, more than 95 per cent of disposables (coffee filters, nappies, loo paper, food packaging and paper handkerchiefs) are made from unbleached recycled materials.

Animal testing

Animal testing has emerged as one of the key issues for the cosmetics and toiletries industry. Substantial progress has already been made. The total number of animals used to test cosmetic and toiletry products halved between 1981 and 1987. But there is still some way to go: in 1987, some 14,500 animals died in experiments to test products like hairsprays, skin creams and shampoos.

Experiments carried out in this sector now represent less than 0.5 per cent of all animal experiments carried out in Britain. 'They're on the decline the whole time,' says the Cosmetic, Toiletry & Perfumery Association. 'Many companies would rather scrap a product than have to do tests using animals.'

Lists of cruelty-free products are available from the British Union for the Abolition of Vivisection (BUAV) and the National Anti-Vivisection Society. But there is controversy about what the term 'cruelty-free' actually means. According to a Euromonitor report, some cosmetics manufacturers may be misleading the public by claiming that their products are not tested on animals. *All* cosmetics ingredients were tested on animals at some stage, because all products must contain preservatives — and all preservatives undergo animal testing before they are passed by a government committee.

Companies operating in this field have a number of different options. They can, for example, make products that:

- contain no animal ingredients

- contain no ingredients tested on animals by the company

SAINSBURY'S POLICY ON ANIMAL TESTING AND COSMETICS/TOILETRIES

The fullest policy statement we received in this area was from Sainsbury's. Since it highlights some of the main issues which need consideration we have reproduced it in full.

'Increasingly, people are concerned that animals are being used to test cosmetics and toiletries and to many people such tests inflict needless cruelty.

'Sainsbury's has long accepted that whilst tests on animals may still in some cases be necessary, e.g. for pharmaceuticals, and indeed are often required by regulatory authorities in the interests of human health and safety, it is unjustified to subject animals to tests for the purpose of developing cosmetic and toiletry products.

'No Sainsbury cosmetics or toiletries are tested on animals. Furthermore, we produce a detailed specification and carefully check the chain of supply of ingredients to be used. We insist that our suppliers establish that no animal tests for cosmetics or toiletry purposes are conducted on our behalf on any ingredient that is to be incorporated into our products. Indeed, no such tests have been conducted for at least 5 years.

'Our own scientific staff regularly monitor suppliers and check products made for us and ingredients used, to ensure that no changes are made which might affect our requirements on animal testing.

'Our ban on animal testing however, does not make us any less confident in the safety and satisfactory performance of our products. Finished products are tested on human volunteers. In future, bacterial tests and cell cultures may be able to be used and research is continuing on alternatives to animal testing which we are watching with interest.

'We are the first major supermarket in the UK to adopt so comprehensive a policy.'

- contain no ingredients tested on animals in the last 5 or 10 years by anybody
- have not been tested, as whole products, on animals.

Many cosmetic companies are now either boosting their use of human volunteers in product testing, or putting money into the development of alternatives. Among the companies helping to support work done by the Fund for the Replacement of Animals in Medical Experiments (FRAME) are **Avon**, **Bristol Myers**, **Johnson & Johnson**, **Marks & Spencer** and **Rimmel**.

Some companies, such as **Elida Gibbs**, dispute that any product is totally 'cruelty-free', given that most components of cosmetic and toiletry products have been tested at some time. The key question for the moment is not whether an ingredient has been tested on animals — but how long ago it was tested.

The Body Shop, for example, will not use ingredients that have been tested in the last five years, while **Beauty Without Cruelty** goes even further and imposes a 10-year limit.

However, there has been concern that if the European Commission succeeds in its plans to test not only new products for health, safety and environmental effects, but also those that have been used — in most cases safely — for many years, the number of animal tests needed will go through the roof.

An additional source of useful information is *The Cruelty Free Shopper* published by the Vegan Society, although the majority of products they list are not available in supermarkets. A list of further suppliers is given at the end of this chapter.

Over-packaging

Conspicuous over-packaging is part and parcel of the cosmetics and toiletries market. As discussed in our Packaging section, the 1990s will see enormous pressure building on all sectors of industry to develop and use more environment-friendly packaging. But there is a tremendous amount of work still to be done in terms of picking the right materials, lightweighting packages, avoiding double packaging, ensuring that products are not only 'recyclable' but recycled, and so on.

Equally, it is important that more environment-friendly products are packaged in more environment-friendly materials. So a recycled paper loo roll, for example, should be packaged in a recycled paper pack. With today's high quality recycled papers and modern printing technology, that need mean no drop in quality of finish or performance.

PRODUCTS SHELF BY SHELF

After-shave, scents and perfumes

90% of aerosols will be CFC-free by the end of 1989, but watch out for over-packaged products and if you can avoid aerosols, do. (See page 200.) As far as cruelty-free products are concerned, more and more are now available, some of which are highlighted in the Table. The supermarkets certainly seem to be much more aware of the animal testing issue than they were.

So far, at least, it is difficult to find cruelty-free perfumes and

OWN-BRAND AFTER-SHAVE, SCENTS AND PERFUMES

Most of the supermarkets specified that although they could guarantee that some or most of their products have not been tested on animals, they could not guarantee that ingredients had not been tested at some time.

Supermarket	Cruelty-free?	Comment
Asda	Yes	Body sprays have no animal ingredients and products are not tested on animals
Co-op	Yes	Products not tested on animals and labelled to say so
Gateway	Yes	Do not insist that products are tested on animals. No products labelled as cruelty-free
M & S	Yes	Products not tested on animals and signs on the shelves to say so
Safeway	N/A	No products in this category
Sainsbury's	Yes	Sainsbury's have a progressive policy on the cruelty-free issue (see page 204)
Spar	N/A	No products in this category
Tesco	N/A (no own brand)	Limited range of fragrances on offer

scents in Britain's supermarkets. Instead, try some of the smaller suppliers listed at the end of this chapter.

Bath products

A number of bath products can contribute to water pollution, but in general — given effective sewage treatment — the problems are minimal. That said, most of these products are unnecessary and we could well manage without them — and simultaneously the packaging in which they come.

Many bath foaming products contain formaldehyde, which you may wish to avoid, particularly if you or your family suffer from allergies. A range of **Creightons** cruelty-free bath products (oil, gel and 'seeds') can be found in **Gateway** stores. Many of the cruelty-free suppliers listed at the end of this chapter sell bath products.

Cotton wool

Most of the supermarkets say that their cotton wool products are chlorine bleached, which raises the dioxin issue again, but they stress that there is no health hazard to the consumer.

Sainsbury's say that they stock hydrogen peroxide bleached products, which do not involve the production of dioxin-contaminated effluents, and **Tesco** — which uses sodium hypochlorite — is encouraging suppliers to switch to what they consider to be a more environment-friendly process, oxygen bleaching. **Asda**'s *Baby Cotton Buds* are already produced by oxygen bleaching and the company says it is also trying to get its cotton wool suppliers to switch to this process.

Deodorants

These products are affected by all the four issues outlined at the beginning of this section. All of them should be free of CFCs by the time The Green Consumer's *Supermarket Shopping Guide* is published.

The fast-movers among supermarkets in getting out of CFCs were the **Co-op**, **Gateway**, **Safeway**, **Sainsbury's** and **Tesco**. Most have switched to hydrocarbon propellants, although some products have been packaged in pump-action sprays which will pump nothing into the air but the product. In general, use either a pump-action spray, dry stick or roll-on. (Or simply wash well!) The Table shows how each supermarket fares in the animal cruelty stakes as well as on packaging.

OWN-BRAND DEODORANTS
AND ANTI-PERSPIRANTS

Supermarket	Cruelty-free?	Packaging
Asda	No Asda brand deodorants are tested on animals. They are planning to label them to say so	All packaging is under investigation
Co-op	Co-op brands are labelled to say the product has not been tested on animals	Co-op brand roll-on in PE plastic, rather than PVC
Gateway	No products in this category	Have considered environmental acceptability of packaging but feel there are few alternatives at the moment
M & S	Do not test products on animals, but do not label them to say so	Actively investigating the environmental acceptability of their packaging
Safeway	No products in this category	Cardboard boxes used for their roll-on anti-perspirant are made from recycled paper*
Sainsbury's	No toiletries or deodorant products are tested on animals. Considering a logo to specify this	Looking for biodegradable or recycled packaging
Spar	They say that Spar anti-perspirant qualifies as cruelty-free, but it is not labelled as such	
Tesco	Own-label products have not been tested on animals	Recycled cardboard is used as much as possible for delivery boxes

* We do not think it should be necessary to use a cardboard container for roll-on deodorants, even though most cardboard containers are made, at least in part, from recycled paper.

Hairsprays

All hairsprays should now be CFC-free. Companies like **Alberto-Culver** and **Bristol-Myers** promoted their products heavily as 'ozone-friendly' early in 1988. 'Great style shouldn't cost the Earth,' said the advertisements for Alberto-Culver's *VO5* products. In fact, the *VO5* range had been CFC-free since 1976, but the company only decided to go public with the fact in February 1988. The impact on its sales was dramatic. But the days when hairsprays can be pushed as 'ozone-friendly' are numbered. Next comes the debate about the use of aerosols themselves (see page 200) and about animal testing.

One of the slower companies to drop CFCs was **L'Oreal**, which did not switch until 1989. This caused a good deal of comment in the TV studios making Green Consumer programmes — since L'Oreal is a popular brand with TV presenters!

Loo paper and paper tissues

Britain uses 1.5 billion loo rolls and 30 million boxes of tissues a year, most of which are based on virgin pulp. (See also Nappies and Sanitary protection products.) The issues here include the following:

- the felling of trees (mainly conifers) for pulp production

- the chlorine-bleaching of many pulps, leading to dioxin pollution and contamination problems

- the energy-intensiveness of pulp and paper manufacturing operations

- the need to develop products that use a much higher proportion of recycled fibre.

It takes one tree to make something like 6,000 loo rolls. Even though many of the trees may be grown overseas, the environmental impact is worth considering. Friends of the Earth expressed alarm, for example, when the US paper giant **Scott** (manufacturers of *Andrex*) were awarded a 900,000 hectare timber concession in Indonesia. FoE understood Scott were considering clearing the natural monsoon forest in order to establish a massive eucalyptus plantation. Eucalyptus is a particularly greedy and thirsty tree, stripping nutrients and water from the soil, while returning relatively little in the way of humus.

Part of the answer is to look out for brands of loo paper that are made from recycled paper — and the higher the proportion of recycled paper the better. Ask for 100 per cent recycled brands. Increasingly, the quality of the product is indistinguishable from that of mainstream brands.

Although a number of the supermarkets offer loo rolls containing a proportion of recycled paper, as the Table shows, the main choices if you are looking for 100 per cent recycled products are **Fort Sterling**'s *Nouvelle* and **Sainsbury's** *Revive*.

Aimed squarely at the Green Consumer, *Nouvelle* comes in four colours — including a tasteful green! 'Nouvelle has all the features demanded by the consumer,' says the company, including 'softness, strength and a long roll, together with the benefit of saving trees.' (The sheet count is the same as for a major brand.)

As with other bleached paper products, the chlorine bleaching issue is important. Look out in the future for brands based on paper which is both recycled and non-chlorine bleached.

One issue which may soon be laid to rest, is the notion that dyed loo paper biodegrades more slowly than undyed paper. Research by leading manufacturers has shown that there is no significant difference. But it is worth remembering that most coloured loo paper is bleached before it is dyed.

Meanwhile, mounting interest in the environment has encouraged a number of manufacturers to look at their products anew. Those who suffered hard loo paper at school can take some comfort from the fact that **Jeyes** have realised that their hard tissue products were made from recycled fibre all along! A number of products, as our Table shows, have a recycled content-range of 20–60 per cent. But manufacturers are increasingly likely to target the 'top end' of the market, aiming for products that are both recycled and of a high quality.

LOO PAPER

SUPERMARKET OWN-BRANDS

Supermarket/Brand	Recycled paper content?	Labelled as recycled?	Packaged in recycled paper?	Chlorine-bleached? (See Note 1)	Comments
Asda Toilet Roll	20%	No	No	Yes	All Asda paper products are chlorine-bleached. They are seeking alternatives and will offer them when available
Co-op Toilet Tissue	50%	Will be labelled with '50% recycled paper'	No	Yes	All Co-op paper products are chlorine-bleached, but this is under review
Fluffy products (stocked by **Gateway**)	100%	Yes	No	Yes	All Gateway paper products are chlorine-bleached, but they are discussing this with suppliers
Iceland	None	No	No	Yes	Iceland say that recycled paper content and chlorine bleaching are areas of concern and are being considered
M & S *St Michael* Toilet Paper	30%	No	No	Yes	All St Michael brand paper products are chlorine-bleached but they are investigating alternatives
Safeway Economy Toilet Tissue	50%	No but hope to	No but hope to	Yes‡	

Continued overleaf

LOO PAPER (continued)

SUPERMARKET OWN-BRANDS

Supermarket/Brand	Recycled paper content?	Labelled as recycled?	Packaged in recycled paper?	Chlorine-bleached? (See Note 1)	Comments
Safeway Standard Toilet Tissue*	About 50%	No	No	Yes‡	Use polythene packaging. Manufactured by Fort Sterling
Safeway Standard Toilet Tissue*	None	No	No	Yes	Use polythene packaging. Manufactured by British Tissues
Safeway Softest Toilet Tissue	None	No	No	Yes	They say that the packaging is biodegradable
Safeway Decorated Toilet Tissue	None	No	No	Yes	They say that the packaging is biodegradable
Revive Recycled Toilet Tissue (**Sainsbury's**)	100%	Yes	No	Yes	
Sainsbury's Economy Toilet Tissue – white	50%	No	No	Yes	Sainsbury's own-label products are still chlorine-bleached but this is under review
pink, peach, green, blue	60%	No	No	Yes	
Sainsbury's Soft Bathroom Tissue range	20–25%	No	No	Yes	As above for Sainsbury's
Sainsbury's Supersoft Toilet Tissue	up to 25%	No	No	Yes	As above for Sainsbury's

Brand	Recycled paper content	Labelled as recycled?	Packaged in recycled paper?	Chlorine-bleached?	Comments
Spar Toilet Paper	50% (min)	No	No	No	Looking into maximising recycled content
Campion (sold by **Gateway**)	50% (min)	No	No	Yes	
Tesco Toilet Tissue	100%	Yes	No	Yes	Tesco are looking for sources of non-chlorine bleached products

MANUFACTURERS' BRANDS

Brand	Recycled paper content	Labelled as recycled?	Packaged in recycled paper?	Chlorine-bleached?	Comments
Nouvelle†	100%	Yes	No	Yes	Made by Fort Sterling
Babysoft	20–60%	No	No	Yes	Made by Stuart Edgar
Checkpoint	60–80%	No	No	Yes	Made by Stuart Edgar
Andrex Toilet Tissue	None	No	Paper but not recycled	Yes	Made by Scott. They are examining alternative methods to chlorine bleaching. Percentage of chlorine-bleached pulp has been decreasing
Dixcel Kittensoft	Minimal	No	No	Yes	Made by British Tissues
Dixcel Family Value	50%	Yes (50% recycled fibre)	No	Yes	Made by British Tissues

Continued overleaf

LOO PAPER (continued)

MANUFACTURERS' BRANDS

Brand	Recycled paper content?	Labelled as recycled?	Packaged in recycled paper?	Chlorine-bleached? (See Note 1)	Comments
Kleenex Velvet Bathroom Tissue	More than 40%	Yes	No	Yes	Made by Kimberly-Clark. All their paper products are labelled 'Caring for the Environment'

1. Just as we were going to press we discovered an interesting ambiguity in the responses to this question. There seems to be some confusion amongst companies about whether or not the use of sodium hypochlorite constitutes chlorine bleaching. Those companies marked ‡ replied to our questionnaire that their products are not chlorine bleached; but either at the time or subsequently they explained that they use sodium hypochlorite. (Those companies which answered 'Yes' may also, of course, be using sodium hypochlorite and themselves defining this as 'chlorine bleaching'.) We investigated and found that the use of sodium hypochlorite is a form of chlorine bleaching; but it is a liquid and can apparently be used in a more controlled way than the gas used in other chlorine bleaching processes. It is therefore considered, to some degree, more environmentally friendly. As a result of our initial findings we are embarking on a detailed report about all bleaching processes.

* Although all Safeway Standard Toilet Tissue comes in the same pack, it is manufactured by two different companies.

† Supermarkets which stock Nouvelle brand loo paper are: Asda, Gateway, Safeway, Sainsbury's, Tesco, Waitrose and some not included in our survey — Morrisons, WM Low, Lo Cost, Nisa, Kwik Save.

As far as paper tissues are concerned, *Fluffy*, stocked by **Gateway**, is 100 per cent recycled paper. A number of products fall in the 20–30 per cent range, including **Asda**'s *Facial Tissues* and **Sainsbury's** *Facial Tissues*. Alternatively, use cotton handkerchiefs.

TISSUES
SUPERMARKET OWN-BRAND

Supermarket/Brand	Recycled paper content	Labelled as recycled?	Packaged in recycled paper?	Chlorine-bleached? (See Note)
Asda Facial Tissue	20%	No	Partly (cardboard outer contains some recycled fibre)	Yes
Fluffy (stocked by **Gateway**)	100%	Yes	No	Yes
Safeway Economy Facials	None	No	Yes	Yes
Safeway Facials	None	No	Yes	Yes
Safeway Facials Mansize	100%	No	Yes	Yes
Sainsbury's Cosmetic Tissues	Up to 35%	No	No	Yes
Spar Facial Tissues	Don't know	No	No	Yes
Tesco Multicoloured Facial Tissue	100%	Yes	Yes	Yes

MANUFACTURERS' BRANDS

Brand	Recycled paper content	Labelled as recycled?	Packaged in recycled paper?	Chlorine-bleached?
Handy Andies	Not stated*	No	High percentage of recycled fibre	Yes
Dixcel Kittensoft	Minimal	No	Cardboard box	Yes
Dixcel Family Value	50%	Yes (50% recycled fibre)	Cardboard box	Yes
Kleenex Tissues	More than 40%	Yes	Cardboard box (some recycled content)	Not stated

* 'Commercially sensitive information'.
NOTE: See Note 1 to Loo Paper table on page 214.

Make-up

Again, the key issues to watch for here are over-packaging and animal testing.

As the Table shows, the supermarkets say that their products are not tested on animals — although it is not clear whether the suppliers are doing such testing. Presumably many of them are. Some of the cruelty-free brands stocked by supermarkets such as **Asda**, the **Co-op** and **Safeway** are listed. There is clearly growing interest in the environmental acceptability of cosmetics packaging, although this is an area where further consumer pressure will certainly be needed.

A growing range of skin care and other cosmetic products are available from the cruelty-free suppliers listed at the end of this chapter. Many such products have not yet found their way into the supermarkets, although **Montagne Jeunesse** products can now be found in **Asda** stores and **Tesco** plans to offer own-brand cruelty-free skincare lotions.

OWN-BRAND MAKE-UP

Supermarket	Cruelty-free?	Packaging
Asda	Products not tested on animals	They have not considered the environmental acceptability of packaging in this area
Co-op	Products not tested on animals	They claim that they do not over-package their make-up
Gateway	Do not require products to be tested on animals	Not stated
M & S	Products are not tested on animals	Actively investigating environmental acceptability of packaging
Safeway	No own-brand products (None of the branded products they offer are labelled as cruelty-free but suppliers assure Safeway that they are not tested on animals)	N/A

OWN-BRAND MAKE-UP (continued)

Sainsbury's	No own-label cosmetics are tested on animals. Moving to label cosmetic products with this but find some too small. Point of sale cards state their policy	Increasingly will be looking into recycled or biodegradable packaging
Spar	No products in this category	N/A
Tesco	No products in this category	N/A

The Green Consumer Guide provoked a letter from the **Dead Sea Mud Company**, which offers *Dead Sea Mud*, (a natural clay from the Dead Sea area) which is used as a face mask, and *Dead Sea Bath Salts*. 'Needless to say,' the company concluded, 'its production is also entirely without cruelty to man or beast. We simply dig it up.' It is apparently useful for treating psoriasis and other common skin conditions.

Nappies (and Baby Care)

If there has been any single issue in this sector which has been pre-eminent since the publication of *The Green Consumer Guide*, it has been the question of the environmental acceptability of disposable nappies. The main issues are:

- the felling of trees for pulp production
- the chlorine-bleaching of some pulps, leading to dioxin pollution and contamination problems
- the biodegradability of the plastics used
- the sheer volume of nappies that go into the waste stream and the pollution problems associated with soiled nappies in landfill sites.

In *The Green Consumer Guide* we recommended that mothers should not worry too much about using disposable nappies, if that meant that they could use their energies more constructively in other areas of green consumerism. But there is now a new class of products on the market — more 'environment-friendly' disposable nappies — and so there is a choice to be made between different brands of nappy.

We certainly use a lot of nappies. An astounding 3.5 billion disposable nappies are used in Britain every year, accounting for 4 per cent of the country's household waste stream. The UK disposable nappy market is thought to be worth around £330 million a year, with sales up 16 per cent between 1988 and 1989. Each baby using disposable nappies uses dozens each week. Sadly, despite the claims of some manufacturers and mail-order catalogue operations, there is no such thing as a 'green' disposable nappy. But some disposables are more environment-friendly than others.

Chlorine-bleached pulp has been used as padding for almost all nappies sold in the UK, both because of its absorbency and strength, and because consumers have been persuaded that they wanted a pure white product.

Peaudouce was first on to the UK market with a non-chlorine bleached disposable nappy, closely followed by **Procter & Gamble**. Peaudouce says that its new fluff pulp process uses more than 90 per cent of the tree, so that twice as many nappies (1,000) can now be manufactured from one fully grown pine tree. This argument has been discounted by some of the company's competitors, who argue that using most of the tree rather than just the trimmings left by other industrial processes, is actually less environment-friendly. Procter & Gamble tested its conventional nappies and found no dioxins, even at a detection limit of 1–2 parts per trillion. Despite that fact, the company decided to launch a more environment-friendly version of its *Pampers* brand.

Both **Peaudouce**'s *Ultra Plus* and **Procter & Gamble**'s *Pampers* products are now off-white in colour, because they are non-chlorine bleached. *Togs*, made by **Swaddlers**, also went chlorine-free early in 1989.

The supermarkets not only began to stock these brand-name, environment-friendly nappies, but also started to develop own-label products. The **Co-op**, **Safeway**, **Sainsbury's** and **Tesco** have all introduced such products. Tesco alone sells over 100 million nappies a year, so the conversion to non-chlorine bleached products will certainly have an impact.

The next issue with disposable nappies will be the biodegradability of the plastics used. **Peaudouce** has announced a biodegradable plastic backing sheet. *Pampers* has followed suit, although **Procter & Gamble** consider **Peaudouce's** claims to be exaggerated. And whether or not that is resolved, there is yet another issue lurking in the wings: the question of whether it is acceptable to dispose of nappies in landfill sites. The total quantity of soiled nappies being landfilled is certainly considerable. It is not at all certain, however, that mothers will be prepared to give up the convenience of disposables, so the challenge must be to produce alternatives that are almost equally convenient and cost-competitive.

One interesting development in the United States involves **Procter & Gamble** and a recycling company, **Rabanco**. They are experimenting with the recycling of disposable nappies! The idea is to wash them before turning the wood-pulp padding into cardboard boxes and building insulation, and the plastic outer layer into refuse bags and flower-pots. Another US company, **Anderson Diaper Co.**, charges $4 a week to pick up used disposable nappies from parents and recycles them for use in fertilisers and other products.

The alternatives on offer in Britain at the time of writing are terry towelling and *Biobottoms*. Terry towelling, or cloth, nappies are available from suppliers like **Mothercare**. *Biobottoms*, on the other hand, are a re-usable nappy covering made from wool. Used with a liner, either disposable or non-disposable, they apparently only need washing every 4-6 nappy changes. They are available from **The Whole Thing**.

Babies tend to get through an awful lot of disposable products these days. Avoid disposable bibs and bottles, for example. Washable plastic bibs will cut down on your laundry load!

Since most baby products are less harsh than the detergents and other products sold for adult use, they are likely to be somewhat less of a problem in terms of environmental impact per fluid ounce. But mainstream baby products are particularly likely to have been tested on animals, so if this is an issue which is important to you, try some of the products from 'cruelty-free'

NAPPIES

SUPERMARKET OWN-BRAND

Supermarket/Brand (disposable nappies)	Chlorine-bleached?	When did they, or will they, change process?	Stock washable nappies?
Asda	Yes	Planning to	No
Co-op	No	April 1989	Yes
Gateway	Yes	Will change	No
M & S	No	July 1989	No
Safeway Ultra	No	April/May 1989	No
Sainsbury's	No	March 1989	No, but are considering
Spar **Spar** Saver	Yes	Will change	No
Tesco	No	April 1989	Yes — Zorbit

MANUFACTURERS' BRANDS (disposable nappies)

Brand	Chlorine-bleached?	When did they, or will they, change process?	
Celatose	No	Early 1989	
Peaudouce	No	January 1989	
Pampers	No	February 1989	
Togs Premium	No	January 1989	
Togs Ultracares	No	January 1989	
Togs Cares	No	January 1989	

suppliers like **Cosmetics To Go**, **Creighton Laboratories** and **Weleda**. They include low-lather *Infant Shampoo* from Cosmetics To Go, tested on human volunteers rather than on animals, and an alternative to talcum powder, *Dusting Powder*, which is based on corn starch. Creighton's offer baby oil, shampoo, lotion, soap, milk bath and dusting powders. Weleda sells products like a gentle *Calendula Shampoo*.

Sanitary protection products

1.5 billion packets of sanitary towels and 1 billion packets of tampons are used in Britain every year. The main issue in the tampon market in the early 1980s was the emergence of toxic shock syndrome (TSS). In 1989, Britain became aware that there was another environmental issue affecting both sanitary towels and tampons: dioxin contamination resulting from chlorine-bleaching of paper pulp. The Table shows which brands are based on which materials. Although some environmentalists have assumed that **Tambrands'** *Tampax* brand, for example, is based on chlorine-bleached paper pulp, the product is made from a mixture of rayon and cotton — and is oxygen bleached.

As far as the biodegradability of sanitary towels and tampons is concerned, the Association of Sanitary Protection Manufacturers says that 'all tampons are biodegradable, as no UK manufacturers have products with non-biodegradable plastic applicators, whilst sanitary towels are some 95 per cent biodegradable, in weight terms'.

The two least biodegradable elements in sanitary towels are the backing sheet (also called the poly-baffle), which provides the barrier layer in the towel, and the silicone-coated release paper strips. Manufacturers are continuing to research and test alternative materials offering increased biodegradability, without compromising consumer comfort or confidence.

In 1989, *Tampax*, the UK's biggest tampon brand, was at the epicentre of a row about the environment. **Tambrands**, the company behind the brand, had launched a major advertising campaign to defuse the concern about the dioxin issue and biodegradability. Its ads said that *Tampax* products had been 'environment friendly since 1937'. The company, which at the time made over 2 million tampons every day in the UK, claimed that its products were 'all 100% biodegradable'.

But the Women's Environmental Network (WEN) retorted that some products, particularly those containing cotton and rayon, might contain pesticide residues. WEN director Bernadette Vallely alleged that all the major sanpro manufacturers are likely to use cotton from China and Brazil, and much of that has been farmed using pesticides like DDT, paraquat and aldrin which have been banned in First World countries. The key phrases here include 'are likely' and 'much of'. The fact is that no one really knows what the situation is, but sanpro manufacturers are unlikely to be able to defuse such concerns simply by launching major press advertising campaigns.

OWN-BRAND SAN-PRO PRODUCTS

Supermarket	Product name	Chlorine-bleached? (see Note)	Comments
Co-op	Co-op Press on Towels Co-op Slim Towels Co-op Pant Liners	Yes Yes Yes	Although they contained chlorine-bleached pulp at the time of our research they were planning to change by July 1989
Gateway	Gateway Caprice (Reg, Super)	No	Introduced this range in August 1989
Safeway	Safeway Press on Towels (Reg, Super and Super Slim)	Yes	At the time of our research plans were under way to introduce non-chlorine-bleached san-pro products
Sainsbury's	Sainsbury's Individually Wrapped Pant Liners Sainsbury's Liberty Press-on Towels, Super Plus	Yes Yes	Working on changing from this process. All other Sainsbury's sanitary towels are now oxygen-bleached
Spar	Spar Press-on-towels (Reg and Super) Spar Individually Wrapped Towels Spar Panty Liners	Yes Yes Yes	They are changing all san-pro products to non-chlorine-bleached pulp. Planned to be on the shelf by July/August 1989
Tesco	Tesco Sanitary Towels (Super and Reg) Tesco Tampons	Yes ‡ Yes ‡	

NOTE: See Note 1 to Loo Paper table on page 214.

BRAND-NAME SAN-PRO PRODUCTS

Company	Brands	Chlorine-bleached? (See Note)	Comments
Johnson & Johnson	Carefree Vespre	Not stated	They did not complete the questionnaire but did respond by letter. It was ambiguous, however, on the question of whether their products are currently chlorine-bleached
Stuart Edgar	Interlude	Yes	They are planning to re-introduce non-chlorine bleaching process
Scott	Libra Bodyform Libra Slims Pennywise	Yes No No	
Tambrands	Tampax Fresh Response	No No	They are made of a mixture of rayon and cotton and are oxygen-bleached
Smith & Nephew Consumer Products	Dr Whites Lil-lets Lilia Golden Babe	No No No No	
Kimberly-Clark	Simplicity Kotex Sylphs	No No No	All Kimberly-Clark products have a symbol 'Caring for the environment' on the back of their packs

NOTE: See Note 1 to Loo Paper table on page 214.

Shampoos

All the chains responding to our questionnaire said that the detergents and other ingredients used in their shampoos were at least as biodegradable as required by current legislation and industry guidelines — which should come as no surprise. Supermarkets such as **Gateway** and **Safeway** said that they did not consider any of their shampoos to be particularly environment-friendly.

As far as cruelty-free products were concerned, some stocked them, others didn't. Those that did were **Asda** (*ABC Shampoos*), the **Co-op** (all own-label shampoos), **Gateway** (all own-label shampoos and **Montagne Jeunesse** products), **Marks & Spencer** (no *St Michael* cosmetics or toiletries are tested on animals), **Sainsbury's** (all own-label products and *Vale of Health Shampoo*), **Spar** (all own-label products) and **Tesco** (own-label products). **Safeway**, on the other hand, said that none of its products were noted for being 'cruelty-free'.

This doesn't mean that Safeway are necessarily worse than everyone else, but it certainly means that it is worth checking with them if you are buying shampoos in their stores. And Safeway does stock the *Natural History Collection*, which has had a joint promotion with the World Wide Fund for Nature (WWF).

Soaps and skin care

Soaps are made from plant oils or animal fats, mixed with alkali. They are generally fairly biodegradable. An expanding range of products that are both free of animal fats and have not been tested on animals is available, although you are more likely to find them through specialist suppliers and health stores than through the supermarkets. Most of these firms offer a wide range of soaps, bath and skin care products. Increasingly, however, some of the specialist suppliers are succeeding in breaking into the supermarkets. Some of **Creighton's** cruelty-free soaps, for example, are stocked by some branches of **Gateway** and **Tesco**.

Suncare products

Supermarkets like suncare products, particularly suntan preparations and sunglasses. They need little display space, and then only for a few months. Both are rapidly expanding markets — and are likely to remain so as concern about the thinning of the ozone layer grows, with the implication that more ultraviolet light will reach the beach where our bodies sizzle in the sun, causing more skin cancers.

Remember, you can get sun-burned even if you are in partial shade — or ten feet under water! The combination of exotic, sun-baked holiday destinations and ozone layer fears have dented sales of low-protection factor products (their share of total UK sales worth £45 million fell from 33 per cent to 24 per cent between 1987 and 1988), while high factor products increased from 21 per cent to 34 per cent.

Tanning accelerators, increasingly used in suncare ranges, are meant to boost the melanin content of your skin. Alternatively, people use tanning pills which contain beta carotenes and canthaxanthene. Apart from the fact that some tend to turn you yellow rather than brown, there has also been concern that canthaxanthene leaves deposits in the back of the retina, impairing night vision.

Many of these products are — or have been — tested on laboratory animals. Indeed, one US firm was recently in the headlines for allegedly using hairless mice to test sun creams. Their heads were covered in masking tape and tin foil and they were then exposed to several hours of intense heat from a sun simulator. Half of the mice died. Future generations will view this sort of 'research' with abhorrence.

Toothpaste

Toothpaste may be the last product to come to mind when you are thinking of environmental pollution, but the acid effluents produced during the manufacture of the titanium dioxide pigments, used as a whitener in almost all toothpastes, are worth thinking about. These effluents make some British rivers and parts of the North Sea more acid. While the **Co-op** actually labels its toothpaste to say which ingredients it contains (it does contain titanium dioxide), most do not.

Although titanium dioxide producers like **Laporte** and **Tioxide** are trying to clean up their act, the Green Consumer may feel that it is appropriate at this stage of the game to switch to clear gel toothpastes (which do not contain titanium dioxide). Most of the toothpastes on offer in supermarkets contain titanium dioxide. Only brands of the gel variety do not, such as **Procter & Gamble**'s *Crest Tartar Control Gel* and **Marks & Spencer**'s own-brand *St Michael Blue Minty Gel* and *Fresh Mint* toothpastes.

Alternatively, you might like to try some of the more natural, herbal brands which are available from specialist suppliers like **Camilla Hepper** or the **Green Farm Nutrition Centre**. *Vicco Vajradanti* toothpaste, from **Mandala Ayurvedic Imports**, contains 18 different herbs to help clean your teeth and maintain healthy gums. It contains no animal ingredients and has not been tested on animals.

Asda and **Co-op** are moving to plastic laminate tubes, which they say are more energy-efficient than 100 per cent aluminium. **Sainsbury's** says its plastic and aluminium tubes can be burned without causing environmental problems.

CONTACTS

Although in most chapters we have focused on the products supplied by the supermarkets, they have lagged behind their smaller competitors in offering cruelty-free products. We are therefore listing some of these smaller suppliers.

Barry M, Unit 1, Bittacy Business Centre, Mill Hill East, London NW7 1BA or on 01-349 2992.

Beauty Without Cruelty Ltd, Avebury Avenue, Tonbridge, Kent TN9 1TL or on 0732 365291.

Body Care, 50 High Street, Ide, Exeter, Devon EX2 9RW or on 0392 217628.

Bodyline Cosmetics, Unit 5, Alders Way, Yalberton Industrial Estate, Paignton, Devon TQ4 7QL or on 0803 555582.

Body Reform, Unit 5, Kingsway Buildings, Bridgend Industrial Estate, Mid Glamorgan CF31 3SD or on 0656 57101.

British Union for the Abolition of Vivisection (BUAV), 16a Crane Grove, London N7 8LB or on 01-700 4888.

Camilla Hepper Sales Ltd, Unit 18/19, Mountbatten Road, Kennedy Way, Tiverton, Devon EX16 6SW or on 0884 258673 and 258923.

Caurnie Soap Company, The Soaperie, Canal Street, Kirkintillock, Scotland G66 1QZ or on 041-776 1218.

Chandore Perfume, 2 Ashtree Avenue, Mitcham, Surrey CR4 3DR or on 01-648 5129.

Cosmetics To Go, 29 High Street, Poole, Dorset BH15 1AB or on 0800 373366 (FREE).

Creighton Products, Water Lane, Storrington, Pulborough, Sussex RH20 3DP or on 09066 5611.

Crimpers Pure Products, 63 – 67 Heath Street, London NW3 6UG or on 01-794 2949.

Culpeper Ltd, Hadstock Road, Linton, Cambridge CB1 6NJ or on 0223 891196.

Dolma Vegan Perfumes, 34 Goodere Drive, Polesworth, Nr Tamworth B78 1B7 or on 0827 893116.

Dr Hawden Trust for Humane Research, 6c Brand Street, Hitchin, Herts SG5 1HX or on 0462 36819.

Faith Products, 52 – 56 Albion Road, Edinburgh EH7 5QZ or on 031-661 0900.

Fund for the Replacement of Animals in Medical Experiments (FRAME), Eastgate House, 34 Stoney Street, Nottingham NG1 1NB or on 0602 584740.

Green Farm Nutrition Centre, Burwash Common, East Sussex TN19 7LX or on 0435 882482.

Honesty Cosmetics, 33 Markham Road, Chesterfield, Derbyshire S40 1TA or on 0246 211269.

Mandala Ayurvedic Imports, Zetland Studios, 7 Zetland Road, Redland, Bristol BS6 7AG or on 0272 427124.

Martha Hill, The Old Vicarage, Laxton, Nr Corby, Northants NN17 3AT or on 078085 259.

Montagne Jeunesse, London Production Centre, Broomhill Road, London SW18 4JQ or on 01-871 5080.

National Antivivisection Society, 51 Harley Street, London W1N 1DD or on 01-580 4034.

Pecksniffs Bespoke Perfumery Ltd, 37 Offington Lane, Worthing, West Sussex BN14 9RG or on 0908 62174.

Pure Plant Products, Grosvenor Road, Hoylake, Wirral, Merseyside or on 051-632 5998.

Vegan Society, The, 33 – 35 George Street, Oxford OX1 2AY.

Weleda (UK) Ltd, Heanor Road, Ilkeston, Derbyshire DE7 8DR or on 0602 309319.

The Whole Thing, 23 Camden Lock, Camden Town, London NW1 8AF or on 01-485 3374.

Household Cleaners

In the average British household 31 days a year are spent cleaning the home, or two hours a day. The cleaning tasks carried out most frequently are dusting, washing the dishes, washing clothes, vacuuming the sitting room and cleaning the loo and bath.

The detergent and household cleaning markets are dominated by a small number of major companies (see page 261 – 3). As far as environmental issues are concerned, detergents have probably 'enjoyed' the highest profile in this section.

Detergents

The detergent industry has done a great deal over the last 30 years to address the environmental and health effects caused by its products. But as more and more chemicals and other products go into the waste stream produced by our modern societies, so there has been a steadily growing concern, particularly on the Continent, about the environmental impact of detergents.

The detergent giants, **Lever Brothers** and **Procter & Gamble**, are seeing companies such as **Ecover**, **Henkel**, **Tesco** and **Ark** launching new product ranges — and promoting them on the basis of their environmental performance. Interestingly, however, Lever has concluded that environmental pressures will not be particularly helpful in giving it a competitive edge, whereas many of the smaller companies have recognised a marketing opportunity.

The emergence of 'green' firms which stress the environmental performance of their products has helped spark change. Previously confined to the health shop, Ecover's range of detergents first broke into the supermarket sector during Green Consumer Week 1988, when **Sainsbury's** began to stock *Ecover Washing Powder* on an experimental basis in a number of London stores.

Next in line was **Tesco**, which responded to the Green Consumer campaign by launching its 'Tesco Cares' initiative in January 1989. Tesco features a number of 'environment-friendly' cleaners and detergents, including a range of Ecover detergents, **Henkel**'s *Bright White* phosphate-free biological automatic washing powder and 'new' phosphate-free *Tesco Cream Cleanser*.

Today, the new 'environment-friendly' products can be found in several hundred supermarkets, particularly urban stores operated by Sainsbury's, Tesco, Asda and Safeway. This trend sparked an increasingly heated 'suds war'. The Soap and Detergent Industry Association, representing over 60 companies, worked itself up into quite a lather over the claims made by Ecover and other Continental detergent companies. At the same time, the supermarkets are now turning around to the manufacturers who make their 'own-brand' products and asking for more environmentally acceptable detergents.

So what are the issues the consumer should take into account when deciding which detergent to use in the washing-up bowl, dishwasher or washing machine, and in household cleaners? The following are some of the points you may want to consider.

Ingredients and Issues

Very few of today's detergents are based on soap, which is made from animal fats or plant oils, and breaks down rapidly in the environment. Unfortunately, unadulterated soap is only an effective cleaner in soft water, so most modern detergents are based on petrochemical surfactants, phosphates which soften the water and other 'builders', which boost the surfactant's cleaning power. Also added are whiteners, brighteners, anti-corrosion chemicals and enzymes.

Surfactants: Detergents contain surfactants that render water more efficient as a cleansing agent and make a major contribution to the quality of modern life. The first surfactants were soaps, which were made by mixing fats and oils extracted from animals or plants with a strong alkali, such as lye (concentrated sodium hydroxide or potassium hydroxide). In hard water areas, however, soaps form scums and deposits, a problem which was one reason for the development of synthetic surfactants. These are often made from petroleum products or plant oils.

Following the introduction in the 1940s of early 'hard' surfactants, particularly of alkyl benzene sulphonate (ABS), foaming rivers became a common sight in Britain and elsewhere. Many sewage plants were buried under mountains of foam while in the United States, it was not uncommon for surfactants to find their way into underground water, resulting in foaming tapwater. ABS was eventually dropped, but such problems ensured that 'biodegradability' became a household word as controls were introduced. The detergent industry and its suppliers developed alternative materials which biodegrade more rapidly and introduced these voluntarily, ahead of UK and EEC legislation.

Today, the big detergent manufacturers continue to use surfactants derived from petrochemicals, arguing that they are perfectly safe for the consumer and the environment, while some 'green' detergent makers have dropped petrochemicals in favour of surfactants derived from coconut, palm, linseed, soya, groundnut or rape oils. They argue that the petrochemical industry causes a good deal of pollution — an argument which is hard to dispute in the wake of the *Exxon Valdez* disaster. So in addition to any pollution caused by surfactants directly, they are produced by an industry which, in green eyes, is suspect.

All detergents and cleansing products are required by law to biodegrade rapidly. Under UK legislation, surfactants must have an average of at least 80 per cent biodegradability, measured on at least 14 daily samples over 19 days. The surfactants, in fact, achieve this rate of biodegradation within three hours, a much shorter time than they would spend passing through the average sewage treatment works.

Ecover's products have been heavily promoted as '100% biodegradable', a claim that caught the detergent giants on the hop. **Procter & Gamble** says that the implication that 'non-green' detergents are not biodegradable is grossly misleading. All commercially available surfactants have been biodegradable since the early 1970s. To counter the green challenge, the Soap and Detergent Industry Association is now encouraging member companies to label their products as biodegradable. The real question is *how fast* particular products biodegrade.

While it is probably true that the substances used by the green firms break down faster than the petrochemical surfactants used by the big detergent companies, it's not clear that the environmental benefits are particularly significant in areas with effective sewage treatment facilities. Remember, a much higher proportion of homes in Britain are linked to the sewage system than is the case in much of Europe, although some 14 per cent of Britain's sewage is still, unbelievably, discharged untreated into our estuaries and seas. Phosphates, it is worth noting, can pass through even properly run sewage works.

Phosphates: Most detergents on the market contain what the industry calls 'builders', which make the water softer and more alkaline — and let surfactants work better. Some industrial cleaning compounds are little more than pure phosphate. Domestic laundry powders contain higher levels of surfactant than such high-phosphate industrial products, but also depend heavily on phosphate builders. Phosphates constitute around 20 – 25 per cent by weight of most washing powders — and an even higher proportion of dishwasher powders. Liquid clothes-washing products contain less phosphate, but often compensate by including 3 – 4 times more surfactants.

Detergents are not the only source of phosphate in rivers and other waters: sewage, farm run-off, effluents from intensive livestock units and agricultural fertilisers account for three-quarters of the phosphate found in UK rivers. Wherever it comes from, however, phosphate can cause eutrophication, a process which in nutrient-poor waters can help to provide the conditions to support more plants, fish and other organisms. On the other hand, too much phosphate in slow moving rivers or lakes causes algae to 'bloom' too fast, stripping the water of oxygen and suffocating or poisoning most other organisms. Some of the poisons are produced by algae to help them compete with other algae. At its worst, eutrophication can turn slow-moving water bodies into green mires of slime and dead fish.

The eutrophication of Lake Erie in the 1960s was one of the eco-disasters that helped spark the 'environmental revolution' in North America. Eutrophication caused by detergents is not a major problem in most parts of Britain today, however, even in vulnerable areas like the Norfolk Broads, but greater problems in other European countries have sparked action. Land-locked Switzerland has banned phosphates in detergents, while Italy, Holland and West Germany severely restrict the quantities that can be used.

As a result, a growing number of Continental brands are phosphate-free and, as our supermarkets begin to go green, they are inevitably turning up on British shelves, too.

As phosphates are used to soften the water you use to wash clothes, you can probably do without them if you live in a soft water region like Wales. If you live in a hard water area, the phosphate substitutes should work fine. If not, you may need to invest in a water-softener. The easiest way of finding out the hardness of your water is to call your local water authority. Longer term, water authorities should start to print water hardness information on the water bills they send out. The map overleaf shows the approximate hardness of water in different areas of the country.

Instead of phosphates, Ecover uses zeolites, which are similar to pumice stone, and citrates to provide a water-softening effect. Zeolites are minerals and therefore do not biodegrade, but cause no harm even in large quantities.

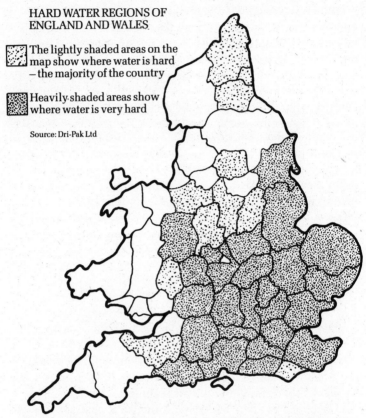

HARD WATER REGIONS OF
ENGLAND AND WALES

The lightly shaded areas on the
map show where water is hard
– the majority of the country

Heavily shaded areas show
where water is very hard

Source: Dri-Pak Ltd

Despite industry claims that phosphate-free products are more expensive and, in some cases, less effective than normal detergents, they are selling well. Further product lines have been launched by new entrants like **Nitor** and **Ark**, which should help bring prices down.

Mainstream companies like **Lever** and **Procter & Gamble** expect the opening up of the Single European Market from 1992 to have an important influence on the perceived environmental acceptability of detergents. 'Phosphate may not be a problem in the UK,' as Lever put it, 'but it could be made into a UK problem because of a combination of publicity from Germany and commercial exploitation.' Both companies expect a steady tightening of environmental standards.

NTA and EDTA: As the environmental pressures have built up on phosphates, detergent manufacturers have tried to find alternatives. Unfortunately, most of the substitutes have turned out to have problems of their own. NTA (nitrilotriacetate) was tried in the 1970s, but was subsequently banned. Later on the ban was lifted and it was tried again in the 1980s — and then was banned again. This was because it combines with toxic metals already in the environment and 'remobilises' them so that they can be carried into our drinking water or food, especially fish and shellfish. NTA is still used, however, in countries — like the Netherlands and Switzerland — where phosphate-based products have been banned. We were told by industry sources that NTA was not used in the UK.

Another compound that is used is ethylene diamine-tetraacetate (EDTA), which stabilises bleaches in detergent products. It causes similar environmental problems to NTA.

Bleaches: Sodium perborate and sodium percarbonate are two oxygen bleaches used in washing powders, both to remove stains and to prevent the yellowing of laundry.

Both types of bleach are equally effective, but most manufacturers have tended to prefer sodium perborate for complete washing powders. A key reason is that sodium percarbonate degrades in the pack unless a stabiliser is added. EDTA (see Table) is used to stop the bleach working too quickly during the washing process, but — as we have seen — is environmentally suspect.

Because German research has also suggested that perborate bleaches can result in boron contamination of rivers, **Ecover** decided to use a percarbonate bleach — without EDTA. This has necessitated developing a two-part washing powder, where the percarbonate bleach is only added for white washes. Ecover points out that the bleach added to mainstream washing powders often goes down the drain without being used.

Enzymes: Confusingly, washing powders containing enzymes are usually marketed as 'biological', which does not mean that they are environment-friendly. Enzymes are added to washing products to help break down stubborn stains based on proteins, like blood or chocolate. When Lever switched to the use of enzymes in *New System Persil*, a consumer revolt forced the company to offer the choice between the old-style *Persil* and the new product. A significant number of consumers preferred — and remained loyal to — the old-style Persil.

From the late 1960s enzymes were added to the list of laundry detergent additives, and by 1970 as many as 75 per cent of the volume of detergents sold in the US market contained one or more enzymes. Protein- and starch-digesting enzymes were produced by carefully cultivated varieties of the bacterium *Bacillus subtilis*. Initially, enzymes caused respiratory allergies in some production workers handling them in large quantities, but improved industrial hygiene measures have just about eradicated such problems.

Green firms like **Ecover** spurn enzymes, arguing that they can cause allergies. The big detergent makers counter by quoting large-scale testing with housewives which showed no difference in the incidence of skin problems between users of biological and non-biological powders. One point to note about enzymes is that they can help make your washing more energy-efficient.

Brighteners and whiteners: Optical brighteners are used to make washed clothes look whiter. They belong to a group of compounds which were also used in food products like flour and sugar until a ban was introduced. When used in washing powders, they attach themselves to fabrics during the washing process. Once the clothes are dry, they work by converting invisible ultraviolet light into visible blue light. These substances are not major pollutants, but companies like **Ecover** argue that they can lead to skin sensitisation and allergy problems. The Soap & Detergent Industry Association counters that 'there is no evidence that brighteners commonly used in detergents have ever caused skin sensitisation.'

Preservatives: Powdered detergents are not prone to microbial contamination, but liquid products may be. Aside from asking consumers to store liquid detergents in the fridge or to use them up inside a week, the main option is to use preservatives. The preservative used by **Ecover** is the only petrochemical ingredient the company employs. 'Although it occurs in many plants and animals,' the company explains, 'it cannot be obtained from these sources and has to be manufactured.'

Packaging: Trends in packaging are discussed in Chapter 4. In the clothes-washing sector, the basic trend, fuelled by the introduction of liquid formulations, is towards the use of more plastic packaging. The trend towards light-weight packaging economises both on the use of raw materials and on the use of energy in manufacture and distribution, although the resulting growth in the use of plastics is causing concern among environmentalists. **Lever**, for example, has introduced a plastic pack for its Sun dishwashing powder. Environmentally, it makes sense to avoid all such plastic packs, unless — and until — they are available on a refillable basis (see under Fabric softeners, below) or until proper plastic recycling facilities are available.

Ecover makes a feature of its washing powder pack, which it notes is made of cardboard produced with recycled paper (true of everyone's else's pack, too). But it also carries a cut-price Friends of the Earth (FoE) membership offer. By March 1989, this had already pulled in over 2,000 new FoE members.

Ecover does use plastic (polyethylene) bottles for packaging its liquid products. They will eventually be packed in a new type of carton, the company says. Ecover avoids PVC, and Lever (which believes that a ban on PVC may be on the cards in the future) and Procter & Gamble also avoid PVC 'wherever possible'. Lever predicts that recycled plastics will be used, via co-extrusion technology, to make some '50 per cent of plastic packs in the next 10 years'.

New plastics are being tested which are made from sugar and biodegrade very rapidly, but Ecover has calculated that on current pricing such materials would double the cost of its washing up liquid. Longer term, however, the cost should come down fairly substantially. The trend towards greater product *concentration* is also likely to be important in packaging terms. The introduction of several concentrated fabric softener brands, for example *Comfort*, *Lenor* and a number of own-label products, gives three times the number of uses for any given size of pack. In such cases, it is critically important that the required dosing is clearly identified on the pack, to avoid waste.

WASHING POWDERS*

MANUFACTURERS' BRANDS

Company	Brand	Contains phosphates?	Contains petro-chemical based surfactants?
ACDO (The Astley Dye & Chemical Company)	Acdo Soap Powder	Yes (5%)	No
Ark	Ark Concentrated Washing Powder	No	No
Ecover	Ecover (The Unique) Washing Powder	No	No
	Ecover Washing Powder without Bleach	No	No
Faith Products: no powders; liquid formula detergents only			
Henkel, distributed by **British Tissues**	Henkel Bright White	No	Yes
Lever Brothers[3]	New System Persil Automatic	Yes	Yes
	Original Non-Biological Persil Automatic	Yes	Yes
	Persil	Yes	?
	Surf	Yes	Yes
	Surf Automatic Powder	Yes	Yes
	Lux	No	No

Length of time to biodegrade (active ingredients only)	By what %?	Use NTA or EDTA?	Use bleach?	Use enzymes?	Optical brighteners?	Packaging information†
See note[1]	Not stated	EDTA	Yes	No	Yes	White lined chipboard
5 days	96–100%	No	Yes	No	No	Recycled cardboard
5 days (OECD tests)	100%	No	Yes	No	No	Recycled cardboard — FoE subscription offer on-pack
5 days	100%	No	No[2]	No	No	Recycled cardboard — FoE subscription offer on-pack
19 days	95%	No	Yes	Yes	Yes	Recycled cardboard
'Industry standard'	Not stated	Not stated	Yes	Yes	Yes	?
'Industry standard'	Not stated	Not stated	Yes	No	Yes	?
'Industry standard'	Not stated	Not stated	Yes	No	Yes	?
'Industry standard'	Not stated	Not stated	Yes	Yes	Yes	?
'Industry standard'	Not stated	Not stated	None[4]	Yes	Yes	?
'Industry standard'	Not stated	No	None	No	No	?

Continued overleaf

WASHING POWDERS* (continued)

MANUFACTURERS' BRANDS

Company	Brand	Contains phosphates?	Contains petro-chemical based surfactants?
Procter & Gamble	Ariel	Yes	Yes
	Ariel Automatic	Yes	Yes
	Bold 3	Yes	Yes
	Daz	Yes	Yes
	Daz Automatic	Yes	Yes
	Dreft	Yes	Yes
	Dreft Automatic	Yes	Yes
	Fairy Automatic	Yes	Yes
	Fairy Snow	Yes	Yes
	Tide	Yes	Yes
Robert McBride Group	Green Force	No	Yes

SUPERMARKET OWN-BRAND

Supermarket	Brand	Contains phosphates?	Contains petro-chemical based surfactants?
Co-op	Co-op Blue Biological Washing Powder (High Suds)	Yes	Yes

Length of time to biodegrade (active ingredients only)	By what %?	Use NTA or EDTA?	Use bleach?	Use enzymes?	Optical brighteners?	Packaging information†
'Fully'[5]	Not stated	EDTA	Yes	Yes	Yes	Recycled cardboard
'Fully'[5]	Not stated	EDTA	Yes	Yes	Yes	Recycled cardboard
'Fully'[5]	Not stated	EDTA	Yes	Yes	Yes	Recycled cardboard
'Fully'[5]	Not stated	EDTA	Yes	Yes	Yes	Recycled cardboard
'Fully'[5]	Not stated	EDTA	Yes	Yes	Yes	Recycled cardboard
'Fully'[5]	Not stated	No	No	No	No	Recycled cardboard
'Fully'[5]	Not stated	No	No	Yes	No	Recycled cardboard
'Fully'[5]	Not stated	EDTA	Yes	No	Yes	Recycled cardboard
'Fully'[5]	Not stated	EDTA	Yes	No	Yes	Recycled cardboard
'Fully'[5]	Not stated	EDTA	Yes	No	Yes	Recycled cardboard
3 days[6]	95%	No	Yes	Yes	Yes	Chipboard cartons made from 75% recycled paper

Length of time to biodegrade (active ingredients only)	By what %?	Use NTA or EDTA?	Use bleach?	Use enzymes?	Optical brighteners?	Packaging information†
19 days	80%	No	Yes	Yes	Yes	Recycled cardboard

Continued overleaf

WASHING POWDERS* (continued)

SUPERMARKET OWN-BRAND

Supermarket	Brand	Contains phosphates?	Contains petro-chemical based surfactants?
Co-op (contd)	Co-op Non-Biological Auto Wash Powder	Yes	Yes
	Co-op Biological Automatic with Fabric Conditioner	Yes	Yes
Gateway	Swift	No	Yes
M & S	Super Concentrated Automatic Washing Powder — Biological Action	Yes[7]	Yes
	Super Concentrated Automatic Washing Powder — Non-Biological	Yes[7]	Yes
	Super Concentrated Automatic	Yes	Yes
Safeway	Safeway Low Temperature Automatic	Yes	Yes
	Safeway Automatic, Non Biological	Yes	Yes
Sainsbury's	Sainsbury's Biological Automatic	Yes	Yes

Length of time to biodegrade (active ingredients only)	By what %?	Use NTA or EDTA?	Use bleach?	Use enzymes?	Optical bright-eners?	Packaging information†
19 days	80%	No	Yes	No	Yes	Recycled cardboard
19 days	80%	No	Yes	Yes	Yes	Recycled cardboard
18 days	100%	No	Yes	No	Yes	Recycled cardboard
'Industry standard'	Not stated	EDTA	Yes	Yes	Yes	Polyethylene pail which they say can be re-used in a number of ways[8]
'Industry standard'	Not stated	EDTA	Yes	No	Yes	Polyethylene pail which they say can be re-used in a number of ways[8]
'Industry standard'	Not stated	EDTA	None	Yes	No	Polyethylene pail which they say can be re-used in a number of ways[8]
5 days	Not stated	EDTA	Yes[9]	Yes	Yes	Recycled cardboard cartons
5 days	Not stated	EDTA	Yes[9]	Yes	Yes	Recycled cardboard cartons
10–19 days	min 85%	No	Yes	Yes	Yes	Recycled cardboard

Continued overleaf

WASHING POWDERS* (continued)

SUPERMARKET OWN-BRAND

Supermarket	Brand	Contains phosphates?	Contains petro-chemical based surfactants?
Sainsbury's (contd)	Sainsbury's Blue Detergent	Yes	Yes
	Sainsbury's Biological	Yes	Yes
	Sainsbury's Soap Powder	Yes	Yes
Spar	Spar Blue Washing Powder	Yes	Yes
	Spar All Temperature Automatic Powder	Yes	Yes
Tesco	Tesco Automatic — Phosphate-free	No	Yes
	Blue Washing Powder	Yes	Yes
	Tesco Automatic Biological Washing Powder	Yes	Yes
	Tesco Automatic Non-Biological Washing Powder	Yes	Yes

Length of time to biodegrade (active ingredients only)	By what %?	Use NTA or EDTA?	Use bleach?	Use enzymes?	Optical brighteners?	Packaging information†
10 – 19 days[10]	min 83%	No	Yes	No	Yes	Recycled cardboard
10 – 19 days[10]	min 85%	No	Yes	Yes	Yes	Recycled cardboard
10 – 19 days[10]	min 85%	No	Yes	No	No	Recycled cardboard
'Industry standard'	Not stated	No	Yes	No	Yes	Inner carton is printed chipboard with adhesive and outer carton contains recycled material
'Industry standard'	Not stated	No	Yes	No	Yes	As above
19 days	More than 80%	None	Yes	Yes	Yes	Recycled cardboard. By the end of 1989 the cardboard will be made from 100% recycled pulp[11]
'Industry standard'	Not stated	EDTA	Yes	No	Yes	Recycled cardboard
'Industry standard'	Not stated	No	Yes	Yes	Yes	Recycled cardboard
'Industry standard'	Not stated	No	Yes	No	Yes	Recycled cardboard

Continued overleaf

WASHING POWDERS* (continued)

SUPERMARKET OWN-BRAND

Supermarket	Brand	Contains phosphates?	Contains petro-chemical based surfactants?
Tesco (contd)	Tesco Biological Washing Powder	Yes	Yes

* The information contained in this table is drawn from the response to a detailed questionnaire we sent to the companies. If there are some companies who have not completed the questionnaires accurately, we cannot accept responsibility.

† Where companies have stated that their washing powders come in cardboard boxes, we have assumed some recycled paper content; however if they have specified the quantity of recycled paper we have included this.

1. Acdo have said that soap has always been biodegradable and is therefore not subject to standard tests.

2. Ecover offer separate bleach on this product so that it is not used unnecessarily. The bleach they offer separately is percarbonate, which cannot be included in powders because it activates the other ingredients.

3. Lever Brothers responded to our detailed questionnaire about the ingredients in their products. They did not, however, respond in the format that we requested, because they felt that our approach could be 'misleading or superficial'. This means that we have had to interpret the information they provided and there are some gaps.

Length of time to biodegrade (active ingredients only)	By what %?	Use NTA or EDTA?	Use bleach?	Use enzymes?	Optical brighteners?	Packaging information†
'Industry standard'	Not stated	No	Yes	Yes	Yes	Recycled cardboard

4. No bleach is listed in their summary of ingredients.
5. Procter & Gamble have responded that all their powders are fully biodegradable. This will mean that they fulfil the OECD requirements on timing, but they have supplied no evidence which suggests that the powders biodegrade faster than required by law.
6. They specify that it is a maximum of 3 days if it goes through efficient sewerage treatment.
7. They say there is 30% less phosphate than in 'conventional powders'.
8. They say their washing powders are highly concentrated (using one-third volume for the same wash performance) and therefore use less packaging. Consumers must read the packet carefully, however, so that they do not use more powder than is necessary.
9. They say 'non-perborate'.
10. They say that it only takes 3 – 5 days under natural conditions.
11. Tesco have a full description of the purpose of each ingredient on the pack.

Washing-machine powders and liquids

Once, washday was Monday: now we spread the load through the week. The average British family now washes clothes more frequently, but at lower temperatures. Market research shows that the average family washes five loads a week, almost half of which are done at 40°C and only 6 per cent are washed at high temperatures. Overall, however, the result is that we are using more energy, more water and more detergents.

This market is also seeing rapid changes in the type of product you can buy. The low-suds detergent market is growing at around 10 per cent a year and leading firms like **Lever** and **Procter & Gamble** have launched liquid versions of their major washing powder brands. These liquid products now account for over 30 per cent of the market.

A number of supermarkets now offer low-phosphate (**Marks & Spencer**) or phosphate-free (**Co-op**, **Gateway**, **Safeway**, **Sainsbury's** and **Tesco**) washing powders. The Co-op said it was negotiating with **British Tissues** to develop a phosphate-free washing powder.

A number of other manufacturers, including **ACDO**, are now cutting the amount of phosphate in their products. **Henkel**, the West German detergent giant, was the first major company to break into the UK market with a phosphate-free powder, called *Bright White*, although the first phosphate-free product on the UK market was **Ecover's** *Washing Powder*. Ecover claims that its products biodegrade fully in just five days. Furthermore, the washing powder does not contain perborate bleach. Instead a percarbonate bleach is supplied separately for use with white washes only. The bleach activates at a relatively low temperature, 40°C. Ecover also offers *Liquid Clothes Wash*, which can be used with the company's *Alternative Bleach*.

Faith Products offers a liquid formula detergent — *Clear Spring* — for use either in washing machines or when washing clothes by hand. It is promoted as fully biodegradable and free of phosphates and enzymes, and is effective in hard or soft water. For woollens, **Lever's** *Lux Flakes* — based on pure soap — and *Persil Soap Powder* are mainstream environment-friendly products.

Washing-up liquid

It is worth noting that washing powders have been seen as more of a problem than washing-up liquids, which are generally little more than surfactants with added colouring and perfume.

The products offered by **Ecover** (*Washing-up Liquid*) and **Faith Products** (*Clear Spring*) pioneered in the 'green' market, but a range of other products is now appearing. Given the level of confusion prevailing in this area, it is perhaps worth noting that phosphates, bleaches and enzymes are not found in UK washing-up liquids, despite consumer fears to the contrary.

One bone of contention: the major detergent manufacturers have been disputing the claims of some 'green' firms that their new products are not based on petrochemical surfactants. They point out that the chemicals used in washing up liquids to make surfactants more water-soluble are ethoxylates. Because they are based on ethylene oxide, which in turn originates from the petroleum industry, they ask whether the claims being made are fair. We have been around and around this one, eventually concluding that it may represent a small Achilles heel for green products — but ultimately not a potentially fatal one!

The main angle of attack developed by green suppliers has been to highlight the use of petrochemical surfactants by manufacturers like **Lever** and **Procter & Gamble**. **Ecover** has also stressed that it uses surfactants based on renewable resources like palm or coconut oil. Ecover's *Washing Up Liquid* cleans effectively without producing a mass of foam. It is based on a coconut oil surfactant and contains milk whey, which helps keep your hands in good condition. **Ark**'s *Washing-up Liquid* made by West Germany's **Wundi**, was launched on the UK market in mid-1989. Unlike Ecover's products, however, Ark's contain paraffin. By no means finally, **Werner & Mertz** import *Frosch Dish Washing Detergent* from West Germany, which is advertised as formaldehyde-free and is packed in polythene.

Now the supermarkets are swinging in. The **Co-op** says it started stocking environment-friendly detergents because of growing consumer demand. It has launched its own *Environment Care* range.

Remember, some dishwashing liquids (such as *Fairy Liquid*) are very much more concentrated than others. Product concentration helps cut packaging, transportation and energy costs. You may want to check how long your bottle lasts!

Dishwasher detergents

AEG argues that using a dishwasher on an economy programme need use no more energy and water than doing the washing up by hand. But dishwashers need to be carefully chosen and run to ensure that their environmental performance is acceptable. Don't overdo the detergent: powdered dishwasher detergents may contain up to 40 per cent phosphate. Try a phosphate-free brand and, whichever brand you use, test out different quantities to see which work best in particular circumstances.

Faith Products has added a dishwasher liquid and rinse aid to its 'Clear Spring' range. Both are phosphate-free and have not been tested on animals. '*Clear Spring* can shift two day old lasagne from Wedgwood, as well as any of its rivals,' they say. Ecover should have a competing product on the market by the time of The Green Consumer's *Supermarket Shopping Guide*'s publication. (See also **Werner & Mertz** page 249.)

Fabric conditioners

An interesting development in this sector has been the introduction of refill packs in countries such as West Germany and Spain. Since **Procter & Gamble** launched its refill system for its *Lenor* fabric softener in Germany during 1988, 25 per cent of Lenor sales have been in refill packs. This has become a major battleground for suppliers like Henkel, Lever and Procter & Gamble — and the refill pack really ought to be tried in Britain.

The idea is that liquids are sold in concentrated form and in smaller packages, and are then diluted to the correct strength with water. In Spain, the products are largely sold on the basis of convenience, but in environment-conscious West Germany refill packs have been popular because they cut the amount of plastic waste.

Wherever possible, dry clothes made from natural fibres in the fresh air and you will have no need for fabric conditioners. Such products are also used to control static electricity in man-made fibres, however, so you may want either to switch away from man-made fibres, or to try out **Ecover**'s *Fabric Conditioner*. This is based on a coconut oil surfactant and is suitable for all types of fabric.

Bleaches and Disinfectants

Around 80 per cent of households buy bottled bleaches, which are usually very strong chemical products. They are used for cleaning sinks, loos and drains. The two main types of bleach in this sector are 'chlorine' and 'oxygen' bleaches. While manufacturers say there is little to choose between them in ecological terms, some environmentalists are concerned that the chlorine bleaches are related to highly toxic organochlorine compounds.

Sodium hypochlorite bleaches are the most commonly available chlorine product. They can emit dangerous chlorine gas if mixed with acids, so they must carry a label warning: 'Never mix liquid hypochlorite bleach with acidic toilet cleaners'. But it is worth noting that they break down fairly rapidly in the environment to produce harmless sodium chloride — better known as common salt — and oxygen.

Given that chlorine bleaches kill bacteria by liberating a highly reactive form of oxygen when mixed with water, their chemical action is not radically different from that of the second class of bleaches, the 'oxygen' or 'peroxide' bleaches — of which hydrogen peroxide is the most powerful. The most commonly used in this sector is sodium perborate, also found in clothes washing products (see page 235).

To date, there is little obvious difference between the environmental performance of the major bleach brands. In undiluted form they can obviously be extremely toxic to fish and other organisms, but if you put them down your loo they should be highly diluted before they get anywhere near them.

As with many other cleansing products, use bleaches sparingly if you want to cut back on your contribution to water pollution. Bleach manufacturers often encourage you to use their products to kill bacteria down your drains. We would suggest that you ignore this advice, unless there is an odour problem. And if your house has a septic tank, be wary about using bleach in sinks or loos. You risk knocking out the microbes which break down the wastes in the septic tank.

Lever has dominated the market with its *Domestos* brand for some years, a sodium hypochlorite product. Some supermarkets, such as **Marks & Spencer**, do not sell bleaches. At the time of writing, **Safeway** had not yet done anything to improve the environmental performance of its bleaches, but said it plans to introduce a bleach in a biodegradable plastic bottle. **Gateway** also has plans in this area. The **Co-op** says it is looking for an alternative to hypochlorites for use in its own-brand bleaches.

As far as other disinfectants used in this sector are concerned, the 'phenolic' disinfectants are toxic to fish. That should be no problem if the diluted disinfectant passes through an efficient sewage treatment works, and in any event these products are mainly found at the 'heavy' end of the disinfectant spectrum. **Johnson Wax** provides a range of disinfectants which are promoted as both non-phenolic and PDCB-free. PDCB (paradichlorobenzene) is an important water pollutant which is now banned in a number of European countries.

It is worth noting, however, that *no* household disinfectants contain PDCB. **Jeyes** — the largest UK disinfectant manufacturer — pioneered the move away from phenolic to alternative products. **Reckitt & Colman** also produce non-phenolic disinfectants, as do **Robert McBride**, **British Products Sanmex**, **AIN** and **CWS**.

Drain cleaners

In general, the supermarkets stock bleaches, but not drain-cleaners. The exception is **Tesco**, which sells a **Rentokil** enzyme-based product for septic tanks. Some do stock **ICI**'s *Soda Crystals*, however, based on sodium carbonate decahydrate. The product is relatively non-toxic and has been used for over 100 years, among other things for softening bath water. Water in its natural state already contains sodium and carbonate salts, so the addition of sodium carbonate from Soda Crystals is very unlikely to cause environmental problems (see pages 258 – 9).

Don't pour strong bleaches like sodium hypochlorite down the drain — they can knock out the bacteria which break down waste products naturally. One home-made recipe involves flushing the offending drain with boiling water in which you have dissolved a quarter cup of baking soda and 50 ml (2 oz) of vinegar.

Lavatory cleaners

Surprisingly, the British are the most fanatical race when it comes to cleanliness in the lavatory bowl. For anyone looking for simple, effective solutions, vinegar is a tried and tested loo cleaner. A key issue in this sector revolves around PDCB, which is still contained in some lavatory cleaners — and most toilet blocks.

The products available range from specialist cleaners (liquids and powders designed for cleaning the loo), through in-cistern devices (designed to be put in the cistern, colouring and/or cleaning the water flushed into the pan) to pan blocks or 'in-the-bowl' devices. We advise using such unnecessary cleaners as sparingly as possible — and the Green Consumer may want to avoid in-cistern, pan and in-the-bowl devices altogether.

The **Co-op**'s liquid lavatory cleaner, toilet blocks and rim blocks are all PDCB-free. Its *Toilet Ducks* are also PDCB-free. The Co-op removed PDCBs in 1987 and is reviewing the labelling of products in this sector. **Marks & Spencer** does not stock loo cleaners, but its *St Michael* rim blocks do not contain PDCB. **Safeway** says it plans to move away from all product ingredients that may be toxic — and that none of its products contain PDCB. **Johnson Wax**'s *Lifeguard* toilet care range is PDCB-free, as are **Lever**'s *Frish*, **Reckitt & Colman**'s *Harpic*, **Sainsbury's** *Fresh* and **Jeyes**'s *Sanilav* ranges. When **Tesco** began to go green, it reduced the amount of PDCB in its toilet blocks, with the eventual goal of removing it altogether.

One loo cleaner imported from West Germany is **Werner & Mertz**'s *Frosch Bio Toilet Cleaner*. This removes lime, rust or scale, even under the rim. The product is packed in polythene, which is considered the most environment-friendly plastic in Germany. The company also makes *Frosch Vinegar Cleaner*, for use in cleaning your loo, bath, taps, refrigerators or pans.

Ecover's *Toilet Cleaner* is based on a coconut oil surfactant and acetic acid, or vinegar. The acetic acid has a descaling, scouring and disinfecting effect. The product does not 'kill 100% of all known germs', Ecover says. 'Such products will also destroy the beneficial bacteria in septic tanks which help to break down household wastes and detergents.' If you have a septic tank, take note. And you may also want to try **Ark**'s *Toilet Cleaner*, which came on to the market in mid-1989.

Abrasives, Descalers and Metal Cleaners

Ingredients and Issues

Among the ingredients found in such products are phosphate, ammonia, ethanol, sulphamic acid, phosphoric acid and sodium hydroxide. These may be corrosive, toxic or irritant. As a general rule, the stronger the product, the more likely it is to cause pollution during production, use or disposal.

Descalers

These are used to remove the deposits of limescale that build up in kettles, irons, baths, showers, sinks and toilets, especially in hard water areas. Calcium, which occurs naturally in tap-water, is deposited as scale when water is heated.

Kettle descalers are generally based on formic or sulphamic acids, which are corrosive and toxic if swallowed. If your kettle gets furred up, its energy efficiency will fall sharply. Use *Oz Safe Kettle Descaler*, recommended for use on both metal and plastic kettles and jugs, coffee machines and tea makers.

The descalers sold for sinks and baths are often based on citric and phosphoric acids. Citric acid is relatively mild, whereas phosphoric acid can cause skin or eye injuries. (See under Lavatory cleaners.)

In hard water areas, steam irons can quickly become heavily scaled, cutting their energy efficiency. *Oz Steam Iron Cleaner* is a safe, non-toxic cleaner which removes the scale from the inside of your iron and from the steam holes.

Showers are more energy- and water-efficient than baths, but the jets can scale up in hard water areas if you are not careful. *Oz Shower Jet Cleaner* safely cleans and unblocks shower jets and heads.

Metal cleaners

Among the ingredients found in metal cleaners are acidified thiorea and sulphuric acid, raising questions about corrosiveness and toxicity. Ordinary cleaners may be corrosive and/or toxic. **Johnson Wax**'s *Goddard's Metal Care* range is about as environment-friendly as you will get from a mainstream producer. *Brasso* and *Silvo* are also formulated without thiorea. *Copper Glo* is **Homecare Products'** answer to non-toxic, cruelty-free copper cleaning and polishing. It also works on brass, chrome and stainless steel. (See also *Soda Crystals* box, page 258.)

Oven cleaners

Many oven cleaners are based on sodium hydroxide, more commonly known as caustic soda. This is corrosive and irritant. Caustic soda can react with other household cleaners, particularly acids or ammonia. Mix caustic soda with ammonia solutions, for example, and clouds of toxic ammonia gas may be released. If you're looking for a safe, simple solution, try baking soda mixed with water.

Hob Brite from **Homecare Products** is a cream cleanser formulated for ceramic, glass and halogen cooker tops. It is promoted as non-toxic, phosphate-free and cruelty-free. If you are looking for a safer cleaner for your microwave, try *Microwave Plus* from **Homecare Products**.

Sink and other surface cleaners

As far as phosphate is concerned, surface cleaners typically contain a fairly small amount, around 5 per cent. On their own, surface cleaners are not a major threat, but a growing range of alternative products are now available. The **Co-op** has launched an *Environment Care* range of products, which includes surface cleaners. **Marks & Spencer** does not sell surface cleaners, but says it is actively developing environment-friendly ranges. **Safeway** has asked **Robert McBride** (see 'Behind the Brands', page 263) to supply a cleaner aimed at the Green Consumer.

Ecover's *Cream Cleaner*, based on a coconut oil surfactant, is suitable for all domestic surfaces such as sinks, baths (including acrylic baths), stainless steel, formica, paintwork, tiles, pots and pans. A German range of household cleaning products introduced in 1989 is made by **Nitor**. The first product to be launched was Nitor's *All-purpose Cleaner*, promoted as the 'Greener Cleaner'. The product is phosphate-free and comes in a polyethylene container. A general household cleaner is also available from **Ark**. *Oz Bathroom Cleaner*, which is made by **DDD** and is available from most supermarkets, removes limescale from baths, taps, sinks and tiles. It is non-toxic, non-caustic, biodegradable and not harmful to animals. Unusually, too, the DDD pack highlights the product's biodegradability, although the package itself is still made of non-biodegradable plastic. *Shiny Sinks*, available from **Homecare Products**, is non-toxic, phosphate-free and cruelty-free. This soft-abrasive cream cleanser removes hard water deposits, rust stains and metal tarnish as it cleans. Used regularly, it prevents the build-up of lime scale. (See also Soda Crystals box page 258.)

Air Fresheners, Polishes and other products

Air fresheners

All air-fresheners on the UK market should now be CFC-free. But air fresheners are still an example of an unnecessary product. It is surely better to keep your kitchen, bathroom or loo clean and open the window — rather than use a product which merely hides the smell instead of getting rid of it.

Beeswax polishes

Bees are vital pollinators in the countryside — and beekeepers are ever-alert to pesticide problems which may damage or kill their swarms. Support bees by buying beeswax products, like those stocked by **Asda** (*Asda Paste Polish, Asda Aerosol Polishes*), **Co-op** (*Furniture Polish with Beeswax, Leos Silky brand*), **Gateway** (*Gateway Summer Beeswax Polish*), **Sainsbury's** (*Mansion Natural Wood, Sainsbury's Furniture Polish, Lord Sheraton Pure Beeswax Balsam*), **Marks & Spencer** (*St Michael Furniture Spray*) and **Safeway** (*Safeway Beeswax*).

Floor cleaners

Floor cleaners are hardly a major environmental threat. But don't overdo them. There are a number of more 'environment-friendly' brands on the market. **Ecover**'s *Floor Soap* is suitable for all floors. Alternatively, try **ICI**'s *Soda Crystals* (see page 258), which can be used to clean vinyl flooring, mats, brushes and brooms.

Hand cleaners

Not something that most of us use often, but if you end up with oiled or greasy hands you may want to try a cleaner that is not based on white spirit. Like other petrochemical products, white spirit can contribute to indoor pollution and, outdoors, to photochemical smogs. Try **Ecover**'s *Heavy Duty Hand Cleaner*. This will remove oils, grease and dirt. In this case, the coconut oil surfactant is combined with wood pulp to provide a gentle scouring agent.

Window cleaners

Hardly a major environmental problem either, these come in three basic forms — emulsions, trigger packs and aerosols. Some products, like *Windolene*, come in all three forms. Most aerosol products should now be CFC-free, but trigger packs are

SODA CRYSTALS ·

Soda Crystals have been used in the home for over 100 years. They are non-flammable, of low toxicity, give off no harmful fumes and are generally considered safe. Indeed, many people use them to soften their bath water. ICI says that they are 'the strongest safe cleaner' and suggests that they can replace many less environment-friendly products and make others go further. They are good at removing grease, which makes them ideal for cleaning sinks, floors, walls, waste pipes and drains. They also help clean stained and blackened pans and cooking dishes, hobs, ovens and cooker hoods. As a washing agent, they add a sparkle to glass and silver, while removing stubborn tannin and caffeine stains from the insides of tea and coffee pots and mugs. One way to clean tarnished silver is to soak it in a Soda Crystal solution to which has been added a good handful of tin foil — or milk bottle tops!

Used as an economical water softener in automatic washing machines, they make soap and detergents go further and clean more efficiently. And when it comes to stain busting, use Soda Crystals to remove blood, ink, fruit juice, tea, coffee, cocoa or milk stains. The only catch: don't use them on aluminium, which they can darken.

Among their many uses, claim ICI, are the following:

Cleaning drains
Reviving limp parsley
Extending the performance of washing powder
Defurring kettles

Cleaning silver
Setting jelly
Keeping hot water bottles hotter
Preventing chopped apples from going brown
Removing moss and lichen from patios and
garden ornaments
Cleaning grease and dead flies from car
windscreens
Loosening dirt from clothes
Tenderising meat
Cleaning beehives
Softening corns and chilblains
Making crystal sparkle
De-sliming sponges
Repelling insects and mice
Soothing insect bites
Cleaning blinds
Removing chewing gum from carpets
Cleaning brewing equipment
Removing bird droppings

As always, however, there is no such thing as a free
lunch. In some countries — including the USA, Turkey,
Kenya and Tanzania — it may be possible to dig natural
sodium carbonate out of the ground. But in Europe sodium
carbonate is made by adding ammonia and brine to
limestone, and is a highly energy intensive business. So
don't use more than you have to!

probably a more environment-friendly alternative (because they contain no CFCs and no hydrocarbons) and are equally effective.

Some products contain white spirit, which means that you should be careful to use them only in well-ventilated areas. West Germany's **Werner & Mertz**, whose motto is 'For the Environment's Sake', promotes its *Frosch Spirit Glass Cleaner* — based on alcohol — as an 'environment-friendly' product. **Ark** also now offers a window cleaner, launched in mid-1989.

BEHIND THE BRANDS

Next time you pick a detergent, think about the environmental acceptability of the manufacturer as well as the acceptability of the product. Unfortunately, it's often difficult to spot which companies make which products, because brand advertising spotlights the product rather than the manufacturer. So here are some background facts on a dozen detergent and cleaner manufacturers.

The Green Pioneers

ACDO, a small manufacturer with a turnover under £5 million, sees environmental questions as 'very important' in helping its products stand out. It has carried the Vegetarian Society symbol on its packs since early 1989 and its soap-based washing powder contains no synthetic detergents. Its phosphate content has been cut to 5 per cent.

Ark is a hybrid organisation, combining environmental and commercial objectives. Its imported range of environment-friendly detergents, sold by a commercial subsidiary called **Ark Products**, was launched on the UK market during the summer of 1989.

DDD, which reports a £10m turnover, produced its environmental policy in 1988. It reformulated its *Stain Devil* range to eliminate possible toxic ingredients, while its *Stain Salts* cut the consumer's need to use phosphates.

Ecover, distributed in the UK by **Full Moon**, is the best-known green supplier and has forced the pace in the detergents sector by its visible success in attracting the Green Consumer and by launching its cunningly worded *Green Paper* with Friends of the Earth in spring 1989. It has removed some of the ingredients (including phosphates) which are used by mainstream manufacturers but considered environmentally undesirable by Ecover. While there is currently a good deal of debate about the environmental importance of different rates of biodegradability, Ecover's products are designed to fully biodegrade in five days — faster than the industry standard of just over two weeks.

Full Moon has carried out joint promotions with Friends of the Earth on Ecover's *Washing Powder* and its turnover is rising from £2 million to an expected £10 million in 1989.

Homecare Products, on the other hand, comes in at £750,000. Homecare's product range is promoted as 'cruelty-free' (i.e. not tested on animals), including *Shiny Sinks*, *Hob Brite*, *Bar Keeper's Friend* and *Copper Glo*. But it increasingly features environmental themes in its promotional literature. The company says it audits its use of energy and materials, and its products are packed in cardboard tubes, rather than plastic packs. Natural acids such as citric acid are used in Homecare cleaning products.

Faith Products, with a turnover between £250,000 and £500,000, has been another important pioneer. Its products are cruelty-free and its the *Clear Spring* laundry liquid was the first British phosphate-free liquid to reach the market. The company has used environmental issues as a key element in its promotions for the *Clear Spring* range and as an important element in promotions for its *Faith in Nature* range.

Nitor, like Werner & Mertz (see below), is a German company which has spotted the opportunity to export 'environment-friendly' products to Britain. Nitor's first product on the UK market, introduced in 1989, was its *All-purpose Cleaner*, promoted as the 'greener cleaner'.

Two Giants

Although the spotlight of media attention may have concentrated on the new entrants to this market, the detergents sector is still dominated by two companies: Lever Brothers and Procter & Gamble.

Lever, which now has a £300 million UK turnover, adopted its first overall environmental policy in 1983, pulling together individual environmental statements produced over the previous couple of decades.

'Our products are designed to have no adverse environmental impact,' Lever says. 'As consumers have shown little or no interest in this aspect in the past, such information has not been considered necessary.' But, it admits: 'This situation may change.' In particular, Lever argues that, while phosphate problems have not been a major issue in Britain, they 'could be made into one because of publicity from Germany'.

While Lever feels that its customers are unlikely to be interested in its environmental performance, it has done a great deal to clean up its act over the years. Through recycling the water used in its detergent powder factories, Lever cut its effluent load eight-fold. On the product front, its *Concentrated Comfort* gives three times the number of uses from a given size of pack.

Procter & Gamble has an even larger UK turnover, £630 million in 1988. It also argues that its detergents, which include the best-selling *Fairy Liquid*, *Dreft*, *Tide*, *Daz*, *Ariel* and *Bold*, are 'in the forefront of industry biodegradability level achievement'. The company has plans to set up a Green Ribbon Panel, to ensure that its product range is not only environment-friendly but is seen to be so.

On the manufacturing side, the scale of some of the industry's unsung achievements is illustrated by the fact that between 1976 and 1986 Procter & Gamble's overall energy usage dropped by 38 per cent as production volume jumped by 50 per cent.

Emerging Middleweight Challengers

Between the green Davids of the detergent sector and the would-be green Goliaths, there are a number of medium-sized companies that are devoting a great deal of effort to making sure that their products are more environment-friendly.

Amway is a $1.5bn (approximately £1 billion) door-to-door selling company founded 30 years ago by two Americans. Its catalogue makes much of the fact that its products do not contain CFCs and that its cleaners are based on biodegradable surfactants. Its *Dish Drops* product, for washing dishes, is promoted as 'environmentally safe', while its *Car Wash* contains no phosphates. It is not clear, however, whether Amway's entire range has been formulated with the environment in mind. As usual, it's worth asking about each product as you buy.

The Robert McBride Group's interest in environmental affairs reflects the fact that it is part of the BP Group. It says that it is strongly committed to environment-friendliness and continuously views its business through a 'green filter'. It provides phosphate-free products.

Johnson Wax is probably the most environmentally conscious of all the major companies in this area. Its policy stresses that it is 'committed to develop and market products which are environmentally sound and which, when usage instructions are followed, will not endanger the health and safety of consumers and users.' The company removed CFCs from its aerosol products as long ago as 1976 and, in 1988, led the way in labelling its UK products as 'ozone friendly'. Green issues now figure in all new product development briefs.

The **Jeyes Group** is likely to be one of the surprise new entrants into the green product market. The company's 'good citizen' policy dates from 1972, when it was part of the Cadbury-Schweppes group. Jeyes removed paradichlorobenzene (PDCB) from its products in 1976 and changed the active ingredient of its loo cleaners from hydrochloric acid to citric acid in 1981. All its products are phosphate-free. Jeyes may well launch its own complete range of more environment-friendly products.

Werner & Mertz with a DM350 million (around £110 million) turnover, offers the *Frosch* range of household cleaning products, which are phosphate-free and biodegradable within 3 days. The range, launched in the UK in 1989, includes a neutral cleaner, vinegar cleaner, spirit glass cleaner, toilet cleaner, cream cleaner and washing-up liquid. Werner & Mertz note that the environmental pressures in West Germany, Austria and Switzerland have helped push manufacturers there well ahead of British firms.

All the companies we quizzed not only thought environmental issues important, but also considered that they were likely to become even more pressing. We asked whether they thought that the Single European Market, which will emerge after 1992, would help to push things forward. 'I hope so,' says John Sharman, Director of **Homecare Products**. Everyone else said: 'Yes'.

WHAT YOU CAN DO

1 Most detergents do not work so well in hard water. Ask your water authority about the hardness of your water. You may need a water softener.

2 Cut down on the amount of detergent you use. The average family washes five loads of clothes a week rather than one, so we may often be washing clothes that are nearly clean anyway.

3 Try out some of the 'environment-friendly' products.

4 Look for concentrated products, which save on packaging. (In Germany, some washing products are now sold in refillable containers. They should be tried here.)

5 Wash at lower temperatures, to save energy.

6 Dry clothes outside whenever possible. It saves on energy and fabric conditioner.

Household Goods

Without thinking about it, we use an enormous array of products around the house which would have seemed semi-magical to our great-grandparents, from batteries to clingfilm. At the same time, however, most of us fail to think of the environmental shadows cast by some of these products.

Whether you are responsible for doing the housework or the DIY jobs which pile up in any household, you may want to look for products which are more environment-friendly. We provide some initial ideas, but would be delighted to hear from you if you can add some practical additional steps to our initial short-list!

Adhesives

All of us, at some time or other, get stuck in to tasks which need glues or other adhesives. Ask most people what they think the main problems are with these products and they will mention solvent abuse, particularly by children and young adults. Or maybe they will mention the danger of 'superglue' products sticking people to their environment, or bits of the same person to other bits!

But there are pollution considerations here too. Products like petrol, white spirit, paraffin and solvents are hydrocarbons, all of which contribute to one of the most important air pollution problems we now face in our cities — photochemical haze. Initially, these noxious hazes were mainly found in cities which had a lot of cars and bright sunshine. The unburnt hydrocarbons emitted by the vehicles were changed by solar radiation into ozone and other chemicals which, at near-ground level, can damage our health and plant life.

Although the main focus has been on exhaust emissions, it is worth recalling that many glues are based on petroleum-based solvents. As some of the more obvious and easier-to-tackle sources of hydrocarbon emissions are dealt with, there will be growing interest in what the Americans call 'fugitive emissions' — caused by leaks, occasional use of hydrocarbon products and so on.

The supermarkets have moved at different speeds in this area, so far entirely in response to the solvent abuse issue. Some, like the **Co-op**, **Sainsbury's**, **Spar** and **Tesco**, say they do not stock own-label glues and adhesives, but this leaves open the question of whether they stock mainstream branded products. **Safeway** says it has eliminated all petroleum-based solvents and **Marks & Spencer** says it is using water-based materials to replace petroleum-based solvents. Both **Asda** and **Gateway** said they stocked *Bostik Solvent Free Adhesive*, while Asda also reported that it stocked *Tipp-Ex School and Study Water Based Correction Fluid* and *UHU Non-Toxic Glue Pen*. Asda did say, however, that such products are not available in all its stores — so you may have to scout around.

Clearly, fears about solvent abuse are coincidentally driving developments in the direction of more environment-friendly products. But don't count on the trend continuing under its own steam. Insist on environment-friendly adhesives which will help to prevent the whole planet coming to a sticky end.

Aluminium foil

The production of aluminium is energy-intensive: 4 – 6 tonnes of oil are used for every tonne of aluminium. So use aluminium foil sparingly, if at all. And, if you do use it, save and re-use as much as you can. Aluminium can be recycled, although the emphasis so far has been on relatively heavy products like cans and pans. Longer term, however, it would be good to see aluminium recyclers also taking quantities of foil or milk bottle tops.

Batteries

When we first wrote *The Green Consumer Guide*, we concluded that 'batteries may not be the No. 1 environmental problem, but they are environmentally undesirable.' Each year, Britain gets through some 400 million batteries — and the overall impact of their production is considerable.

Many batteries also contain hazardous materials such as mercury and cadmium. As a result, the incineration of domestic wastes containing batteries can cause air pollution problems. Indeed, the Danes, who incinerate a fair amount of their waste, have banned mercury oxide batteries, to ensure that they do not end up in incinerators. It seems to be uneconomic at the moment to recycle batteries, although Sweden and Switzerland have developed battery collection schemes. So what should the Green Consumer do? Here are some immediate dos and don'ts.

Do: Use mains power wherever possible. Remember that manufacturing batteries can take up to 50 times more energy than they produce.

Do: Switch to rechargeable batteries if you have any equipment that uses a lot of batteries.

Do: Buy 'green' batteries — which didn't exist in Britain when *The Green Consumer Guide* was first published. Look for batteries that are mercury- and cadmium-free.

Do: Lobby to have batteries collected and stored, against the day when suitable recycling technologies become available.

> **Don't:** Use old batteries with new ones. The new batteries try to recharge the old, cutting their useful life.

> **Don't:** Throw batteries away outdoors — put them in the dustbin.

> **Don't:** Put mercury hearing-aid batteries in the dustbin. Return them to the manufacturer — or to your local surgery. And ask your surgery what they will do with the spent batteries!

As we noted in *The Green Consumer Guide*, there are a number of different types of battery, containing different levels of potentially hazardous materials. The following are the major ones:

● **Zinc carbon batteries** are the most common small batteries and contain very small amounts of mercury in the form of mercuric chloride, and smaller amounts of cadmium. They are used in radios, cycle lamps, torches, shavers, clocks, calculators and TV remote control units.

● **Zinc chloride batteries** are a modern version of zinc carbon batteries. Because of the leakage problems associated with zinc carbon batteries, zinc chloride batteries are based on a dry, harmless powder. They are used in the same types of equipment as zinc carbon batteries.

● **Alkaline manganese batteries** offer a far superior performance in most applications. But they contain more mercury than zinc carbon batteries. Remember, too, that when manufacturers claim that their alkaline batteries 'last up to six times longer', they are comparing them to zinc batteries. When used in less demanding applications, where zinc-based batteries tend to perform better, alkaline batteries last up to three times as long. Alkaline batteries are used in personal stereos, camera flashguns and portable hi-fis.

- **Button cells** require materials of the highest energy density because they are so small. Mercuric oxide and silver oxide are preferred materials. Silver oxide is more expensive, however, and can have a shorter shelf-life, so the more toxic mercury oxide has tended to win out. Button cells are not recycled: the silver contained in a silver oxide watch battery is worth no more than 1p. Mercury cells are used in hearing aids and some cameras, and should be properly disposed of. Health authorities take back hearing aid batteries (ask what they intend to do with them!), while **Duracell** say they also take back mercury cells. Camera shops do not.

- **Nickel-cadmium rechargeable batteries** obviously contain toxic cadmium, generally at the 7 – 15 per cent (70,000 – 150,000 ppm) level. Rechargeable batteries can be recharged as often as 500 times. Although more expensive initially, rechargeable batteries can work out cheaper in the long run. They have to be recharged several times during the normal life of an equivalent alkaline battery, however, and they must also be used very carefully, or their life is shortened. As a result, they have so far won only a small share of the consumer market.

- **Lithium batteries** are more expensive, but hold long-term promise. Lithium offers higher voltages in small batteries than do such materials as silver and mercury. **Kodak** have claimed that their lithium batteries last 'up to ten times' longer than normal zinc carbon batteries and 'twice as long' as current high performance 9-volt alkaline batteries.

Hot on the heels of our suggestion that consumers should try out 'green' batteries if and when they appeared on the UK market, a German battery manufacturer — **Varta** — launched its mercury-free products in Britain in December 1988. The

BATTERIES

Brand	Sizes	Energy output (Volts)	Mercury content (Parts per million)	Cadmium content (Parts per million)	Lead content (Parts per million)	Comments
ZINC CARBON BATTERIES						
Varta (Blue)	HP2	1.5	< 1	118	505	
	HP7	1.5	< 1	193	825	
	HP11	1.5	< 1	114	490	
Ever Ready (Blue)	HP2 (R20B)	1.5	60	16	2200	
	HP7 (R14B)	1.5	70	17	2200	
	HP11 (R6B)	1.5	150	18	2500	
	PP3 (PP3B)	9.0	120	<10	50	
Philips	HP2 (R20)	1.5	30	100	500	Mercury and cadmium content will be further reduced by end of 1989
	HP7 (R6)	1.5	40	100	500	
	HP11 (R14)	1.5	40	100	500	
	PP3 (6F22)	9.0	100	30	*	
ZINC CHLORIDE BATTERIES						
Varta (Silver)	HP2	1.5	< 1	< 2	45	'Environment Friendlier' symbol on all packs except PP3, with explanation about mercury and cadmium content. Also, backing cards are of recycled material.
	HP7	1.5	< 1	< 3	65	
	HP11	1.5	< 1	< 2	45	
	PP3	9.0	55	68	206	

Ever Ready (Silver Seal)	HP2 (R20S)	1.5	< 1	< 10	1700	
	HP7 (R14S)	1.5	< 1	< 10	2000	
	HP11 (R6S)	1.5	< 1	< 10	2200	
	PP3 (PP3S)	9.0	< 1	< 10	10	
Kodak	HP2 (KDHZ)	1.5	< 1	< 2	45	Packs (except PP3) carry a green '0% mercury' flash
	HP7 (KAAHZ)	1.5	< 1	< 3	65	
	HP11 (KCHZ)	1.5	< 1	< 2	45	
	PP3 (K9VHZ)	9.0	55	68	206	
Philips (Greenline)	HP2 (R20)	1.5	< 1	100	500	Information on the mercury content given on pack
	HP7 (R6)	1.5	< 1	100	500	
	HP11 (R14)	1.5	< 1	100	500	
	PP3 (6F22)	9.0	< 1	30	*	

ALKALINE BATTERIES

Varta (Black)	HP2 (LR20)	1.5	235	< 6	110	'Mercury Reduced' flash, with explanation on pack. Also backing card is of recycled material
	HP7	1.5	220	< 5	100	
	HP11	1.5	235	< 6	110	
	PP3	9.0	145	< 4	65	
Ever Ready (Gold Seal)	HP2 (LR20)	1.5	2000	< 1	70	
	HP7 (LR14)	1.5	2000	< 1	70	
	HP11 (LR6)	1.5	2000	< 1	80	
	PP3 (6LF22)	9.0	1500	< 1	50	
Kodak	HP2 (KD)	1.5	< 250	< 6	110	'Environment Friendly' flash on pack
	HP7 (KAA)	1.5	< 250	< 5	100	
	HP11 (KC)	1.5	< 250	< 6	110	
	PP3 (K9VO)	9.0	< 250	< 4	65	

Continued overleaf

BATTERIES (continued)

Brand	Sizes	Energy output (Volts)	Mercury content (Parts per million)	Cadmium content (Parts per million)	Lead content (Parts per million)	Comments
Philips (Green Alkaline)	HP2 (R20)	1.5	200†	1 – 4	70	Information on the mercury and cadmium content, given on pack
	HP7 (R6)	1.5	200†	1 – 4	60	
	HP11 (R14)	1.5	200†	1 – 4	60	
	PP3 (6LR61)	9.0	200†	1 – 4	*	
RECHARGEABLE BATTERIES						
Varta	HP2	1.2	*	120000	*	Rechargeable batteries are recyclable: packs carry a recycling symbol
	HP7	1.2	*	123000	*	
	HP11	1.2	*	121000	*	
	PP3	8.4	*	129000	*	
Ever Ready	HP2 (RX20)	1.2	*	78700	*	
	HP7 (RX14)	1.2	*	120200	*	
	HP11 (RX6)	1.2	*	136400	*	
	PP3 (RX22)	8.4	*	Not stated	*	
Mem-Tek	HP2	1.2	*	140000 appx	*	
	HP7	1.2	*	140000 appx	*	
	HP11	1.2	*	140000 appx	*	
	PP3	8.4	*	140000 appx	*	

< less than
* Company responded with a 'zero'; however trace elements will always be found.
† This figure will be correct from the end of 1989. Until then, the mercury content will be marginally higher.

company, Europe's largest battery-maker, saw its share of supermarket battery sales jump from under 2 per cent to over 13 per cent in just a few months.

This success then prompted other manufacturers, among them **Ever Ready**, **Panasonic** and **Philips**, to launch their own 'green' batteries. Ever Ready took the next step, by announcing that it would also remove cadmium from its batteries, a move rapidly emulated by its competitors. **Duracell**'s alkaline manganese batteries are labelled 'Reduced mercury, No cadmium, Respecting the environment'. Environmental issues, the company told us, will be 'of primary importance' in the battery market.

Interestingly, however, the success of such firms then spurred a counter-attack from **Vidor**, a company which had not responded in time and had seen its market share fall as a result. It attacked the claims made by companies like Varta, noting that batteries were not, in any case, an environment-friendly product. Clearly, as the pace of developments takes off, more manufacturers will have to be scrupulous in their assessment of what really makes a product more environment-friendly.

As our Table shows, different batteries supplied by different manufacturers contain very different levels of mercury, cadmium and lead. Lead is not such a source of concern as mercury and cadmium but some manufacturers are nevertheless beginning to reduce the lead content of their batteries. It is also worth noting that one part per million (1 ppm) of most materials is a vanishingly small amount. 1 ppm is equivalent to one drop of water in 16.5 gallons, or one minute in two years. That said, these heavy metals are hazardous materials and we should do everything in our power to ensure that the levels we discharge into the environment — or which are discharged on our behalf by industry — are kept to an absolute minimum. On these figures, none of the batteries can properly be described as 'environment-friendly', although the major brands have certainly cut — or will shortly cut — their mercury and cadmium content.

The Table also shows that there can be a marked discrepancy between battery manufacturers in terms of on-pack information. This can clearly be seen when comparing **Kodak** and **Varta** zinc chloride batteries. The make-up of both batteries is identical, but Kodak have a '0% mercury' flash on their pack, whilst Varta have an 'environment-friendlier' flash with an explanation on the back that the batteries are mercury- and cadmium-free. Differences such as these can confuse and may even mislead the consumer. A standardised form of labelling environment-friendly products is needed (see page 326).

Neither **Iceland** nor **Marks & Spencer** stock batteries, green or otherwise. **Asda** says that its batteries comply with EEC standards, but plan to cut mercury and cadmium levels substantially by the end of 1989. The **Co-op** says that environment-friendlier batteries are 'available' to any Co-op stores wanting to stock them, which doesn't necessarily mean that your local Co-op will have them! Ask for them. **Gateway**, on the other hand, says it stocks both **Varta**'s *Silver* range (mercury-free) and **Ever Ready**'s *Silver Seal* batteries, which are mercury- and cadmium-free. **Safeway** stocks Varta batteries, as does **Sainsbury's**, which also stocks the *Silver Seal* range. **Tesco** does not sell any batteries promoted as 'environment-friendly', but does sell own-label mercury-free batteries.

Candles

We don't seem to have as many power strikes as we used to, although some critics of electricity privatisation suggest this may soon change. Don't stock up on candles, but if you are buying candles anyway, you may want to avoid those made from animal fat. A number of stores, among them **Asda**, **Co-op Leos** and **Gateway**, said they stock *Deeko* candles, which are made from petroleum products like paraffin wax, and styrene (derived from vegetable oil). **Gateway** and **Sainsbury's** both sell the *Price*'s brand, also based on paraffin wax and styrene. **Safeway** said it sells Kosher candles, under the *Bolsius* label, while **Tesco** reported that none of its candles are made from animal tallow. There is clearly a trade-off here between animal welfare and the issues associated with the petroleum industry.

Clingfilm

The debate still rages on whether PVC is environmentally friendly or not (see page 56) and even though scientists have said that the plasticisers used in clingfilms do not pose a health risk, some supermarkets have decided that they will give the consumer the choice between PVC and non-PVC brands. **Asda**'s own-label product is PVC-free, as are **Iceland**'s, **Gateway**'s, **Marks & Spencer**'s, **Safeway**'s and **Tesco**'s.

The **Co-op** stocks three types of clingfilm: PVC (with a 'low-migration' pledge), PVDC (for use in microwaves) and PE (non-PVC). Interestingly, too, **Spar** is re-introducing its own Spar PVC-free clingfilm, withdrawn last time around because of poor product performance and lack of sales.

Kitchen towels

(See pages 209 – 15 for Loo paper and Tissues.)

Our survey showed that the supermarkets are stocking an increasing number of products based on recycled fibre. The kitchen towels offered by **Kleenex**, **Safeway** and **Tesco**, all of which are made with 100 per cent recycled fibre, are certainly the most impressive to date. **Sainsbury's** *Economy Kitchen Towels* are a close runner-up. None of the products on offer as yet are packaged in recycled paper, which is surely the logical next step, and all the supermarkets say that their kitchen towels do contain some percentage of chlorine-bleached fibre. At this stage of the game, that is probably inevitable.

KITCHEN TOWELS

SUPERMARKET OWN-BRAND

Supermarket/Brand	Recycled paper content	Labelled as recycled?	Packaged in recycled paper?	Chlorine-bleached? (see Note)
Asda Kitchen Roll	20%	No	No	Yes
Horizon Kitchen Towels (stocked by **Gateway**)	Small %	No	No	Yes
Iceland	Nil	N/A	No	Yes

Continued overleaf

KITCHEN TOWELS (continued)

SUPERMARKET OWN-BRAND continued

Supermarket/Brand	Recycled paper content	Labelled as recycled?	Packaged in recycled paper?	Chlorine-bleached? (see Note)
M & S St Michael Kitchen Towel	30%	No	No	Yes
Safeway Kitchen Towels*	Yes, but content not guaranteed	No	Not stated	Yes‡
Safeway Kitchen Towels*	100%	No	Not stated	Yes
Safeway Kitchen Towels Economy	50%	No	No	Yes‡
Sainsbury's Economy Kitchen Towels	About 75%	No	No	Yes
Sainsbury's Kitchen Towels (except Extra Thick)	30 – 50%	No	No	Yes
Spar Kitchen Roll	50% (minimum)	No	No	Yes
Tesco Kitchen Towel	100%	Yes	No	Yes
MANUFACTURERS' BRANDS				
Country Collection Kitchen Towels	100%	No	No	Yes
Dixcel Family Value	50%	Yes (50%)	No	Yes
Dixcel Kittensoft	Minimal	No	No	Yes
Fiesta Kitchen Towel	Not stated†	No	No	Yes
Kleenex Kitchen Towels	100%	Yes	No	Yes‡
Nouvelle Kitchen Towels	100%	No	No	Yes‡
Scottowel Kitchen Towel	Not stated†	No	No	Yes

Note: See Note 1 to Loo Paper table on page 214.
* Safeway Kitchen Towels are manufactured by two different companies.
† Companies replied that this was 'commercially sensitive information'.

Kitchenware

Among the issues to watch out for here are the use of tropical hardwoods and of plastics, particularly those containing cadmium pigments.

When we asked the supermarkets whether they used tropical hardwoods in their products, in the handles of cooking utensils, for example, **Asda**, **Iceland**, **Marks & Spencer**, **Safeway**, **Sainsbury's** and **Spar** came up with a clean bill of health. In the case of Iceland, this was because the company does not sell cooking utensils, while in Spar's case the company replied that none of its kitchen utensils has a wooden handle of any sort. Safeway said that it had investigated its kitchenware products, to see if there was a problem, but found that none of the products it sells has a tropical hardwood handle.

The **Co-op**, on the other hand, supplies two product ranges which use tropical hardwoods: teak salad bowls and stainless steel saucepans with teak handles. The Co-op said it expected to phase the products out by the end of 1989. **Tesco** said it still uses some teak, but that the wood was supplied from well managed, sustainably run forests in Burma and Indonesia.

As far as plastic kitchenware is concerned, the 'housewares' market is highly fashion-conscious, with the 'in' colours changing constantly. One thing that has been slow to change, however, is the industry's enthusiasm for cadmium pigments. Cadmium has been favoured by the plastics industry not only because it helps to produce brilliant red, orange and yellow colours, but also because it does not break down during high-temperature processing. The concern is that cadmium is a toxic heavy metal which can hang around in the environment indefinitely.

The UK plastics industry resisted moves to get cadmium out of its products, although it looks as though an EEC Directive will cut the allowable levels of cadmium quite dramatically. In the meantime, **Curver Consumer Products**, a subsidiary of the giant Dutch company **DSM** and second only to **Addis** in the UK market, turns out 160 products in a range of colours — none of which contains cadmium. The products include bowls, dustbins, kitchenware, storage bins and boxes, vacuum flasks and jugs, coolbags and an assortment of baby products.

Curver was surprised to find that its UK competitors had not taken cadmium out of their products, as the Dutch industry had in the early 1980s. 'In the Netherlands,' the company's managing director pointed out, 'we began to go through this stage seven years ago, when the first restrictions were proposed by Sweden. I never thought that UK manufacturers hadn't followed what happened there so long ago.'

So far, there are two options open to the Green Consumer with such products: look for the Curver brand; or ask your supermarket manager to confirm that the plastic products you are considering buying are cadmium-free.

We asked the supermarkets whether they stocked cadmium-free plastic kitchenware, and, if not, whether they would change. Their answers are summarised in the Table. **Iceland**, the **Co-op** and **Safeway** come out top on this question. Iceland and the Co-op seemed to lead the field by a wide margin.

PLASTIC WARE

Supermarket	All plastic ware cadmium-free?	Time of change
Asda	No	By end of 1989
Co-op	Yes	Has always been the case
Gateway	No	By end of 1989
Iceland	Yes	At least 5 years ago
M & S	No	By January 1990
Safeway	Yes	1988 (changed suppliers in order to do this)
Sainsbury's	No	
Spar	N/A	
Tesco	N/A	

Remember that when supermarkets say they have no own-label product in this category, they almost certainly sell products made by other companies. While own-label products are the easiest to 'green', the supermarkets will increasingly have to think through whether they are comfortable stocking brand-name products seen as less environment-friendly than they might be.

Light bulbs

A pretty poor showing here. None of the supermarkets gave us information which really seemed to measure up to what is needed. Many different factors must be taken into account in judging the energy efficiency of a bulb, including its wattage, the 'lumens' it produces and its life expectancy.

Energy efficiency will be an increasingly pressing priority in the 1990s, yet most of the supermarkets have so far given little thought to the energy efficiency of the light bulbs they sell. They continue to rate it as a second-order target, behind price and product life.

Safeway says it sells the *Mazda Double Life* range, however, which is promoted on the basis of its energy efficiency. But **Sainsbury's** noted that it dropped an energy-efficient bulb a couple of years ago because of poor sales. On the basis of the information supplied, it looks as though the best place to find energy-efficient bulbs is the **Co-op**, where *Osram Double Life*, *Ring Extra Life* and *Philips SL* are stocked. This area seems to be a prime target for *Which?*-style comparative testing, both on life expectancy and energy efficiency.

Moth balls and moth proofers

Moths can be a pest if they get into your wardrobe, and the moth-proofers you use to discourage them may be petroleum based. Herbal products are on the market, so we asked the supermarkets whether they stocked them. None did, and none of the supermarkets stocked moth-proofer aerosols, herbal or non-herbal, that were labelled as CFC-free.

Plastic refuse bags

Finally, we asked if the supermarkets stocked refuse bags made from recycled plastic. Their answers are shown in the Table. Only **Iceland** has a product that apparently meets the bill, although a number of other supermarkets are either considering introducing one — or in the process of developing one. **Tesco** does use bags made from recycled plastics, but these are not offered to its customers.

PLASTIC REFUSE BAGS

Supermarket	Brand of refuse bag made from recycled plastic	Comments
Asda	None	Possible introduction in 1989
Co-op	None	Under review
Gateway	None	Trimmings and production waste fed back into bags at manufacture*
Iceland	Iceland Refuse bags Bejam Refuse bags	Introduced in 1986
M & S	None	Developing range
Safeway	None	Under review
Sainsbury's	None	Discussing with suppliers
Spar	None	Under review
Tesco	None†	

* Gateway say that they do not use secondary recycled granulated polymers but do feed back trimmings and production waste into the manufacture of plastic bags.
Comment: It is quite possible the other brands do this as well, although they did not mention it.
† Tesco use these refuse bags themselves but they are not on sale to customers because of variable quality.

How green are the companies that produce your favourite brands? Our profiles of 76 of the companies that supply the supermarkets draw on the results of SustainAbility's Manufacturers' Survey, carried out in the early part of 1989. In most cases, the profiles also give you the main brand names with which these companies are associated.

Many of the companies did not disclose their annual turnover, but even those that did, account together for a total annual turnover of well over £100 billion! The overall conclusion must be that these companies could have a massive impact in terms of greening Britain's economy, but that they still have a long way to go.

Even though this sample was self-selected, in the sense that the companies listed below decided to answer our questionnaire, only just over a third (36 per cent) of the companies had a written environmental policy statement at the time of our survey. Nearly two-thirds, clearly, did not. The position elsewhere in British industry is much worse than these figures would suggest.

While many companies, including some of those listed below, are now making considerable headway on the unleaded petrol issue, they must set themselves much more ambitious targets in terms of energy efficiency, waste management and recycling, and environmental promotions.

3M UNITED KINGDOM plc

Turnover: £423 million (1988).
Product sectors: Soaps, detergents, cleaners and scourers. Clear tape adhesives.
Brands: Scotch, Scotchbrite.
Written environmental policy: Yes. Published in the early 1970s.
Energy efficiency: Across the company's major production plants the energy programme has maintained (or reduced) energy costs per unit volume to 1986 levels.
Waste and recycling: Several programmes, past and present, e.g. incineration of non-woven waste materials and reclamation of heat for use in-plant.

Company cars: All new cars ordered since start of 1989 must be able to accept unleaded petrol. All existing cars will be converted at the next service interval so they too can run on unleaded petrol.
Environmental promotions: Have discussed 'environmentally friendly' aerosol products with Friends of the Earth.

ACDO (THE ASTLEY DYE & CHEMICAL Co Ltd)
Turnover: Under £5 million.
Product sectors: Soaps, detergents, cleaners and scourers.
Brands: Acdo.
Written environmental policy: Yes. Also have a 'no animal testing' policy.
Energy efficiency: New, more efficient energy saving machinery.
Waste and recycling: No programme. Claim that all their paper and card used to be taken for recycling but now no one seems interested.
Company cars: 25% unleaded. Company policy to convert or ensure all new fleet vehicles run on unleaded.
Environmental promotions: Have worked with the Vegetarian Society.

A. G. BARR plc
Turnover: £73 million.
Product sectors: Soft drinks, mixers and mineral water.
Brands: Irn-Bru, Tizer, Jusoda, St Clements.
Written environmental policy: No.
Energy efficiency: Maximise boiler efficiency. Use low energy lighting in most areas.
Waste and recycling: Have a waste recovery and recycling programme on all sites. Recover and re-use scrap from bottle-making process.
Company cars: 85% unleaded. In future they will ensure that those cars capable of using unleaded actually use it.
Environmental promotions: Participated in the Waste Managment Advisory Committee which included environmentalists, but this was dissolved a while ago. Keep Britain Tidy Group. Contact with Friends of the Earth via the British Soft Drinks Association (BSDA) in the past. Involved, via BSDA, in the promotion of bottle banks.

ALBERTO CULVER Co (UK) Ltd
Turnover: £26 million.
Product sectors: Hair care. Dental care.
Brands: VO5 range, Jojoba, Balsam, Natural Silk Shampoo, Jordan toothbrushes.
Written environmental policy: No.
Energy efficiency: An employee suggestion scheme is in operation and had achieved large energy savings during the past 18 months. Employees rewarded for successful suggestions.
Waste and recycling: All plastic storage drums professionally steam-cleaned to enable re-use. Use of recycled computer paper.
Company cars: 70% unleaded. All new cars to run on unleaded.
Environmental promotions: None.

AMWAY (Kingsway Rowland)
Turnover: $1.8 billion worldwide.
Product sectors: Household goods. Personal hygiene. Health and fitness goods (catalogue sales).
Written environmental policy: Yes.
Energy efficiency: Plastic scraps ground down and re-used to manufacture further plastic bottles. Bottles are not PVC and produce non-polluting ash when burnt.
Waste and recycling: The solvents in inks used in print shop, together with packaging and scrap paper, are used to heat buildings in Ada, Michigan (company manufacturing plant).
Company cars: Company fleet uses unleaded petrol.
Environmental promotions: They sponsored: the Icewalk expedition to the North Pole which aimed to raise consumer awareness of the depletion of the ozone layer and environmental pollution; the Plant-A-Tree programme in USA and UK; and pocket packs with the Royal Society for Nature Conservation (RSNC), a UK activity.

ARK PRODUCTS
Turnover: No figure available at time of going to press.
Product sectors: Range of imported household cleaners.
Brand Name: Ark.
Written environmental policy: Yes.
Energy efficiency: Not disclosed.
Waste and recycling: Not disclosed.
Company cars: Not disclosed.
Environmental promotions: See organisations listings.

BEAUTY WITHOUT CRUELTY Ltd
Turnover: £1,460,000 (1988). £1,700,000 (anticipated for 1989).
Product sectors: Toiletries, cosmetics.
Brands: BWC range.
Written environmental policy: No. But has had cruelty-free policy since 1968.
Energy efficiency: 30% energy saved through the introduction of factory partitioning.
Waste and recycling: No programme.
Company cars: 20% of vehicles able to run on unleaded fuel. All new vehicles will run on unleaded.
Environmental promotions: Zoo Check project to raise funds to save the dolphin. Have also been involved with RSPCA and Humane Research Trust.

BENCKISER Ltd
Turnover: DM2bn (1988).
Product sectors: Soaps, detergents, cleaners.
Brands: Finish dishwasher products, Vanish, Calgon, Impact, Scaleaway, Micromet.
Written environmental policy: Not disclosed.
Energy efficiency: Not disclosed.
Waste and recycling: Not disclosed.

Company cars: Not all their present cars are able to run on unleaded, but all replacement cars will be.
Environmental promotions: Not disclosed.
Comments: Benckiser did not fill in the questionnaire but they did provide the above information in a letter.

BENDER AND CASSEL Ltd

Turnover: £1,196,000
Product sectors: Soups.
Brands: Becas, John Lusty.
Written environmental policy: No.
Energy efficiency: Not disclosed.
Waste and recycling: Re-using production materials.
Company cars: 100% diesel.
Environmental promotions: None.

BENSON'S CRISPS plc

Turnover: £14,698,725.
Product sectors: Crisps (potato) and snacks.
Brands: X.L. Crisps.
Written environmental policy: No.
Energy efficiency: 1987 Award winners: PEP awards.
Waste and recycling: Not disclosed.
Company cars: Not disclosed. They say they only use rented cars.
Environmental promotions: Save the Hedgehog campaign through organic crisps.

BIRDS EYE WALL'S Ltd

Turnover: £520,000,000.
Product sectors: Frozen foods: beef, chicken, ice cream.
Brands: Menu Master, the Captain's Table, Country Club vegetables and puddings, Cornetto, Feast, Elite, Mr Whippy, Walls.
Written environmental policy: Yes. Introduced in 1988.
Energy efficiency: Run a continuous major energy saving programme.
Waste and recycling: Are conducting trials to break down waste to usable gas.
Company cars: 25% unleaded. All company vehicles will be able to run on unleaded as soon as conversions can be carried out. Those which cannot be converted will continue on leaded petrol until replacement. 95% will be lead-free within two years.
Environmental promotions: Through Unilever (parent company). Not disclosed.

BRANDY DOG FOOD (JOHN MACKLE-MOY Ltd)

Turnover: £5 million.
Product sectors: Pet foods.
Written environmental policy: No.
Energy efficiency: No programme.
Waste and recycling: No programme.
Company cars: 60% unleaded.
Environmental promotions: None.

BRECON (SPADEL Ltd)
Turnover: £100 million (approx.).
Product sectors: Natural mineral water.
Written environmental policy: No.
Energy efficiency: In-plant energy saving schemes. Indefinite re-use of hot caustic cleaning baths for cleaning glass bottles.
Waste and recycling: Recovery of 600 tonnes of plastic caps for reprocessing ever year. Containers for the collection of recyclable or problem waste.
Company cars: No programme.
Environmental promotions: Welsh Wildlife Appeal

BRITISH ALCAN ALUMINIUM plc
Turnover: £779 million.
Product Sectors: Aluminium foils. Plastics. Aluminium cans for beverages.
Brands: Alcan Bacofoil, Bacofoil, Alcan (food bags, freezer bags, refuse bags, bin bags, microwave bags), Silverwrap, Baco Wise Buy Plastics.
Written environmental policy: No.
Energy efficiency: Use of hydropower to minimise use of fossil fuel. Large reductions in amount of energy required to smelt aluminium. Continuous programme of technical innovation to produce more 'product' per tonne of aluminium.
Waste and recycling: All production waste recycled. Six aluminium recycling plants. British Alcan Extrusions uses 80% recycled metal. Founder member of Aluminium Can Recycling Association.
Company cars: All changing to unleaded during next 12 months.
Environmental promotions: Aluminium Can Recycling Association, National Trust, National Trust for Scotland.

BRITISH TISSUES Ltd
Turnover: £120 million.
Product sectors: Loo papers. Tissues. Kitchen towels.
Brands: Dixcel/Fern, Bronco. Distribute Henkel Bright White Washing Powder.
Written environmental policy: Yes. Issued in June 1987.
Energy efficiency: Two extended energy surveys in conjunction with the Department of Energy reduced consumption by 5%. Operation of energy monitoring and targeting system through Paper and Board Federation.
Waste and recycling: Use large tonnages of recycled fibre in tissue production processes (40,000 tonnes per year).
Company cars: Most of car fleet already can — and does — run on unleaded fuel.
Environmental promotions: Links with WWF and regional water authorities.

BROOKE BOND Ltd
Turnover: £400 million.
Product sector: Instant coffee and drinking chocolate. Extracts, meat and vegetable. Chutney, pickles and relishes. Sauces and cooking aids. Tea.

Brands: Red Mountain, Choice, Coffee Time, Oxo, Fray Bentos, Hayward's, Ragu, PG Tips, Brooke Bond, Orange Label, Microchef and some Walls canned meat.
Written environmental policy: No.
Energy efficiency: Say they have saved energy in several areas but were not specific.
Waste and recycling: Conversion of waste material into boiler fuel in some factories.
Company cars: The majority run on unleaded.
Environmental promotions: National Trust, Woodland Trust, WWF.

CADBURY Ltd
Turnover: £480 million.
Product sectors: Confectionery.
Written environmental policy: Yes.
Energy efficiency: As a result of a large capital investment programme carried out over the last ten years many small low output plants have been replaced by fewer, more energy efficient, high output plants.
Waste and recycling: Pelletised waste paper used as fuel for boiler plant but proved uneconomic. Recovery of process vapour from milk evaporators for use as boiler feed water.
Company cars: Commercial vehicles all run on diesel fuel.
Environmental promotions: WWF-Cadbury chocolate wildlife bar, each sale resulting in a donation to WWF.

CAMPBELL GROCERY PRODUCTS Ltd
Turnover: £50 million.
Product sectors: Juices, non-alcoholic drinks. Meat, canned, bottled, ready-made meals and snacks. Sauces and cooking aids.
Brands: Prego sauces, V-8 soups, Campbell's.
Written environmental policy: No.
Energy efficiency: Reduction of gas and water usage.
Waste and recycling: No programme.
Company cars: Do not know percentage able to run on unleaded fuel. Nothing has been done to ensure future cars take unleaded.
Environmental promotions: None.

CELATOSE plc
Turnover: £42 million (UK)
Product sectors: Nappies. Sanitary goods.
Brands: Softline disposable nappies, Softline Sanpro.
Written environmental policy: No.
Energy efficiency: Lighting consumption reduced by 40%.
Waste and recycling: Half of the pulp off-cuts from the processing operations are recirculated into the production process.
Company cars: No cars, but when replacing the fleet vehicles they will 'prefer' vehicles capable of running on unleaded fuel.
Environmental promotions: None.

CONTINENTAL WINE EXPERTS Ltd

Turnover: £10 million.
Product sectors: Wines.
Written environmental policy: No.
Energy efficiency: None but currently planning a programme.
Waste and recycling: Card/paper waste collected and sold for recycling. Cans compacted and sold for recycling until a few years ago. No significant quantities of cans any more.
Company cars: 50% unleaded. Company policy is to purchase only cars which can run on unleaded.
Environmental promotions: No programme.

CORSAIR TOILETRIES Ltd

Turnover: Not disclosed.
Product sectors: Hair care. Deodorants and anti-perspirants.
Brands: Corsair, Supersilk.
Written environmental policy: No.
Energy efficiency: No programme.
Waste and recycling: No programme.
Company cars: 25% unleaded.
Environmental promotions: None.

DDD Ltd

Turnover: £10 million.
Product sectors: Soaps, detergents, cleaners, scourers and descalers.
Brands: Stain Devil Range, Oz descalers, Chempro.
Written environmental policy: Yes. To be incorporated in 1988 annual accounts.
Energy efficiency: Not disclosed.
Waste and recycling: Investigated, but not found to be economically viable.
Company cars: 75% unleaded. Policy is to convert where possible and purchase vehicles capable of using unleaded.
Environmental promotions: None.

DECLON DIVISION OF McKECHNIE plc

Turnover: Not disclosed.
Product sectors: Soaps, detergents, cleaners and scourers.
Brands: Kingfisher sponges.
Written environmental policy: None.
Energy efficiency: They have installed new energy-saving heater equipment.
Waste and recycling: Foam is frequently recycled to make chipfoam.
Company cars: Cars use unleaded where possible.
Environmental promotions: None.

DOVES FARM

Turnover: Not disclosed.
Product sectors: Flours, breads and biscuits.
Brands: Doves Farm
Written environmental policy: Yes. Introduced some years ago.

Energy efficiency: No programme.
Waste and recycling: Recycled paper in some packaging.
Company cars: 100% unleaded.
Environmental promotions: Soil Association, Henry Doubleday Research Association, British Organic Farmers.
Comments: Winner of the Grocer Green Awards in 1989 in the branded products category.

DURACELL Ltd
Turnover: £70 million.
Product sectors: Batteries.
Brands: Duracell.
Written environmental policy: Introduced in 1981, but is being updated in with all other documentation as a result of a management buyout in 1988.
Energy efficiency: None.
Waste and recycling: Mercuric oxide cell collection and recycling programmes.
Company cars: 75% unleaded.
Environmental promotions: None in the U.K.

ECOVER
(Company name in UK is Full Moon, but more commonly referred to as Ecover. See profile on page 260)
Turnover: Not disclosed.
Product sectors: Washing-up liquid, washing powder, toilet cleaner, floor soap, cream cleaner, fabric conditioner, wool wash liquid, heavy duty hand cleaner.
Written environmental policy: No.
Energy efficiency: No programme.
Waste and recycling: Experimenting with the recycling of containers.
Company cars: 50% unleaded.
Environmental promotions: Link up with Friends of the Earth.

ELIDA GIBBS
Turnover: £150 million.
Product sectors: Dental care. Shaving goods. Soaps, bath goods. Deodorants and anti-perspirants. Hair care. Air fresheners.
Brands: Mentadent P, S.R., Signal, Erasmic, Astral, Ponds, Vaseline, Pears, Lynx, Sure, Impulse, Vivas, Sunsilk, All-Clear. Dimension, Timotei, Cream Silk, Harmony, Wood Nymph, Mirair
Written environmental policy: Yes. 1988 policy which covers environment as well as consumer safety.
Energy efficiency: Low energy lighting in new factory. Steam generation changed from oil to gas.
Waste and recycling: No programme.
Company cars: Estimate 40%. Conversion to unleaded is recommended and will be paid for by the company. It will be recommended that new car purchases will run on unleaded petrol. Target is 100% unleaded vehicles.
Environmental promotions: Have worked with several groups on environmental issues.

FAITH PRODUCTS Ltd
Turnover: £250,000 – £500,000
Product sectors: Detergents and disinfectants.
Brands: Clear Spring (not for sale through supermarkets), 'Cruelty-Free', Faith in Nature.
Written environmental policy: No.
Energy efficiency: No definite answer, but have low energy lighting and thermostatically controlled heating in well insulated offices.
Waste and recycling: Use of shredded paper as protective packing material.
Company cars: 100% unleaded.
Environmental promotions: Green Kitchen Stand at the Ideal Home Exhibition, organised by Friends of the Earth and SustainAbility. WWF.

FARQUHAR NORTH & Co Ltd
Turnover: Not disclosed.
Product sectors: Meat and fish spreads, pastes and pâtés
Brands: Far-North.
Written environmental policy: No.
Energy efficiency: Some savings in electricity and steam oil.
Waste and recycling: Recovery of waste cardboard.
Company cars: Gradual change to unleaded, as opportunity arises.
Environmental promotions: None.

FROZEN QUALITY Ltd
Turnover: £25 million.
Product sectors: Frozen foods and vegetables.
Brands: Froqual range.
Written environmental policy: No.
Energy efficiency: Contract packers have a programme.
Waste and recycling: Recycling of cardboard waste.
Company cars: 60% run on unleaded. All new cars must run on unleaded.
Environmental promotions: None.

FULL MOON see ECOVER

GENERAL FOODS LTD
Turnover: £268 million.
Product sectors: Cereals. Cakes. Puddings. Instant and ground coffee. Custard powder. Juices. Ice cream, jelly. Canned meat, ready-made meals and snacks. Milk, yoghurt. Jams, treacles and syrups. Sauces. Soups. Herbs and spices.
Brands: Birds, Maxwell House, Mellow Birds, Café Hag, Master Blend, Kenco, Ice Magic, Kitchen Classics, Cuppa's.
Written environmental policy: No.
Energy efficiency: Use of spent coffee grounds for steam generation and conversion to gas.
Waste and recycling: Bottle banks, litter bins and recycling cardboard.
Company cars: Company fleet being changed over to unleaded petrol.
Environmental promotions: Local Authority (Cherwell District Council).

GILLETTE UK Ltd

Turnover: over £113 million.
Product sectors: Shaving goods. Hair care. Skin care. Deodorants and anti-perspirants.
Brands: Double Edge, Contour, GII, Blue II, Gillette, Adorn, Casual, Dry Look, Toni, Aapri, Natrel Plus, Right Guard, Silkience, Styling, ZR.
Written environmental policy: Yes. Latest version introduced in March 1985.
Energy efficiency: All windows double-glazed at the Isleworth plant; boilers at Isleworth changed from heavy oil to gas.
Waste and recycling: Water-cleaning process set up so that water used in cooling can be re-used.
Company cars: Over 50%. Insist that all new cars can run on unleaded.
Environmental promotions: None.

HEDGEHOG FOODS Ltd

Turnover: See Benson's Crisps plc
Product sectors: Potato crisps, snacks and snack bars.
Written environmental policy: See Benson's
Energy efficiency: See Benson's
Waste and recycling: Recycling of office paper.
Company cars: 100%.
Environmental promotions: Soil Association, Farm Organic, 'EKO' Organic (continent), British Hedgehog Preservation Society, Wild Life Hospital, National Barn Owl Release Scheme.

HENDRY BROTHERS (LONDON) Ltd

Turnover: £5 million.
Product sectors: Meat, canned, bottled, ready-made meals and snacks.
Brands: Casserole
Written environmental policy: No.
Energy efficiency: No programme.
Waste and recycling: Information provided was insufficient to be sure they have a programme.
Environmental promotions: Have done some.

H. J. HEINZ Co Ltd

Turnover: £415.5 million.
Product sectors: Baby foods. Health foods and drinks. Meat, canned, bottled, ready-made meals and snacks. Pasta products. Pet foods. Chutneys, pickles, relishes. Puddings. Salad creams and dressings. Sauces and cooking aids. Spreads, paste and pâté. Canned and bottled vegetables. Vinegar.
Brands: Heinz, Weight Watchers, Spaghetti Varieties, 9-Lives.
Written environmental policy: No. (They produced a statement after receiving the questionnaire.)
Energy efficiency: Oil consumption cut by 25% at main factory.
Waste and recycling: Vegetables and fruit waste used for pig feed; cardboard, tin plate, copper and polythene sold for recycling.
Company cars: 10% unleaded. Considering switching to unleaded for all new cars. Executives encouraged to use unleaded.

Environmental promotions: RSPB, WWF, Marine Conservation Society, National Trust. WWF Heinz Guardians of the Countryside in 1988.
Comments: Won the Grocer Green Award in 1988, as the company with the widest series of initiatives.

HOMECARE PRODUCTS — HOMECARE TECHNOLOGY Ltd
Turnover: £750,000.
Product sectors: Surface cleaners and scourers.
Brands: Shiny Sinks, Hob Brite, Bar Keeper's Friend, Copper Glo.
Written environmental policy: No.
Energy efficiency: Naturally lit offices using skylights.
Waste and recycling: No programme.
Company cars: 80% unleaded. New vehicles will take unleaded.
Environmental promotions: BUAV and Animal Aid.

JEYES GROUP Ltd
Turnover: Not disclosed.
Product sectors: Disinfectants, antiseptics, bleaches, loo cleaners. Air fresheners.
Brands: Ibcol, 3 Hands, Jeyes Fluid, Zal, Medicol, Izal, Plus 80, Jeyes Bloo, Sanilav, Herbal.
Written environmental policy: Yes.
Energy efficiency: High efficiency boilers installed at one plant and other measures taken to boost energy efficiency of cooling product equipment.
Waste and recycling: Recycling of plastics.
Company cars: 93% unleaded. All new cars must use unleaded.
Environmental promotions: John Jeyes Lecture under the auspices of Royal Society of Chemistry. 'Advances towards a better environment', created in 1977. The 1989 award went to the researcher who postulated the hole in the ozone layer theory.

JOHNSON & JOHNSON Ltd
Turnover: Not disclosed.
Product sectors: Baby care (powder, soap, lotion, bath oil, shampoo, cotton buds). Wipes. Sanitary goods. Over-the-counter medicines. Dental care.
Brands: J-Cloth, Carefree, Vespre, Band-Aid, KY Jelly, Dentotape, Reach toothbrushes
Written environmental policy: Did not say if they had one, but Johnson & Johnson has been rated in the top three companies with respect to 'Responsibility to the Environment' in the last seven years by *Fortune* magazine's annual corporations assessment survey.
Energy efficiency: Not disclosed.
Waste and recycling: Not disclosed.
Company cars: Not disclosed.
Environmental promotions: Not disclosed.
Comments: Johnson & Johnson did not fill in the questionnaire but they did provide the above information in a letter.

JOHNSON WAX Ltd

Turnover: Not disclosed.
Product sectors: Air fresheners. Loo cleaners, disinfectants. Insecticides. Polishes, metal cleaners. Soaps, detergents, scourers. Pet care.
Brands: Glade Dry, Glade, Lifeguard, Raid, Pledge, Living Wood, Klear, Wax Free Sparkle, Goddard's Metal Care, Shout, Goddards, Brillo.
Written environmental policy: Yes. 1st April 1986, updated October 1988.
Energy efficiency: Offices redesigned to save fuel and lighting costs. Changed from boiler fuel to gas and lighter oil. Heat exchanges in moulding plant used to heat water for washrooms.
Waste and recycling: Recycling of plastics, paper, cardboard and wire wool. Returned and damaged products are re-used where possible.
Company cars: 98% unleaded. New cars will be unleaded.
Environmental promotions: Business in the Community, National Trust, Friends of the Earth, Woodland Trust, British Trust for Conservation Volunteers, Habitat Scotland, Surrey Voluntary Services Council.
Comments: A joint core sponsor for The Green Kitchen Stand at the Ideal Home Exhibition in 1988, organised by SustainAbility and Friends of the Earth.

JOHN WEST FOODS Ltd (part of UNILEVER)

Turnover: £119 million (1988).
Product sectors: Canned fish. Fruit. Meat. Pâtés. Vegetables. Microwave ready meals. Spices.
Brands: John West.
Written environmental policy: Yes. Part of Unilever group and follow group environment policies.
Energy efficiency: No programme.
Waste and recycling: No programme.
Company cars: Conversion to unleaded in progress.
Environmental promotions: Indirectly through local canners, government and authorities.

KRAFT FOODS Ltd

Turnover: Not disclosed.
Product sectors: Cheese. Oils, margarine. Pasta products. Salads and dressings.
Brands: Dairylea, Philadelphia, Golden Churn, Vitalite, Mello, Kraft Singles and Slices, Kraft Dressings.
Written environmental policy: Yes. Last issued in January 1988.
Energy efficiency: Energy usage reductions at both UK factories.
Waste and recycling: Paper board and foil sold for recycling.
Company cars: 99% unleaded. All new cars purchased are able to run on unleaded.
Environmental promotions: Knowsley Borough Council — Kraft Fields Project.

LEVER BROTHERS Ltd

Turnover: £300 million.
Product sectors: Soaps, detergents, cleaners and scourers.

Brands: Persil, Surf, Lux, Stergene, Comfort, Squeezy, Sunlight, Sun Dishwasher, Sun Rinse Aid, Jif, Domestos, Frish, Lifebuoy, Knight's Castile, Shield.
Written environmental policy: Yes. 1983 statement was based on individual environmental aspect statements of previous 10–20 years. Updated in 1988.
Energy efficiency: Additional meters and monthly monitoring. 'Pinch' technology now applied to all new plants.
Waste and recycling: Process water recycling in detergent powder factories, reducing effluent load eight-fold. Installation of waste heat boiler to generate steam from, for example, waste packaging materials.
Company cars: 70% unleaded. All vehicles will be capable of taking unleaded petrol by the end of 1989.
Environmental promotions: Through the SDIA (Soap & Detergent Industry Association) they have worked with the Broads Authority, University of East Anglia, Department of the Environment, Water Research Centre, Freshwater Biological Laboratory, Water Authorities.

LYONS TETLEY Ltd
Turnover: Not disclosed.
Product sectors: Tea. Coffee. Cereals. Cereal bars. Dessert mixes. Chocolate products (home baking).
Brands: Tetley, Lyons, Quick Brew, Choice Leaf, Red Label, Silver Label, Orange Label, J. Lyons Special Reserve, Ready Brek, Applefords Cluster, Lyons Home Classics, Lyons Parfait, Lyons Polka Dots.
Written environmental policy: Yes. Allied Lyons statement of April 1988, currently being updated.
Energy efficiency: Introduction of computer-controlled heat management programmes to effect a 50% reduction in fuel usages.
Waste and recycling: Packaging waste sold for recycling.
Company cars: Fleet currently being converted to unleaded. Vans and heavy goods vehicles operate on diesel.
Environmental promotions: Sponsored the establishment and maintenance of a bird sanctuary in the Wash.

MARS CONFECTIONERY
Turnover: Over £400 million.
Product sectors: Confectionery.
Brands: Mars, Milky Way, Bounty, Topic, Galaxy, Maltesers, Twix, Opal Fruits, Tunes, Locket, M&Ms, Marathon, Revels, Ripple, Tracker, Skittles, Bolisto, Minstrels, Applause, Mars Ice Cream, Mars Milk.
Written environmental policy: No, but apply the Mars five principles (Efficiency, Responsibility, Mutuality, Quality and Freedom) to environmental issues.
Energy efficiency: Yes. The use of energy is continuously monitored. Factories are insulated and heat recovered from steam at the end of processing is used to pre-heat the factory water.
Waste and recycling: Scrap, damaged product and raw material waste are sent away for use in pig feed. All plant machinery is sold off for scrap to be recycled.

Company cars: Since 1988 all new vehicles have been adjusted to run on unleaded. By 1990 all company vehicles will run on unleaded.
Environmental promotions: Sponsored the MARS ENVIRONMENTAL AWARD. Also support an award scheme run through local schools to improve the school environment.

MONTAGNE JEUNESSE
Turnover: £250,000 approx.
Product sectors: Cosmetics and shampoos.
Brands: Montagne Jeunesse.
Written environmental policy: Yes. Introduced in 1988.
Energy efficiency: No programme, but use natural and fluorescent lighting.
Waste and recycling: Re-use packaging and scrap paper internally.
Company cars: Only two, both too old to convert to unleaded. New cars will run on unleaded.
Environmental promotions: Contacts with BUAV, RSPCA, FoE and Greenpeace for the promotion of a Christmas gift set. The Vegan Society.

PASCOE'S Ltd
Turnover: £3 million.
Product sectors: Pet foods
Brands: Complete Dog Food, Pascoe's.
Written environmental policy: No.
Energy efficiency: No programme.
Waste and recycling: Waste and reject products are converted to pig food.
Company cars: 100% unleaded.
Environmental promotions: Links with the Game Conservancy Trust.
Comment: Pascoes considered their dog food to be particularly good from an environmental point of view because 'the end product (faeces) of our product (dog food) is "kickable", which helps dog owners clean it up'!

PEAUDOUCE (UK) Ltd
Turnover: £40 million.
Product sectors: Nappies and wipes. Cotton wool.
Brands: Peaudouce.
Written environmental policy: No.
Energy efficiency: No programme.
Waste and recycling: Recycling of raw materials during production process.
Company cars: 75% unleaded. All replacement vehicles must be able to run on unleaded.
Environmental promotions: No.
Comments: Peaudouce precipitated the green nappy war and were the first manufacturer on to the market in the UK with non chlorine-bleached nappies.

PEDIGREE PETFOODS
Turnover: Not disclosed.
Product sectors: Pet foods.

Brands: Chappie, Bounce, Pal, Pedigree Chum, Mr Dog, Kitekat, Katkins, Whiskas, Sheba, Brekkies, Thomas Cat Litter.
Written environmental policy: No, but consider that the nature of their product implies environmental considerations.
Energy efficiency: Use of insulation. Recycling heat from sterilisers.
Waste and recycling: Waste materials are burnt off-site, using a high-temperature incinerator. The heat from this is used to sterilise waste raw materials for pig food.
Company cars: 25% unleaded. Target is 100% by 1990.
Environmental promotions: Society of Companion Animal Studies, Melton Town Council, Leicestershire and Rutland Trust for Nature Conservation, Bobo and Zizi educational campaign, Melton wetlands project.

PILLSBURY UK Ltd
Turnover: £47 million.
Product sectors: Cakes, pudding mixtures and convenience puddings. Herbs and spices. Baking aids. Canned and bottled vegetables.
Brands: Borwicks, Niblets, Mexicorn.
Written environmental policy: No.
Energy efficiency: Reclamation of energy from waste hot water.
Waste and recycling: Insufficient information.
Company cars: 10% run on unleaded. All new vehicles and those of a year or less old are being converted to run on unleaded fuel.
Environmental promotions: None.

POLY-LINA Ltd
Turnover: £30 million.
Product sectors: Plastic bin liners and refuse bags.
Brands: Tuflina, Poly-Lina, Linabin, Binmatex, Polyfresh.
Written environmental policy: No.
Energy efficiency: No programme.
Waste and recycling: In house recycling of production scrap for re-use in manufacture of refuse sacks.
Company cars: 75% unleaded. Company rule is to use unleaded where possible. All new cars will be able to run on unleaded; existing cars being converted.
Environmental promotions: None.

PREMIER BRANDS UK Ltd
Turnover: Not disclosed
Product sectors: Biscuits and cereal bars. Chocolate and chocolate spread. Cocoa and drinking chocolate. Condensed and powder milk. Yoghurt. Tea.
Brands: Cadbury's, Bournville, Bournvita, Marvel, Typhoo, Fresh Brew, Melrose's, Ridgeways Speciality Teas, Chivers, Hartley, Roses, Moorhouse.
Written environmental policy: No.
Energy efficiency: Use gas from landfill sites to produce steam. Installation of high efficiency gas-fired heating systems.

Waste and recycling: Installation of waste fired boiler to raise steam from factory waste instead of prime energy sources. Recycling of waste paper and glass.
Company cars: Fleet being steadily converted to run on unleaded fuel. Commercial vehicles run on diesel.
Environmental promotions: None.

PROCTER & GAMBLE
Turnover: £630.1 million (1988)
Product Sectors: Detergents. Household goods. Nappies.
Brands: Tide, Daz, Ariel, Fairy Snow, Bold, Dreft, Fairy Liquid, Flash, Lenor, Bounce, Vortex, Camay, Fairy Toilet Soap, Zest, Pampers.
Written environmental policy: Yes. Titled 'Responsibility to the Environment' and published in 1970 Annual Report.
Energy Efficiency: In the ten-year period 1976–1986, P & G's energy efficiency programmes cut by 38% overall energy usage as product volume increased by 50%.
Waste and recycling: All processes are designed to maximise the recycling of by-products and recovery of residual materials. Plants have on-going programmes to continually improve this aspect of operation.
Company cars: 50% unleaded. Encouraging conversion by accepting change-over costs.
Environmental promotions: WWF sponsorship, tied with Pampers.

QUINTINS SNACK FOODS Ltd
Turnover: £2.5 million.
Product sectors: Potato crisps and snacks.
Written environmental policy: No.
Energy efficiency: Use of waste heat. Installation of energy-efficient equipment.
Waste and recycling: Not disclosed.
Environmental promotions: None.

REAL MEAT Co Ltd
Turnover: £800,000.
Product sectors: Meat.
Written environmental policy: No.
Energy efficiency: No programme.
Waste and recycling: No programme.
Company cars: Cars being converted to unleaded where possible.
Environmental promotions: The company is a member of Compassion in World Farming (CIWF), Friends of the Earth and Greenpeace.

RECKITT & COLMAN
Turnover: £1.49 billion (worldwide).
Product sectors: Air fresheners. Insecticides. Loo cleaners, disinfectants. Antiseptics. Soaps, detergents, cleaners and scourers. Dental care. Hair care. Skin care. Over-the-counter medicines. Bath goods.
Brands: Airwick, Haze, Moods, Floret, Harpic, Dettol Cleen-O-Pine, Dettox, Gumption, Blue Bag, Robin, Goldilocks, Windolene, Steradent, Cossack, Supersoft, Nulon, Disprin, Disprol, Lemsip, Solmin, Dettol, Valderma, Haliborange.

Written environmental policy: No. But they say they examine all products and packaging and to put into action the necessary modifications to remove from the products items which give rise to environmental concern.

Energy efficiency: Energy consumption has been reduced by up to 50% over the last 6 years. They have not specified how this has been achieved.

Waste and recycling: Not disclosed.

Company cars: 98% unleaded. All vehicles which can be converted have been converted. All new cars will run on unleaded. Company pumps supply unleaded petrol only.

Environmental promotions: Friends of the Earth.

RHM FOODS (incorporating JAMES ROBERTSON & SON)
Turnover: Not disclosed.

Product sectors: Flours, cornflour and blancmange. Cereals. Cakes. Pudding mixtures. Chocolate and chocolate spreads. Juices. Canned and bottled meat and vegetables. Ready-made meals and snacks. Jams. Salt, sauces and cooking aids. Soft drinks. Stuffings and crumbs.

Brands: McDougalls, Force Wheatflakes, De L'Ora Fruit Juice, Chesswood, Keiller, Saxa, Cerebos, Bisto, Quorn (see page 147), One-Cal, Capri Sun, Norfolk, Paxo.

Written environmental policy: No.

Energy efficiency: Energy audits are carried out at the company's operating sites.

Waste and recycling: Recycling programmes relating to waste glass, board and paper.

Company cars: Transport fleet runs on diesel. Policy dictates that all other vehicles should be converted to unleaded petrol.

Environmental promotions: Conservation Foundation (nationally), bottle bank initiative (nationally), local community efforts relating to company sites.

THE ROBERT McBRIDE GROUP (Part of BP Group)
Turnover: £153 million.

Product sectors: Detergents and disinfectants.

Written environmental policy: Yes.

Energy efficiency: Individual heat recovery programmes.

Waste and recycling: Insufficient information.

Company cars: Cars being converted to run on unleaded. All new cars will run on unleaded.

Environmental promotions: Groundwork Trust.

ROWNTREE MACKINTOSH CONFECTIONERY
Turnover: Not disclosed.

Product sectors: Confectionery.

Brands: Kit-Kat, Aero, Yorkie, Lion, Munchies, Smarties, Fox's Glacier Mints, After Eight Mints, Quality Street, Black Magic.

Written environmental policy: No policy, but claim to take environmental considerations into account.

Energy efficiency: Increased efficiency through the use of gas in some of the ovens.

Waste and recycling: Several water recovery schemes are in operation. Some recycling of paper and cardboard.
Company cars: Progressively moving towards unleaded.
Environmental promotions: None mentioned.

RUBICON PRODUCTS Ltd
Turnover: Not disclosed.
Product sectors: Soft drinks, mixers and mineral water.
Written environmental policy: No.
Energy efficiency: No programme.
Waste and recycling: No programme.
Company cars: None is able to run on unleaded.
Environmental promotions: None.

SCOTT Ltd
Turnover: £258 million.
Product sectors: Loo papers, tissues, kitchen towels. Wipes. Sanitary goods.
Brands: Andrex, Scotties, Handy Andies, Scottissues, Scottowels, Fiesta, Baby Fresh, Body Form, Libra, Libra Slims.
Written environmental policy: Yes. Introduced in February 1978.
Energy efficiency: Installation of clean coal burning technology.
Waste and recycling: Paper machines fitted with waste heat recovery plants which generate hot water.
Company cars: Company policy to run on unleaded fuel.
Environmental promotions: Parent company Scott Paper Co has donated and traded forest lands in the USA in support of conservation efforts.

SECTO Co Ltd
Turnover: £1 million (and over).
Product sectors: Insecticides. Air fresheners.
Brands: Secto Fly Killers, Astral.
Written environmental policy: No.
Energy efficiency: Savings on heating fuel by fitting thermostats for automatic cut off.
Waste and recycling: Recycling of paper, cardboard and metal.
Company cars: 100% unleaded. All new vehicles will be required to run on unleaded.
Environmental promotions: None.

SMITH, ANDERSON & Co Ltd
Turnover: £40 million.
Product sectors: Recycled paper bags.
Written environmental policy: No.
Energy efficiency: Use of water power.
Waste and recycling: Paper is made from recycled fibres, which involves buying large quantities of waste paper.
Company cars: 80% run on unleaded.
Environmental promotions: None.
Comments: Sells recycled paper bags to some supermarkets.

SMITH & NEPHEW CONSUMER PRODUCTS Ltd
Turnover: £70 million.
Product sectors: Over-the-counter medicines. Wipes. Skin care. Sun care.
Bath goods. Deodorants and anti-perspirants. Sanitary goods.
Brands: Airstrip, Elastoplast, Tender Touch, Nivea, Limara, Dr White's,
Lilia, Lil-Lets, Golden Babe.
Written environmental policy: No.
Energy efficiency: Waste-derived fuel project nearing completion.
Waste and recycling: Cardboard containers used for delivery of goods
returned to supplier. Cooling water and steam recycled. Recycle reject
Polythene bottles. Recycle aluminium foil waste. Recovery of solvents for
adhesive manufacture.
Company cars: 15% run on unleaded.
Environmental promotions: Insufficient information.

S. H. PHILLIPS & Co Ltd
Turnover: £5 million.
Product sectors: Cake, pudding mixtures and flour.
Brands: Krisbat, Goldensheaf.
Written environmental policy: No.
Energy efficiency: No programme.
Waste and recycling: Waste food ingredients sold to animal feed
producers.
Company cars: 75% run on unleaded. Appropriate vehicles being
converted.
Environmental promotions: Insufficient information.

SPONTEX
Turnover: Not disclosed.
Product sectors: Soaps, detergents, cleaners and scourers.
Brands: Catering Cloth, Moppet, Sponge Cloth, S-Sponge, Bathbrite,
Brisk, Polistar, Tough Scourer, Twinclean, Washups, Shamois,
Decoraters, Dripstrip, Calypso, Handymop, Hypermop, Range of car
sponges.
Written environmental policy: No.
Energy efficiency: Reduction of waste and investment in equipment to
allow economic use of a cleaner fuel.
Waste and recycling: Investigated the recycling of rejected products.
Company cars: 50% unleaded.
Environmental promotions: Insufficient information.

ST IVEL Ltd
Turnover:£750 million.
Product sectors: Dairy. Fruit juices
Brands: Gold, Shape, Real, Prize, St Ivel.
Written environmental policy: No. Are presently producing one.
Energy efficiency: Water recovery and energy efficiency equipment.
Waste and recycling: Cardboard waste sent for reprocessing. Glass is
recycled. Some dairy waste is used for animal feed.
Company cars: 20% run on unleaded.
Environmental promotions: Sponsorship of regional groups.

STUART EDGAR Ltd
Turnover:£37 million.
Product sectors: Loo papers, tissues, kitchen towels. Foils. Clingfilms. Sanitary goods. Nappy liners. Bath goods. Hair care. Deodorants and anti-perspirants. Sun care.
Brands: Towncape, Stuart Edgar, A-Z, Fanty, Tropic Foil, Big 50, Little Chef, Interlude, Babysoft, Pampered, Kimono, Riviera.
Written environmental policy: No.
Energy efficiency: Switched from oil fires to gas heating.
Waste and recycling: Waste reduction programme.
Company cars: 90% run on unleaded. All company cars converted. New ones must run on unleaded.
Environmental promotions: None.

THOMAS'S (A division of MARS GB Ltd)
Turnover: Not disclosed.
Product sectors: Pet care (food and accessories).
Brands: Aquarian, Atlantis, Marrobone, Thomas, Biscrok, Smacko.
Written environmental policy: Yes. Based on three principles: efficiency, mutuality and responsibility (no more details than this were given).
Energy efficiency: Gas consumption reduced by 20%. New factory site designed for more efficient use of energy. Timers fitted to lighting, additional lagging of pipes, building heavily insulated.
Waste and recycling: Recycling of paper. Recycling of raw materials as far as possible. All effluent is treated and hot air emissions are passed through a bio-filter process.
Company cars: 95% run on unleaded. Ensure that vehicles are adjusted to run on unleaded as far as possible.
Environmental promotions: Royal Society for the Protection of Birds (RSPB), WWF.

UB BRANDS (UNITED BISCUITS)
Turnover: £500 million.
Product sectors: Biscuits, cereal bars and cakes.
Brands: McVities, Crawfords, Carrs Table Water.
Written environmental policy: No.
Energy efficiency: Initiatives taken, details not disclosed.
Waste and recycling: Initiatives taken, details not disclosed
Company cars: Details not disclosed.
Environmental promotions: Member of INCPEN (The Industry Council for Packaging and the Environment).

VAN DE BERGH & JURGENS Ltd (Part of Unilever)
Turnover:£324 million.
Product sectors: Oils and margarines.
Brands: Flora. Krona, Delight, Blue Band, Stork, Elmlea, Crisp and Dry.
Written environmental policy: Yes. Part of Unilever Group and follow group policy.
Energy efficiency: Reduction in the use of steam in factories.
Waste and recycling: Equipment installed to recycle waste produced during the production processes.

Company cars: 100% run on unleaded.
Environmental promotions: Promotions done on their behalf by parent company, but no details given.

VARTA Ltd
Turnover: £22 million.
Product sectors: Batteries.
Brands: Varta.
Written environmental policy: Yes. Published June 1988.
Energy efficiency: Have a policy, but no details of achievements disclosed.
Waste and recycling: Battery recycling and collection in Scandinavia and Germany.
Company cars: 75% run on unleaded. All new vehicles must be able to use unleaded. All existing vehicles were altered by March 31st 1989.
Environmental promotions: Promotion in supermarket involved giving away copies of *The Green Consumer Guide* with a pack of batteries; sponsored the Green Kitchen Stand organised by SustainAbility and Friends of the Earth; and sponsored the Grocer Green Awards.

WELCH & SONS Ltd
Turnover: Over £2 million.
Product sectors: Confectionery.
Written environmental policy: No.
Energy efficiency: Reduction in fossil fuel consumption.
Waste and recycling: No programme.
Company cars: 10% run on unleaded.
Environmental promotions: None.

WELLA (Intercosmetic GB Ltd)
Turnover: £50 million.
Product sectors: Hair care and cosmetics.
Brands: Wella.
Written environmental policy: Yes.
Energy efficiency: No programme.
Waste and recycling: All cosmetic waste treated so as to be environmentally safe and acceptable to local authority standards.
Company cars: 90% unleaded. All cars being converted to unleaded. All new vehicles automatically run on unleaded.
Environmental promotions: None.

WERNER & MERTZ
Turnover: DM350 million (approx).
Product sectors: Cleaning products and detergents.
Brands: Frosch.
Written environmental policy: Yes, but not published at time of going to press.
Energy efficiency: Initiatives taken, no details disclosed.
Waste and recycling: Internal recycling of chemical ingredients. External recycling of paper and polyethylene bottles etc.
Company cars: 100% run on unleaded.
Environmental promotions: None.

WHOLE EARTH FOODS Ltd

Turnover:£3 million.
Product sectors: Spreads. Beans. Sauces, relishes, dressings. Soft drinks. Pasta. Peanut butter.
Brands: Whole Earth.
Written environmental policy: No.
Energy efficiency: No programme.
Waste and recycling: Recycling of glass jars.
Company cars: Some vehicles modified to run on unleaded.
Environmental promotions: Friends of the Earth, Soil Association, Organic Farmers and Growers, Vida Sana (Spain), Nature and Progress, EKO (Holland).

THE WRIGLEY COMPANY Ltd

Turnover: £40 million.
Product sectors: Confectionery.
Brands: Wrigley, Freedent, Orbit, Plen T Pak, P.K., Hubba Bubba.
Written environmental policy: No.
Energy efficiency: No programme.
Waste and recycling: No programme.
Company cars: 80% run on unleaded. All cars that can be, are being converted to unleaded.
Environmental promotions: None, but planted 10 acres of trees in the factory grounds.

COMPANIES FROM WHOM WE HAVE NOT
RECEIVED A COMPLETED QUESTIONNAIRE

Our questionnaire was sent by registered post to some 300 companies, each one addressed to an individual whose name had been supplied by the organisation shortly before we sent out the material. We were extremely pleased with the response rate, but in order to demonstrate the range of manufacturers which can play an important role in the greening of supermarkets, we are listing some of those companies from whom we did not receive a completed questionnaire. Their silence may be due to the loss of their reply in the post. Alternatively, there may have been a change in personnel. We apologise if any company has been included when the questionnaire was, unknown to us, completed by a parent company.

Some of the companies below did express a desire to complete the questionnaire but we never in fact had it back. Occasionally, companies told us it was against their policy to divulge the information we requested. These firms are marked with a star. Since we believe a free flow of information between producers and consumers is essential in improving the overall environmental performance of both retailers and manufacturers, this was naturally disappointing. We would of course welcome responses from these and any other companies on a voluntary basis to assist us in our research and possibly to be included in a more comprehensive and detailed survey of manufacturers' green policies and requirements.

Food Products

ADAMS FOODS
Product sectors: Non-alcoholic juices.
Brands: Just Juice.

ALLIED FOODS ICE CREAM CO
Product sectors: Dairy foods. Ice cream.
Brands: Pendletons, Jeffreys, Vive, Tops.

ANCHOR FOODS
Product sectors: Dairy foods: butter, cheese, cream milk products and yoghurt.
Brands: Anchor, Gervais, Danone.

ANGLO BELLAMY WILKINSON
Product sectors: Confectionery.

ASHE CONSUMER PRODUCTS
Product sectors: Health drinks. Dental and mouth care. Hair care. Baby care. Sun care. Over-the-counter medicines. Air fresheners. Insecticides.
Brands: Sucron, Saxin, Bisks. Amplex, Ice Mint, Gold Spot, Lanoline. Matthews Fullers Earth Cream, Gordon Moore's, Punch and Judy, Eugene, Sebbix. Vitapointe. Maws baby care products, Changetime. Pro Plus, Kruschen Salts. Vapona, Cooper. Monastery Herbs.

BAHLSEN BISCUITS (UK) Ltd
Product sectors: Biscuits and cereal bars. Bread and breadsticks. Nuts and nut kernels. Crisps and snacks. Cake.
Brands: Bahlsen cakes.

BARKER & DOBSON GROUP plc
Product sectors: Confectionery.
Brands: Bensons and Keiller, Barker & Dobson.

BASSETT FOODS plc
Product sectors: Confectionery.
Comments: They told us they did not see the relevance of the questionnaire.

BAYER UK Ltd
Product sectors: Health food and drinks. Soaps, detergents, cleaners and scourers. Over-the-counter medicines. Insect repellants, insecticides.
Brands: Natrena, Limmits, Sionon, Vita Fiber. Mafu. Alka-Seltzer, Actron, Aspirin. Autan, SOS Next Generation Cleaners.

BEECHAM BOVRIL BRANDS
Product sectors: Custard and custard powder. Health food and drinks. Extracts, meat and vegetable. Milk products and yoghurt. Puddings and suets. Sauces and cooking aids. Soft drinks, mixers and mineral water.
Brands: Ambrosia, Lucozade, Ribena, C-Vit, Bemax, Bovril, Horlicks, Shloer.

B. E. INTERNATIONAL FOODS Ltd
Product sectors: Pasta products.
Brands: Doll.

BEVELYNN
Product sectors: Juices, non-alcoholic drinks. Oils, margarines and lards.
Brands: Hellas, Frediani.

BIG T Ltd
Product sectors: Tea.
Brands: Big T.

BP NUTRITION Ltd Luda Pet Food Ltd
Product sectors: Pet foods.
Brands: Complete, Lowe's brand.

BRIDGE FARM DAIRIES Ltd
Product sectors: Milk products and yoghurt.
Brands: Dairy Time.

BRITISH PEPPER & SPICE CO Ltd
Product sectors: Herbs and spices. Baking aids.
Brands: Millstone, Eastern Star.

BRITISH VINEGARS
Product sectors: Oils, margarine and lard. Vinegar and non-brewed condiments.
Brands: Dufrais, Sarsons.

BRITVIC CORONA
Product sectors: Soft drinks, mixers and mineral water.
Brands: Britvic, Corona, Pepsi-Cola, 7-Up, Quosh, Tango, Top Deck, Canada Dry, R.Whites, Shandy Bass, Barbican, Lucozade, Ribena.

BUITONI FOODS
Product sectors: Spreads, pastes and pâté.
Brands: Princes.

BURTON'S BISCUITS
Product sectors: Biscuits and cereal bars. Confectionery.

BURTON'S SNACKS
Product sectors: Crisps (potato) and snacks.

CAMPSIE SPRING SCOTLAND
Product sectors: Soft drinks, mixers and mineral water.
Brands: Campsie.

CAROB CONFECTIONERY
Product sectors: Health food and drinks. Jams, treacle and syrup.
Brands: Carob.

CARR'S FOODS Ltd
Product sectors: Biscuits and cereal bars. Cake.
Brands: Lu Biscuits, Dan Cake, Otto Man.

CAWSTON VALE
Product sectors: Juices, non alcoholic drinks.

CHAMBOURCY
Product sectors: Milk products and yoghurt. Salads, salad creams and dressings.
Brands: Chambourcy.

CHILTERN HILLS
Product sectors: Soft drinks, mixers and mineral water.

CIRIO Co Ltd
(Distributed by Crombie Eustace Ltd)
Product sectors: Oils, margarine and lard. Pasta products. Vegetables, canned and bottled. Vinegar and non-brewed condiments.
Brands: Bertolli Olive Oil, Cirio.

COCA-COLA SCHWEPPES
Product sectors: Soft drinks, mixers and mineral water.
Brands: Coca-Cola, Schweppes, 5-Alive, Kia-Ora, Roses Lime, Appletise, Tropical Spring, Malvern Water.

COLMAN'S OF NORWICH
Product sectors: Baby foods. Juices, non alcoholic drinks. Gravymakers and browning. Horseradish sauce and creams, mint sauce and jellies. Mustard. Sauces and cooking aids.
Brands: Robinsons, Jif Lemon, Home Style.

CORONET CAKE Co
Product sectors: Cake.
Brands: Coronet Cakes.

COW & GATE Ltd
(Baby Products Division)
Product sectors: Baby foods.
Brands: Cow & Gate.

*CPC (UK)
Product sectors: Cornflour and blancmange. Custard and custard powder. Oils, margarine and lard. Extracts, meat and vegetable. Salads, salad creams and dressings. Sauces and cooking aids. Soups. Stuffings and crumbs.
Brands: Brown and Polson, Mazola, Knorr, Hellmanns.
Comments: Replied explaining that the questionnaire would take too long to answer and that some of the information required is confidential.

CROOKES HEALTHCARE Ltd
Product sectors: Baby foods. Health food and drinks.
Brands: Farleys, Breakfast Timers, Oster.

CROSSROADS FOODS
Product sectors: Pasta products.
Brands: Helios.

CROWN FOODS
Product sectors: Frozen foods.
Brands: Sunbird Oven Ready Chicken.

*C. SHIPPAM Ltd
Product sectors: Fish (smoked, canned and bottled), caviar. Meat, canned, bottled, ready-made meals. Snacks. Spreads, pastes and pâté.
Brands: Shippams.
Comments: They told us they would not be completing the questionnaire since some of the information is confidential.

DAIRY CREST FOODS
Product sectors: Juices and non alcoholic drinks. Cheese. Milk products and yoghurt.
Brands: UHT Milk Products. Country Life. Clover. UHT Portions.

DIETARY FOODS Ltd
Product sectors: Health food and drinks.
Brands: Sweet'n Low.

DOUWE EGBERTS
Product sectors: Coffee.
Brands: Full Aroma, Moccona.

EDWARD BAKER Ltd
Product sectors: Pet foods.
Brands: Omega pet foods.

ELKES BISCUITS
Product sectors: Biscuits and cereal bars.
Brands: Elkes.

EVIAN (AGENCIES) Ltd
Product sectors: Juices, non alcoholic drinks, soft drinks, mixers and mineral water.
Brands: Evian, Badoit, Eva range.

F. DUERR & SONS Ltd
Product sectors: Jams, treacle and syrup.
Brands: Duerr's.

F.E. BARBER Ltd
Product sectors: Biscuits and cereal bars. Cereals. Oils, margarine and lard. Vegetables, canned and bottled.
Brands: Coral Reef.

FELIX PAVIA & SON Ltd
Product sectors: Pasta products.
Brands: Lily Brand, Italian Pasta Products.

FINDUS
Product sectors: Frozen foods — fish, meat, chicken, vegetables.

FOX'S BISCUITS Ltd
Product sectors: Biscuits and cereal bars.

GALBANI (LONDON) Ltd
Product sectors: Cheese. Sausages, bacon, open pack meats and pies.

G. COSTA & Co Ltd
Product sectors: Fish (smoked, canned and bottled), caviar.
Brands: Iceland Water Seafoods.

GOLDENFRY FOODS
Product sectors: Gravy makers and browning. Sauces and cooking aids.

GOLDEN WONDER
Product sectors: Biscuits and cereal bars. Choice meat, canned, bottled, ready-made meals and snacks. Nuts and nut kernels. Crisps (potato) and snacks.
Brands: Pot Noodles. Wotsits. Golden Wonder

GRANT'S SCOTTISH CANNED FOODS
Product sectors: Meat, canned, bottled, ready-made meals and snacks.
Brands: Grant Bros.

GREEK & PURE QUALITY FOODS Ltd
Product sectors: Milk products and yoghurt.
Brands: Greek and Pure.

GROCER'S SUPPLY Ltd
Product sectors: Cereals. Cake. Pudding mixtures and convenience puddings.
Brands: General Mills Big 'G' Breakfast Cereals. Betty Crocker.

HAMMONDS
(Division of Pillsbury UK Ltd)
Product sectors: Mint sauce and jellies. Sauces and cooking aids. Vinegar and non-brewed condiments.
Brands: Mr Men.

HANKOW BATCHELOR TEA Co Ltd
Product sectors: Tea.
Brands: H and B.

HARRIS BACON GROUP
Product sectors: Sausages, bacon, open pack meats and pies.

HARRIS-LEEMING BAR
Product sectors: Sausages, bacon, open pack meats and pies.
Brands: Vale of Mowbray.

HAZLEWOOD & CO PRODUCTS Ltd
Product sectors: Cornflour and blancmange. Custard and custard powder. Fruit, canned and bottled. Horseradish sauce and creams, mint sauce and jellies. Mustard. Chutney, pickles and relishes. Crisps (potato) and snacks. Salads, salad creams and dressings. Sauces and cooking aids. Vinegar and non-brewed condiments.
Brands: Morpac brand, Krunchie.

HEY UK Ltd
Product sectors: Soft drinks, mixers and mineral water.
Brands: Trendy, Pops, Hey, Citra.

HILLSDOWN Ltd
Product sectors: Fruit, canned and bottled. Meat, canned, bottled, ready-made meals and snacks. Pet foods. Vegetables, canned and bottled.
Brands: Morton, Smedley, Lockwoods, Wilson's of Scotland, Morrell.

HOMEPRIDE FOODS Ltd
Product sectors: Cornflour and blancmange. Cereals. Cake decorations. Cake, pudding mixtures and convenience puddings. Custard and custard powder. Colours, flavours and essences. Flour. Horseradish sauce and creams, mint sauce and jellies. Ice cream. Jelly. Sauces and cooking aids. Herbs and spices. Baking aids. Stuffings and crumbs.
Brands: Pearce Duff, Granny Smith range, Royal range, Homepride range, Harvest Gold.

HP FOODS
Product sectors: Gravy makers and browning. Jelly. Mint sauce and jellies. Pasta products, canned. Chutney, pickles and relishes. Sauces and cooking aids. Soft drinks, mixers and mineral water. Vegetables, canned and bottled. Vinegar and non-brewed condiments.
Brands: Symingtons. HP Epicure, HP Water.

HUNTERS FOODS Ltd
Product sectors: Nuts and nut kernels. Crisps (potato) and snacks.
Brands: Christies.

JACOBS SUCHARD Ltd
Product sectors: Confectionery.
Brands: Toblerone, Côte d'or, Suchard, Meltis, Milka.

JAMES ROBERTSON & SONS
(subsidiary of RHM)
Product sectors: Cake. Pudding mixtures and convenience puddings. Rice and semolina. Jams, treacle and syrup.
Brands: Viota Cake Mix range, Economix Sachet Packs. Viota.

JOHN DUNHILL
Product sectors: Coffee, ground and/or filter papers.

KELLOGG Co of GB
Product sectors: Cereals.
Brands: Corn Flakes, Frosties, Crunchy Nut Corn Flakes, Rice Krispies,

Ricicles, Coco Pops, All-Bran, Bran Buds, Bran Flakes, Sultana Bran, Honey Smacks, Fruit 'n Fibre, Raisin Splitz, Toppas, Special K, Country Store, Summer Orchard, Start, Nutri-Grain.

KP FOODS
Product sectors: Nuts and nut kernels. Crisps (potato) and snacks. Spreads, pastes and pâté (peanut butter).

LA FAVORITE
Product sectors: Colours, flavours and essences. Horseradish sauce and creams. Mustard. Chutney, pickles and relishes. Salads, salad creams and dressings. Sauces and cooking aids. Vinegar and non-brewed condiments.
Brands: Tewkesbury, Dijon.

LEAF (UK) Ltd
Product sectors: Confectionery. Ice cream.
Brands: Mr Freeze.

LINDT SWISS CHOCOLATES
Product sectors: Confectionery.
Brands: Lindt.

LION FOODS
Product sectors: Horseradish sauce and creams, mint sauce and jellies. Mustard. Chutney, pickles and relishes. Sauces and cooking aids. Herbs and spices. Baking aids. Spreads, pastes and pâté (sandwich spread).

LOCATELLI
Product sectors: Cheese. Sausages, bacon, open pack meats and pies — Italian meat products.

LONDON HERB & SPICE Co Ltd
Product sectors: Tea.
Brands: Heath and Heather, Secret Garden.

LYONS BAKERY
Product sectors: Cake.
Brands: Hales.

LYONS MAID Ltd
Product sectors: Ice cream.
Brands: King Cones, Fun Factory, Gold Seal, Napoli.

LYONS MARYLAND COOKIES
Product sectors: Biscuits.

MANDORA ST CLEMENTS Ltd
Product sectors: Soft drinks, mixers and mineral water.
Brands: St Clements, Mandora.

MANLEY RATCLIFFE Ltd
Product sectors: Gelatine. Oils, margarine and lard. Horseradish sauce

and creams, mint sauce and jellies. Mustard. Jams, honey, treacle and syrup. Salads, salad creams and dressings. Sauces and cooking aids.
Brands: Ratcliffe, Richardson.

MANOR BAKERIES Ltd
Product sectors: Cake.
Brands: Cadbury Chocolate Cakes, Swiss Rolls, Mr Kipling.

MASTER FOODS
Product sectors: Rice and semolina. Meat, canned, bottled, ready-made meals and snacks. Sauces and cooking aids. Vegetables, packeted. Snacks.
Brands: Ben's, Tyne brand, Dolmio, Yeoman.

MASTEROAST COFFEE Co Ltd
Product sectors: Coffee, ground and/or filter papers.

MCM (UK) Ltd
Product sectors: Fish (smoked, canned and bottled), caviar.
Brands: Deep Blue canned fish.

MELITTA Ltd
Product sectors: Coffee, ground and/or filter papers. Milk, condensed and powder.
Brands: Compleat.

MORNING FOODS Ltd
Product sectors: Cereals.
Brands: Mornflake Oats.

MULLER DAIRY UK Ltd
Product sectors: Milk products and yoghurt.
Brands: Fruit Corner, Crunch Corner.

NAIROBI COFFEE & TEA Co Ltd
Product sectors: Coffee, ground and/or filter papers. Milk, condensed and powder. Tea.

*NAPOLINA Ltd
Product sectors: Juices, non alcoholic drinks. Oils, margarine and lard. Pasta products. Pasta products, canned. Sauces and cooking aids. Vegetables, canned and bottled.
Comments: They said they were unable to complete the questionnaire in time and that some of the information was confidential.

NESTLÉ
Product sectors: Cocoa and drinking chocolate. Coffee, instant, ground and/or filter papers. Juices, non alcoholic drinks. Soft drinks, mixers and mineral water. Confectionery. Custard and custard powder. Fruits, canned and bottled. Meat, canned, bottled, ready-made meals and snacks. Milk,

condensed and powder. Milk products and yoghurt. Cream. Puddings and suet.
Brands: Carnation, Nescafé, Milky Bar, Fussell's, Nesquik, Ashbourne.

*NESTLÉ CARNATION Ltd

Product sectors: Pet foods.
Brands: Go-Cat, Go-Dog, Nekolit.
Comments: Said that their 'overriding objective is to develop products which contribute to the well-being of mankind.' They were not prepared, however, to answer the questionnaire.

NESTLÉ

CROSSE & BLACKWELL

Product sectors: Gravy makers and browning. Oils, margarine and lard. Meat, canned, bottled, ready-made meals and snacks. Pasta products. Pasta products, canned. Chutney, pickles and relishes. Puddings and suet. Rice and semolina. Salads, salad creams and dressings. Sauces and cooking aids. Soups. Vegetables, canned and bottled.
Brands: Rice and Things, Pasta Choice. Sunflower, Waistline, Branston, Cook-in-the-Pot, Bonne Cuisine.

NESTLÉ FOOD IMPORTS

Product sectors: Cocoa and drinking chocolate. Confectionery. Fruit, canned and bottled. Health food and drinks. Extracts, meat and vegetable. Pasta products. Salads, salad creams and dressings. Sauces and cooking aids. Spreads, pastes and pâté.
Brands: Milo, Libby's, Caro, Maggi, Maggi International. Holbrooks, La Parfait Swiss Pâté.

NEWFORGE FOODS Ltd

Product sectors: Meat, canned, bottled, ready-made meals and snacks. Pet foods. Sauces and cooking aids.
Brands: Spam, Fetch.

NIBBIT INTERNATIONAL (UK) Ltd

Product sectors: Crisps (potato) and snacks.

NORMEAT

Product sectors: Meat, canned, bottled, ready-made meals and snacks.
Brands: Royal Dane, Lanes, Danish Maid.

PARRISH & FENN

Product sectors: Biscuits and cereal bars. Cake. Chocolate and chocolate spreads. Cocktail accessories and cherries. Cocoa and drinking chocolate. Tea. Juices, non alcoholic drinks. Horseradish sauce and creams, mint sauce and jellies. Mustard. Chutney, pickles and relishes. Oils, margarine and lard. Meat, canned, bottled, ready-made meals and snacks. Pasta products. Crisps (potato) and snacks. Jams, treacle and syrup. Puddings and suet. Salads, salad creams and dressings. Sauces and cooking aids. Soft drinks, mixers and mineral water. Cocktail. Soups. Salt, herbs and

spices. Baking aids. Spreads, pastes and pâté. Stuffings and crumbs. Vegetables, canned and bottled, packeted. Vinegar and non-brewed condiments.
Brands: Bradfords, Mackies, Ormo Cakes and Bakeries, Noels, Van Houten Cocoa, Lazy juice, Mrs Elsewoods, Kaufmann, Benedicta, Meica, Gillot, Escoffier, Noels Mustard, Grand Italia range, Gordons, Ormo, Heildelberg, Brassel, Louisiana Gold, Cocktail, Grant's, Erasco, Flodor Crouton D'Or, Foodfinder, Henaff, Jackson's, Mr Funions.

PASTA FOODS Ltd
Product sectors: Pasta products.
Brands: Record Pasta.

PAYNES '
Product sectors: Confectionery. Tea.
Brands: Lift.

PERCY DALTON'S
Product sectors: Nuts and nut kernels. Spreads, pastes and pâté.
Brands: Percy Dalton's (peanut butter).

PIETRO NEGRONI Ltd
Product sectors: Sausages, bacon, open pack meats and pies.
Brands: Negroni.

POLENGHI UK Ltd
Product sectors: Cheese.

POLLSHON PRODUCE
Product sectors: Fruit, canned and bottled. Salads, salad creams and dressings — USA. Vegetables, canned and bottled.
Brands: Wardour Famous Foods.

PURA FOODS GROUP
Product sectors: Oils, margarine and lard.

*QUAKER OATS
Product sectors: Biscuits and cereal bars. Cereals. Pasta products. Pet foods. Salads, salad creams and dressings. Spreads, pastes and pâtés.
Brands: Quaker Cereal Snack Bars, Quaker Breakfast Cereals, Felix, Chunky, Dinner Jackets, Sutherland.
Comments: They said they do not contribute to publications.

RAYNER BURGESS
Product sectors: Cake decorations. Cocktail accessories and cherries. Fish (smoked, canned and bottled), caviar. Colours, flavours and essences. Gravy makers and browning. Oils, margarine and lard. Milk products and yoghurt. Horseradish sauce and creams, mint sauce and jellies. Mustard. Chutney, pickles and relishes. Salads, salad creams and dressings. Sauces and cooking aids.
Brands: Burgess, Jean Rochele, Crusha, Gorgona.

ROBINSON HEALTH CARE

Product sectors: Soft drinks, mixers and mineral water. Sanitary goods.
Nappies, wipes and cotton wool. Over-the-counter medicines.
Brands: Robinsons Barley Water, Cameo, Cosifit, Paddi Pads, Babbettes.
Poppet, Soft and Pure. Fast-Aid (plasters).

RONDIMPORT Ltd

Product sectors: Sausages, bacon, open pack meats and pies.
Brands: Rondanini.

ROSS

Product sectors: Frozen foods — vegetables, fish, meat, pudding, ice
cream. Chutney, pickles and relishes.
Brands: Ross's.

ROSS YOUNGS Ltd

Product sectors: Frozen foods — fish, dairy products, puddings.

ROWNTREE SUN-PAT Ltd

Product sectors: Cornflour and blancmange. Cheese. Chocolate and
chocolate spreads, cocoa and drinking chocolate. Custard and custard
powder. Jelly. Mint sauce and jellies. Nuts and nut kernels. Chutney,
pickles and relishes. Jams, honey, treacle and syrup. Puddings and suet.
Sauces and cooking aids. Soft drinks, mixers and mineral water. Herbs
and spices. Baking aids. Spreads, pastes and pâté.
Brands: Sun-Pat, Rowntree's Cocoa, Creamola, Gales, Pan Yan.

R. TWINING & Co Ltd

Product sectors: Coffee, instant, ground and/or filter papers. Tea.

RYVITA

Product sectors: Cereals. Biscuits.

SALE TILNEY FOODS plc

Product sectors: Fish (smoked, canned and bottled), caviar. Fruit, canned
and bottled.
Brands: Red Sail, Gold Reef.

SCANDINAVIAN SUPPLIERS (LONDON) Ltd

Product sectors: Cocktail accessories and cherries. Chutney, pickles and
relishes.
Brands: Opies Cocktail Delicacies, Felix of Scandinavia.

SEARL CONSUMER PRODUCTS

(distributed by Batchelors Foods Ltd)
Product sectors: Health food and drinks.
Brands: Canderel.

SHARP & NICKLESS
Product sectors: Biscuits and cereal bars.
Brands: Olde English.

SHREDDED WHEAT Co
Product sectors: Biscuits and cereal bars. Cereals. Cake. Puddings and suet.
Brands: Jacobs, Peek Freans, Huntley & Palmers, Shredded Wheat, Shreddies.

SIMPSON READY FOODS Ltd
Product sectors: Meat, canned, bottled, ready-made meals and snacks. Puddings and suet. Vegetables, canned and bottled.
Brands: Goblin, Simpsons, Caterdish.

SMITHS CRISPS Ltd
Product sectors: Nuts and nut kernels. Crisps (potato) and snacks.
Brands: Planters, Big D, Tudor, Smiths Crisps.

SOONER SNACKS Ltd
Product sectors: Nuts and nut kernels. Crisps (potato) and snacks.
Brands: Murphy's Nuts.

SOVEREIGN
Product sectors: Frozen foods — chicken.

SPEARHEAD Ltd
Product sectors: Coffee, ground and/or filter papers. Confectionery. Shaving goods. Loo paper, tissues and kitchen towels.
Brands: Van Nelle Coffee. Daily Bar, Velamints. Schick (disposable razors).

SPILLERS FOODS Ltd
Product sectors: Juices, non alcoholic drinks. Pet foods.
Brands: Five Alive Fruit Juices/ Fanta, Winalot, Kennomeat, Bonus, Spratts, Bonio, Kattomeat, Choosy.

SPL Ltd
Product sectors: Rice and semolina. Fish (smoked, canned and bottled), caviar. Colours, flavours and essences. Health food and drinks. Sauces and cooking aids.
Brands: SPL label, Nutrament, Simon Label.

STUTE FOODS
Product sectors: Chocolate and chocolate spreads. Juices, non alcoholic drinks. Jams, honey, treacle and syrup. Sauces and cooking aids.

SUN VALLEY Ltd
Product sectors: Nuts and nut kernels.

TATE & LYLE
Product sectors: Jams, treacle and syrup.
Brands: Lyle's, Fowlers.

THE CIDER MILLS
Product sectors: Juices, non alcoholic drinks.

TREBOR
Product sectors: Confectionery.

TUCKER FOODS
Product sectors: Crisps (potato) and snacks.

UNI MERCHANTS Ltd
Product sectors: Bread and breadsticks. Rice and semolina. Oils, margarine and lard. Pasta products. Chutney, pickles and relishes. Sauces and cooking aids. Herbs and spices. Baking aids. Spreads, pastes and pâté. Vegetables, canned and bottled.
Brands: Dauphin, Mennucci oil, Di Martino, De Sortis, Padrmasole, Caugant Pâtés, Talpe, Jeco, Alpino.

UNITED PRESERVERS Ltd
Product sectors: Coffee, ground and/or filter papers.
Brands: Lavazza Italian Espresso.

VICO FOODS (UK) Ltd
Product sectors: Vegetables, packeted.
Brands: Mr Mash.

WALKERS CRISPS
Product sectors: Crisps (potato) and snacks.
Brands: Walkers.

WANDER FOODS Ltd
Product sectors: Cocoa and drinking chocolate. Milk products and yoghurt.
Brands: Ovaltine.

WEBBS COUNTRY FOODS Ltd
Product sectors: Frozen foods — chicken.

WEETABIX
Product sectors: Cereals.
Brands: Alpen, Bran Fare, Weetabix.

WELLS (DRINKS) Ltd
Product sectors: Soft drinks, mixers and mineral water.
Brands: Cwm Dale Spring.

WESTLER FOODS Ltd
Product sectors: Meat, canned, bottled, ready-made meals and snacks. Soups.
Brands: Multi-Menu, American Original.

WILTSHIRE TRACKLEMENTS
Product sectors: Mustard.

W. JORDAN (CEREALS) Ltd
Product sectors: Biscuits and cereal bars. Cereals. Flour.
Brands: Jordans Original.

WYETH NUTRITION
Product sectors: Baby foods.
Brands: SMA baby milks.

Non-Food Products

ADDIS
Product sectors: Plastics — kitchen bowls, waste bins etc.

BEECHAM TOILETRIES & HEALTHCARE
(Beecham Group Ltd)
Product sectors: Adhesives. Dental and mouth care. Hair care. Men's
range. Deodorants and anti-perspirants. Bath goods. Skin care. Beecham
Health Care. Baby care. Over-the-counter medicines.
Brands: UHU, Macleans, Aquafresh, Silvikrin. Bristows, Vosene, Falcon,
Restoria. Slazenger Sports range, Brylcreem, Body Mist, Slazenger,
Midas, Fenjal, Badedas, Pure and Simple. 2nd Debut, Ashton and
Parsons, Beechams cold remedies, Cephos powders. Dinnefords grip mix,
Ellimans Embrocation. Eno salts, Germolene, Maclean Indigestion tablets,
Mac Lozenges, Oxy, Phensic. Phyllosan, Quickies, Ralgex, Setlers. Venos,
Vykmin, Yeast Vite.

BIG D
Product sectors: Air fresheners. Insecticides. Disinfectants. Gas re-fills.
De-icers. Polish. Soaps, detergents, cleaners and scourers.
Brands: Big D aerosols.

BRISTOL MYERS Co Ltd
Product sectors: Soaps, detergents, cleaners and scourers. Deodorants and
anti-perspirants. Hair care.
Brands: Mr Muscle, Mum, Fresh and Dry. Vitalis. Score, Natural Balance,
Creme Rinse, Finale, Nice 'N Easy, Loving Care, Born Blonde, Glints.

BRUNEL TRADING Co Ltd
Product sectors: Over-the-counter medicines.
Brands: Child Cherry Cough Syrup, Glycerine, Wallis range, Wallis
Vitamins, Zetavite, Hi Vite, Rusco Label.

BRYANT & MAY Ltd
Product sectors: Matches, lighters, cigarette papers and filters.
Brands: Brymay, Ship, Bo-Peep, Englands Glory, Pioneer, Scottish
Bluebell, Vulcan, Swift, Three Torches, Winners, Cooks, Swan lighters,
Swan, Clipper, Cricket, Hi Lites, Panoramic, Nuevo.

CARR and DAY MARTIN Ltd
Product sectors: Shoe care. Polishes (metal polish, silver polish, wax polish). Window cleaners.
Brands: Carr and Day Martin, Stephensons Olde English.

CHESEBROUGH-PONDS Ltd
Product sectors: Cosmetics.
Brands: L'Onglex polish remover, Cutex polish remover.

CURVER CONSUMER PRODUCTS
Product sectors: Plastic ware — washing bowls etc.

CUSSONS (UK) Ltd
Product sector: Air fresheners. Soap; detergents, cleaners and scourers. Hair care. Bath goods. Baby care. Deodorants and anti-perspirants — men's range. Over-the-counter medicines.
Brands: Racasan (also loo freshener), 1001 Cleaner, Morning Fresh, Imperial Leather, Cold Cream, Cussons, My Fair Lady, IL Gold. Cussons, Roberts Laboratories.
Comments: Their completed questionnaire arrived with the authors too late (July '89) for inclusion in the book.

DALE PRODUCTS
Product sectors: Loo paper, tissues and kitchen towels. Nappy liners. Wipes.
Brands: Dalex, Ladylove, Baby Dream.

DRG STATIONERY
Product sectors: Stationery.
Brands: Basildon Bond, Duke, Lion Brand.

DYLON INTERNATIONAL Ltd
Products sectors: Dyes and fabric care. Descalers. Insecticides. Shoe care, shoe inserts.
Brands: Dylon, Ouest, Doom, Miss Dylon, Bama.

*EVER READY
Product sectors: Batteries.
Comments: Although they were not willing to complete the questionnaire they did provide specific information, for the batteries section.

FISONS plc
(Fisons Consumer Health)
Product sectors: Over-the-counter medicines.
Brands: Radian-B Liniment, Roskens, Sanatogen, Secaderm, Vapex, Zam-Buk.

FOOD BROKERS Ltd
(Helene Curtis)
Product sectors: Hair care. Over-the-counter medicines.
Brands: Helene Curtis, Finesse, Optrex, Strepsils, Complete Care.

GALENCO
Product sectors: Bath goods. Hair care. Skin care.
Brands: Gentle Care, World Wildlife Foam Bath, Pearl, Galenco.

HAVENTRAIL
Product sectors: Air fresheners. Polishes. Oven cleaners. Starch.
Insecticides. Gas refills. Decorations. Hair care. Deodorants and anti-
perspirants. Over-the-counter medicines.
Brands: Provence Household Aerosols, Mr Snow (decorative snow),
Acquiesce, Wild, Expose, Lisa, Mikaela, Jodie, Gemma. Hayley Algi
Spray.

JACKEL INTERNATIONAL Ltd
Product sectors: Baby care.
Brands: Pur by Tommee Tippee (very large range).

*KIMBERLY-CLARK Ltd
Product sectors: Loo paper, tissues and kitchen towels. Sanitary goods.
Cotton wool.
Brands: Kleenex, Ballet, Simplicity, Kotex. Sylphs, Delsey.
Comments: Although they were not willing to complete the questionnaire
they did provide specific information for inclusion in our tables.

LEWIS WOOLF GRIPTIGHT Ltd
Product sectors: Baby care.

LRC PRODUCTS Ltd
Product sectors: Rubber products.
Brands: Marigold (housegloves), Durex (contraception).

NATURAL BEAUTY PRODUCTS Ltd
Product sectors: Skin care. Bath goods. Hair care.
Brands: Body Reform, Frequency.

NICHOLAS LABORATORIES Ltd
Product sectors: Over-the-counter medicines. Bath goods. Depilatory
goods.
Brands: Aspro Clear, Spearmint Rennie, Matey, Shower Fresh, Radox.

PRICE'S PATENT CANDLE Co Ltd
Product sectors: Candles.
Brands: Price's.

PUNCH SALES Ltd
Product sectors: Soaps, detergents, cleaners and scourers. Candles.
Brands: Mista HiJeen, Kinsale.

SANODA Ltd
Product sectors: Air fresheners. Loo cleaners. Soaps, detergents, cleaners and scourers.
Brands: Scentinel, Flush Kleen, Lu, Maid of AllWork, Flashbrite, Scourbrite, Gold Scouring cloths.

STAFFORD-MILLER Ltd
Product sectors: Dental care.
Brands: Sensodyne (toothpaste, toothbrushes and denture products).

STERLING HEALTH
Product sectors: Soaps, detergents, cleaners and scourers. Moth balls. Oven cleaners. Over-the-counter medicines. Nappies and wipes. Fruit juices.
Brands: Andrews Liver Salts, Coldrex Tablets, Hedex, Milk of Magnesia, Panadol Baby Wet Ones, Nappysacks, Delrosa Pure Concentrated.

*SUNDROPS
Product sectors: Insecticides. Moth balls. Soaps, detergents, cleaners and scourers. Over-the-counter medicines.
Brands: Amogas, Stardrops, Starpine, Startips, Starclen, Zoflora, Starpax Home Medicines.
Comments: Considered the questionnaire to be too time consuming, and were concerned with the right of the authors to publish any of the information provided.

*TAMBRANDS Ltd
Product sectors: Sanitary goods.
Brands: Tampax.
Comments: Although they said they could not provide detailed and potentially confidential information they did provide specific information for inclusion in our tables.

THORN EMI
Product sectors: Lightbulbs.

VILEDA Ltd
Product sectors: Soaps, detergents, cleaners and scourers.
Brands: Vileda, Coronet.

WARNER-LAMBERT HEALTH CARE
Products sectors: Dental and mouth care. Over-the-counter medicines. Hair care.
Brands: Efferdent (denture cleaner), Euthymol (toothpaste), Listerine, Anusol, Gelusil, Remegal. Oraldene, Colour Story, Poly Tint, Hi-Lights, Lo-Lights, Papilloten. Henna, Henara, Jojoba.

WELLCOME FOUNDATION
(Wellcome Hygiene services)
Product sectors: Cotton wool.
Brands: Simply Gentle, Macdonald's Simply Gentle.

WHITEHALL LABORATORIES
Product sectors: Over-the-counter medicine. Skin care. Dental care.
Brands: Anadin, Bismag, Bisodol, Dristan, Powerin, Preparation H,
Tramil, Anne French, Immac, Kolynos (denture fixative and toothpaste).

WIGGINS TEAPE (STATIONERY) Ltd
Product sectors: Stationery.

WILKINSON SWORD
Product sectors: Shaving goods.
Brands: Wilkinson Sword (razors, blades, shaving foam and after-shave).

WILLIAM FREEMAN & Co Ltd
Product sectors: Baby care. Hot water bottles.
Brands: W. Freeman, Suba.

ZAMO MANUFACTURING
Product sectors: Disinfectants, bleaches, detergents.
Brands: Zamo.

Into the Green Decade

The world has changed since we wrote *The Green Consumer Guide* — and the pace of development accelerated dramatically while we were researching The Green Consumer's *Supermarket Shopping Guide*.

The task of putting together these Guides has persuaded us not only that consumers are increasingly interested in buying environment-friendly products, but that the supermarkets, manufacturers and growers will respond rapidly if consumer pressure is brought to bear in the right way.

As our Supermarket Survey shows (see pages 67–98), the supermarket groups that scored well in *The Green Consumer Guide* have continued to expand the range of environment-friendly products they offer. Others, including the **Co-op** and **Marks & Spencer**, either were not included or did less well last time — but have since devoted a great deal of effort to improving their performance.

On receiving our questionnaire, for example, the Co-op sent out their own questionnaire to some suppliers, while Marks & Spencer appointed its first 'green issues manager'.

Inevitably, the sheer pace of developments is causing a number of problems. For example, the supermarkets' very enthusiasm in responding to the Green Consumer is now raising tricky questions in relation to the profusion of competing labelling systems.

The labels shown on page 328 are simply a selection of those now appearing on products, some put there by manufacturers, some by retailers, some operating on their own and some in association with public interest groups. Clearly, it is essential that Britain moves towards a Green Label scheme for environment-friendly products, like West Germany's 'Blue Angel' scheme which now covers over 3,000 products.

As we move into the 1990s, the challenge will be to broaden and deepen the greening of Europe which — in most respects — has only just begun. The Green Consumer will play a critically important role in waking up business to the emerging threats and opportunities.

We plan to continue producing both updated editions of our existing Guides and totally new Guides, to help consumers identify the key issues and find appropriate products and services. If you have comments to make on our existing coverage or suggestions for future editions, please contact us at: SustainAbility Ltd, 49 Princes Place, London W11 4QA.

LOOK FOR THE GREEN LABEL

Whether it's Sainsbury's holding the Earth in the palm of their hand, BUAV's rabbit or the Soil Association's organic version of the wool mark, you are going to see a lot more 'environmental' labelling of products. This extraordinary profusion of different labels is both a symptom of the growing determination of business to capture the custom of the Green Consumer and, increasingly, a cause for concern. The consumer may well end up being confused by the competing claims made on behalf of different products.

The same problems have surfaced in the food labelling sector, where there is concern that consumers are perplexed and, at worst misled, by voluntary labelling. So, for example, a strawberry trifle might have 'Free from artificial colours' splashed across the front of the carton. Yet the list of ingredients can show numerous additives, including dipotassium phosphate, adipic acid, potassium sorbate and propylene glycol monosterate. There are also colours which are not counted as 'artificial' because they are chemically identical to natural colours.

Imagine this same approach applied to environmental labelling and you have a recipe for disaster. The problem is that companies are often making their own minds up about what is 'environment-friendly' — and focusing on one issue among a number. So, for example, we might see an 'ozone-friendly' label on an aerosol containing a noxious pesticide or a 'cruelty-free' label on a product that is not biodegradable.

We are convinced that Britain needs a Government-backed Green Label scheme to ensure quality control in this area. If the confidence of consumers is to be maintained, indeed increased, they will need to be assured not only that the green product they are buying actually helps solve environmental problems, but also that it offers everything they would expect from that sort of item.

There is not much point, to take just one example, in buying a mercury-free battery which gives you half the charge of a normal battery — if in the end you use twice the amount of other chemicals.

The vetting of products will need to be carried out by an independent panel, supported by technical assessors, with the standards set with the help of government agencies. As the flood of new product launches grows, so the need for such quality assurance will also increase.

It is important to note that even with a national labelling scheme of this sort, there will still be a strong and continuing need for specialist labels — like a scheme for organic food. But experience in other countries has shown that the development of a Green Label helps to provide the reassurance that is needed at a time of rapid change in consumer markets.

As The Green Consumer's *Supermarket Shopping Guide* went to press, the Government announced its support for an EEC-wide green labelling scheme, although the evidence suggests that the scheme will focus on the environmental impacts associated with a product's use and disposal, with no reference to the effect of the methods of production, packaging and distribution.

Here is a selection of labels you might find on the shelves:

Sainsbury's

Spar

Panasonic batteries

Varta batteries

WWF

World Wide Fund for
Nature (logo appears on
a variety of products)

BUAV
(British Union for the
Abolition of Vivisection)

The Consumer's Guide to Useful Organisations 1989

Ark Trust

498 – 500 Harrow Road, London W9 3QA. Tel: 01-968 6780
Main Aim: To raise awareness about environmental issues and to work towards solutions through a democratically organised membership.
Issues: All environmental problems and their interconnection, especially relating to human health.
Number of Members: 8,000
Membership Fee: £12
What you Get: A membership pack with the Ark manifesto. Membership card. Badge and car sticker.
Sales: In May 1989 they launched 7 household cleaners, which are covered in the detergents' section (see Chapter 14).
Green Consumerism: Aim to encourage the production of environment-friendly products and, if necessary, produce the goods themselves. Ran into major administrative problems in the summer of 1989, as a result of which their commercial objectives seemed likely to be emphasised more than their environmental campaigning objectives.

The Association for the Protection of Rural Scotland (APRS)

14a Napier Road, Edinburgh EH10 5AY. Tel: 031-229 1898
Main Aim: Protection of rural Scotland, including encouraging people to work and live there. Retention of historic bridges. Awards for good design in rural Scotland.
Issues: Environment. Pollution. Waste disposal. Fish farms. Forestry. Roads. Planning. Design in the countryside.
Number of Members: 46 constituent and affiliated members. 3 corporate members. 750 individual members.
Membership Fee: £50 (constituent); £20 (affiliated); £150 or £50 (corporate, depending on size); £8 (individual); £5 (OAP); £100 (life)
What you Get: Annual report. Newsletters. Invitation to award ceremonies. Council meetings.
Sales: Guide (booklet) to sources of information about rights of way in Scotland.
Green Consumerism: No specific ventures as yet.

British Trust for Conservation Volunteers (BTCV)

36 St Mary's Street, Wallingford, Oxon OX10 0EU. Tel: 0491 39766
Main Aim: To involve people in practical conservation work.
Issues: Urban clean-up. Countryside conservation.
Number of Members: 11,000 (last year 9,000 — 22% increase).
Membership Fee: £10; £5.50 (special rate); £14 (family)
What you Get: *The Conserver Magazine*. Summer and winter 'Natural Break' holidays. Annual report. Quarterly newsletter. Local group activities every weekend.
Sales: Sell publications through a catalogue (e.g. practical handbook on how to set up a conservation group). Sell general equipment through a trading company. T-shirts and sweat shirts.
Green Consumerism: No specific ventures, but the BTCV's aim is to help people become more aware of the importance of the environment.

Consumer Association (CA)

2, Marylebone Road, London NW1 4DX. Tel: 01-486 5544
Main Aim: Association for Consumer Research (ACR) is a registered charity which undertakes research and comparative testing of goods and services. Its trading subsidiary, Consumers' Association Ltd (CA), publishes these findings in *Which?* and its other publications. The CA represents the consumer interest and campaigns for improvements in goods and services.
Issues: The CA has campaigned successfully for safer consumer goods and on a wide range of issues, including more and better information on labels, investor protection and increased competition in the market-place. It continues to campaign on reform of shop hours, safety, competition and making suppliers of goods and services, including the privatised industries, more responsive to consumers.
Number of Members: 1,013,600
Membership Fee: Subscription to *Which?* magazine costs £51 a year (details from Subscription Department, PO Box 44, Hertford SG14 1SH).
What you Get: Monthly issues of *Which?*, containing comparative reports on household goods, services, money matters, cars and motoring, DIY, items on food and health. Public interest reports.
Sales: Has published over 50 titles in hardback and paperback of interest to the consumer.
Green Consumerism: Pollution was one of the first major Green subjects covered by reports that have appeared in *Which?* in the last few years. Since then lead in petrol, ozone and aerosols and pesticide residues in food have been covered. At the time of writing, *Which?* also planned a survey on 'going green'.

Council for the Protection of Rural England (CPRE)

Warwick House, 25 Buckingham Palace Road, London SW1W 0PP. Tel: 01-976 6433

Main Aim: Campaigns for the countryside through well informed research and briefing of national and local government and of the media.
Issues: Agriculture and land use. Reafforestation and woodlands. Local planning. Lobbying Parliament on current issues: e.g. transport, road networks and Channel Tunnel.
Number of Members: 38,000 (last year 32,000 — 18.7% increase)
Membership Fee: £8; £11 (joint); £5 (under 25 yrs); £250 (life)
What you Get: *Countryside Campaigner* (3 times a year). Annual Report. Affiliation to local branch. Local events.
Sales: All publications available on request from CPRE
Green Consumerism: Advocate recycling. Promote organic farming (endorsed guidelines of Soil Association). Promote energy conservation through, for example, lobbying of Parliament. One of their publications is entitled *Electricity for Life* and compares the various options available for the generation of electricity.

Friends of the Earth (FoE)

26–28 Underwood Street, London N1 7JU. Tel: 01-490 1555
Main Aim: Protection of the environment and promotion of sustainable alternatives.
Issues: Air, sea, river and land pollution. Ozone depletion, acid rain, carbon dioxide build-up. Tropical deforestation and soil erosion. Biotechnology. Energy related issues, e.g. nuclear, renewable energy and conservation. Pesticides and agriculture. Recycling.
Number of Members: 100,000 supporters. This figure includes members and regular donors. Approximately 60,000 are subscribers (last year 30,000 subscribers — 100% increase).
Membership Fee: £12 (£10 direct debit); £5 (special rate)
What you Get: Quarterly newsletter — *Friends of the Earth Supporter's News*. Details of local groups. Update on current campaigns. Catalogue.
Sales: Catalogue offers a growing range of products.
Green Consumerism: Very successful in this area. They now incorporate a Green Consumer dimension in all their main campaigns. Have had a major impact in the boycotting of: whale products, aerosols containing CFCs, tropical hardwoods from badly managed forests, non-returnable bottles, leaded petrol, food additives, and non-organicallly grown produce. The aerosol issue became a major turning point in displaying the enormous power of the consumer. The *Daily Mail* Ideal Home Exhibition's Green Kitchen was set up by FoE together with SustainAbility.
Recommend: recycled products, Body Shop products, bicycles and public transport, organic and low-additive foods, unleaded petrol and catalytic converters, alternatives to tropical hardwoods, home insulation, draught-proofing and double-glazing. They can see potential for the Green Consumer to have a growing impact in a number of other areas, including: design; health; leisure activities; building materials; DIY; and energy systems.

Greenpeace UK

30 – 31 Islington Green, London N1 8XE. Tel: 01-354 5100
Main Aim: Campaigns against abuse of the natural world through lobbying and non-violent direct action protests, backed by scientific research.
Issues: Toxic waste disposal in rivers, seas and atmosphere. Radioactivity. Endangered species.
Number of Members: 251,000, 150 local groups (last year 100,000 -150% increase).
Membership Fee: £12 (individual); £6 (unwaged); £17.50 (family); credit card membership available on: 01-205 5222
What you Get: Quarterly newsletter — *Greenpeace News*. Special mailing on issues. Events. Merchandising catalogue.
Sales: Catalogue. Orders handled by Traidcraft plc.
Green Consumerism: Have already run a few campaigns targeted at the Green Consumer, including recommendations to boycott: whaleproducts, kangaroo hide running shoes and fish products from Iceland. They have run a campaign for clean cars, recommending catalytic converters.

Henry Doubleday Research Association (HDRA)

National Centre for Organic Gardening, Ryton-on-Dunsmore, Coventry CV8 3LG. Tel: 0203 303517
Main Aim: To carry out research into and promote ecologically sound and sustainable methods of organic gardening and farming, and to save many threatened British seed varieties from extinction.
Issues: Interests are maintained in many regions of the world, with specific research projects focusing on the development of sustainable systems for arid and semi-arid regions. This work falls into two important areas. First, the exploration and conservation of the genetic resources of under-exploited plants. Secondly, the development of novel farms and farming systems to harness these discoveries in an ecologically sound way.
Number of Members: 15,000
Membership Fee: £12 (individual); £7 (concessions); £15 (family/group); £150 (life)
What you Get: Magazines; free gardening advice; free admission to Ryton (organic) Gardens; support from local groups all over Britain; the use of HDRA reference library at Ryton; the HDRA mail order Organic Gardening Catalogue.
Sales: Merchandising catalogue
Green Consumerism: Sell organic produce through their own shop, award-winning café and mail order catalogue. Extensive promotion of environmentally safe produce.

London Food Commission

88 Old Street, London EC1V 9AR. Tel: 01-253 9513
Main Aim: To provide research and advice on all food matters so as to improve public health and education.

Issues: Food quality. Pesticide and fertiliser residues. Additives. Labelling. Improving consumer choice.
Number of Members: 70 national and local organisations.
Membership Fee: Subscription to *The Food Magazine*: £12.50 (individual); £25 (organisation)
What you Get: Independent, scientifically sound advice that puts consumers, the environment and public health interest first.
Sales: Books. *The Food Magazine*.
Green Consumerism: Suggest that Green Consumers have great potential to improve health, consumer choice and the environment by exerting pressure on food suppliers to: a) improve controls over unnecessary 'chemicalisation of food'; b) encourage the production of pesticide-free foods.

Marine Conservation Society

9 Gloucester Road, Ross on Wye, Herefordshire HR9 5BU. Tel: 0989 66017
Main Aim: Seeks to protect the marine environment and to promote its practical management by: lobbying and campaigning on marine issues; research on marine life; and wardening of certain coastal sites.
Issues: Marine pollution. Marine resource depletion. Fisheries conservation. Toxic waste disposal. Nuclear waste disposal.
Number of Members: 4,000 (last year 2,000 — 100% increase)
Membership Fee: £8
What you Get: Quarterly magazine — *Marine Conservation*. Local groups which participate in research projects. AGM and conference. Sales brochure.
Sales: Merchandising catalogue. Publications, including *The Good Beach Guide*. Gifts, T-shirts etc.
Green Consumerism: Have recommended that consumers avoid buying: marine curios, shells (including sea-urchin lights and air plants mounted on shells), oil from basking sharks (used in some products containing animal fats) and TBT paints on yachts or fish farm cages. Also research the quality of our beaches.

National Society for Clean Air (NSCA)

136 North Street, Brighton BN1 1RG. Tel: 0273 26313
Main Aim: To seek the improvement of the environment by promoting clean air, noise reduction and other control measures, having regard to the implications for all aspects of the environment.
Issues: Ozone depletion, acid rain and the Greenhouse Effect. Transportation emissions and noise. Radiation.
Number of Members: 1,000, includes industry and local authorities (last year 650 — 53% increase)
Membership Fee: £11.50 (individual)
What you Get: Quarterly newsletter. NSCA members' handbook. Access to library. Discounts for conferences and workshops.

Sales: Mostly publications.
Green Consumerism: Suggest that consumers avoid: asbestos, polluting fuels and CFCs. Recommend: unleaded petrol, smokeless fuel, noise insulation and energy efficiency.

National Trust (NT)

36 Queen Anne's Gate, London SW1H 9AS. Tel: 01-222 9251
Main Aim: Protects places of historic interest or natural beauty, holding countryside and buildings in England, Wales and Northern Ireland for the benefit of the nation.
Issues: Conservation of buildings (research into acid rain), landscapes, wildlife and flora. Also coastline conservation through Enterprise Neptune: 1990 will mark 25 years of saving the coastline.
Number of Members: 1,660,151 (last year 1,543,000 — 7.6% increase. In July 1989 the National Trust announced that membership had reached 1.75 million, almost double the figure in 1979.)
Membership Fee: £16
What you Get: Magazine (3 times a year). Admission at reduced rates to most properties. National Trust handbook.
Sales: Shops and cafeterias at many of their sites. Most food served is local produce.
Green Consumerism: Stopped selling aerosols which contain CFCs. All their cars run on unleaded petrol.

New Consumer Ltd

52 Elswick Road, Newcastle upon Tyne NE4 6JH. Tel: 091-272 1148
Main Aim: A clean and healthy environment and an international market place that sustains the planet's people and resources. The main sources of information will be their consumer books and guides.
Issues: Establishing market support for ethical products; providing support services for national member consumer organisations and making financial, technical, management and marketing resources available to these organisations.
Number of Members: No details at time of going to press, but membership is being established.
Membership Fee: See above.
What you Get: See above.
Sales: Consumer books and shopping guides. The *New Consumer* magazine.
Green Consumerism: New Consumer's policies fully incorporate environmental considerations. Publications include a consumer shopping guide which evaluates goods against 10 social criteria, including equal opportunities, military contracts, animal testing, apartheid and the environment.

Oxfam

272 Banbury Road, Oxford OX2 7DZ. Tel: 0865 56777
Main Aim: To relieve poverty, distress and suffering in every part of the world, without regard to political or religious beliefs.
Issues: Deforestation and soil erosion. Pesticides and pollution. Relief aid.
Number of Members: No members
Membership Fee: N/A
What you Get: N/A
Sales: Oxfam have a large catalogue of products and publications. In 1989, during World Environment Day, they released a publication entitled *People and the Environment*. They also have Oxfam shops all over the country, which raise funds for the central organisation.
Green Consumerism: Oxfam focuses on the impact on the Third World of unsafe pesticides and some cash crops.

Royal Society for Nature Conservation (RSNC)

The Green, Nettleham, Lincoln LN2 2NR. Tel: 0522 752326
Main Aim: To create a better future for wildlife by campaigns, education, establishment of nature reserves and community action organised through its nationwide network of 48 Local Wildlife Trusts and 50 Urban Wildlife Groups.
Issues: Nature conservation and forestry. Nature conservation and agriculture. Pollution. Waste disposal. Improved European laws on wildlife. Habitat loss.
Number of Members: 204,000 in local wildlife trusts (last year 184,000 — 10.7% increase)
Membership Fee: £6 – £12
What you Get: *Natural World* colour magazine. Local newsletters. Access to nature reserves. Range of local wildlife trust activities.
Sales: Catalogue selling range of products.
Green Consumerism: Research project into alternatives to horticultural peat.

Royal Society for the Prevention of Cruelty to Animals (RSPCA)

The Causeway, Horsham, West Sussex RH12 1HG. Tel: 0403 64181
Main Aim: The prevention of cruelty and the promotion of kindness to animals.
Issues: Animal welfare.
Number of Members: 21,000 (last year 23,000 — 8.7% decrease)
Membership Fee: £8; £250 (life)
What you Get: Postal vote for council. Quarterly magazine, *RSPCA Today*. Campaign literature. Merchandising catalogue.
Sales: Merchandising catalogue. Have also aligned themselves with a petfood manufacturer to raise funds. (Brand name *Duo*, manufactured by **Luda**).
Green Consumerism: Suggest that consumers avoid: fur coats, some meat and all products involving cruelty to animals. They recommend cruelty-

free products. They recognise that there is enormous potential in this area and have produced a brochure to explain the connections between what they do and a number of environmental issues, published during Green Consumer Week in 1988.

Royal Society for the Protection of Birds (RSPB)

The Lodge, Sandy, Bedfordshire SG19 2DL. Tel: 0767 80551
Main Aim: The conservation and protection of wild birds and their habitats through campaigns, education and research.
Issues: Species extinction. Disappearing Britain. Modern intensive agricultural methods. Marine pollution. Land reclamation from wetlands, rivers and seas. Potential estuary loss.
Number of Members: Over 500,000, including Young Ornithologists (last year 423,000 — 18.2% increase)
Membership Fee: £12 (individual); £15 (joint); £18 (family); £6 (OAP)
What you Get: Quarterly magazine — *Birds*. Free admission to reserves. Local members' groups.
Sales: Sales catalogue
Green Consumerism: Alerted people to the fact that feeding salted nuts to birds can be deadly and campaigned against lead fishing weights when it was found that they were killing swans. Keep a look out for the effects of persistent environmental poisons, such as DDT.

Soil Association

86 Colston Street, Bristol BS1 5BB. Tel: 0272 290661
Main Aim: Protection of the environment through the promotion of links between organic agriculture, the environment, food quality and human health.
Issues: Soil degradation, pesticide and fertiliser pollution. Food quality. Countryside problems. Rural deprivation.
Number of Members: 5,500 (last year 4,500 — 22% increase)
Membership Fee: £10
What you Get: *Living Earth Magazine* (quarterly). Advice on organic practices. Events. Conferences. Mail order book service.
Green Consumerism: Actively promote organic practices and organic produce, especially 'safe meat'. They have the most widely recognised symbol guaranteeing that organic standards are being adhered to. Campaigned for real milk and recognise that there is considerable potential for Green Consumer activities.

Tidy Britain Group

The Pier, Wigan, Lancs, WN3 4EX. Tel: 0942 824620
Main Aim: To protect and enhance the amenities of town and country in the United Kingdom, particularly by promoting prevention and control of litter and by encouraging environmental improvement schemes.

Issues: Litter and waste disposal. Environmental education.
Number of Members: Companies and organisations only.
Membership Fee: N/A
What you Get: N/A
Sales: Starting to merchandise
Green Consumerism: Encourage sponsorship of litter bins and recycling.
Are in close contact with The Industry Council for Packaging and the
Environment (INCPEN).

Town and Country Planning Association (TCPA)

17 Carlton House Terrace, London SW1Y 5AS. Tel: 01-930 8903
Main Aim: To campaign for a better environment by means of effective
planning and community participation, with an emphasis on the needs of
the disadvantaged.
Issues: Planning. Urban decline and regeneration. Energy issues.
Transport issues. Revitalisation of the countryside.
Number of Members: 1,350 (last year 1,350 — no change)
Membership Fee: £24
What you Get: Monthly journal, *Town and Country Planning*. Discount
on conferences. Discount on *Planning Bulletin*.
Sales: Publications only.
Green Consumerism: No specific ventures yet.

Traidcraft plc

Kingsway, Gateshead, Tyne and Wear NE11 0NE. Tel: 091-491 0591
Main Aim: A Christian initiative that buys a variety of craft products such
as clothing, foodstuffs, household items, teas and coffees from community
groups in developing countries.
Issues: Challenging the way the rich exploit the poor by demonstrating
that trade with the Third World should be based on justice, concern for
people, partnership between rich and poor,and care for the environment.
Number of Members: N/A
Membership Fee: N/A
What you Get: N/A
Sales: Products available in some shops and through the Traidcraft
catalogues.
Green Consumerism: The buyers of all Traidcraft products take
environmental issues into consideration. Traidcraft also offers a range of
recycled paper products which are made in Europe.

Transport 2000

Walkden House, 10 Melton Street, London NW1 2EJ. Tel: 01-388 8386
Main Aim: To lobby central and local government for more rational
transport policies, in the interests of accident prevention, social justice,
the protection of the environment and the conservation of land and
energy.

Issues: Public versus private transport. Environmental impact of transport systems. Pollution. Equity issues. Disappearing Britain. Environmental conservation. Land conservation. Pedestrian priority: 'Feet First' campaign.
Number of Members: Corporate membership. Also have supporters' scheme (annual subscription and/or donations).
Membership Fee: £5; £2.50 (concessions); £8 (household)
What you Get: Newsletter (quarterly). 20% discount on publications and journal *Transport Retort*. Details of local groups.
Sales: Mostly reports.
Green Consumerism: Lobby for public transport and therefore are against private road transport. Interested in the potential of the Green Consumer.

World Wide Fund for Nature (WWF: formerly World Wildlife Fund)

Panda House, Weyside Park, Godalming, Surrey GU7 1XR. Tel: 0483 426444
Main Aim: To achieve the conservation of natural resources in the UK and other parts of the world by education, public policy, site protection, species conservation and training.
Issues: Species extinction. Loss of habitat. Deforestation. Energy issues and acid rain. Air, sea and land pollution. Land use and rural economy in the UK.
Number of Members: 155,000 (last year 125,000 — 24% increase)
Membership Fee: £15
What you Get: Quarterly newsletter, *WWF News*. Annual catalogue. Membership card and car sticker. Events.
Sales: Merchandising activities are a multi-million pound business which includes catalogues and on-pack promotions.
Green Consumerism: Recognise the enormous potential of the Green Consumer. Advise people to avoid holidays which endanger wildlife and encourage holiday-makers to let them know if they witness any particular problems whilst abroad, e.g. abuse of animals for tourist entertainment. Provided core funding for Green Consumer Week in 1988.

Women's Environment Network

287 City Road, London EC1V 1LA. Tel: 01-490 2511
Main Aim: To provide consumer information for women.
Issues: Health and the environment. Dioxins in nappies and sanitary products. Safety of household products. Women and radiation, e.g. x-rays. Transport and women. Women and the environment in relation to Third World issues.
Number of Members: 2,000
Membership Fee: £10 (individual); £7 (concessionary rate); £20 (founder member)
Sales: Catalogue. Publications.
What you Get: Magazine. Newsletters. Monthly meetings. Seminars.
Green Consumerism: The network's activities revolve around green consumerism. It has recently launched the 'Green Home' campaign, built around a house designed with green issues in mind and a *Green Living* magazine which came out in conjunction with the campaign.

Index of Brand Names

Names in brackets refer to manufacturers.

Index

This index refers to manufacturers and organisations only where they are mentioned in the body of the text; the Manufacturers' Survey (pages 283 – 323) and the Consumer's Guide to Useful Organisations (pages 331 – 40) are not included here since they are organised alphabetically. No reference either is made to the supermarkets which participated in the survey, which appear *passim*.